NEW METHODS OF FINANCING YOUR BUSINESS IN THE UNITED STATES

A Strategic Analysis

OTHER WORKS BY FREDERICK D. LIPMAN

International Strategic Alliances: Joint Ventures Between Asian and U.S. Companies (2nd Edition)

Whistleblowers: Incentives, Disincentives and Protection Strategies

The Family Business Guide: Everything You Need to Know to Manage Your Business from Legal Planning to Business Strategies

International and U.S. IPO Planning: A Business Strategy Guide

Executive Compensation Best Practices

Corporate Governance Best Practices: Strategies for Public, Private, and Not-for-Profit Organizations

Valuing Your Business: Strategies to Maximize the Sale Price

Audit Committees

The Complete Guide to Employee Stock Options

The Complete Guide to Valuing and Selling Your Business

The Complete Going Public Handbook

Financing Your Business with Venture Capital

How Much Is Your Business Worth

Going Public

Venture Capital and Junk Bond Financing

NEW METHODS OF FINANCING YOUR BUSINESS IN THE UNITED STATES

A Strategic Analysis

Frederick D Lipman

Blank Rome LLP, USA

 **World Scientific**

NEW JERSEY · LONDON · SINGAPORE · BEIJING · SHANGHAI · HONG KONG · TAIPEI · CHENNAI · TOKYO

Published by

World Scientific Publishing Co. Pte. Ltd.

5 Toh Tuck Link, Singapore 596224

USA office: 27 Warren Street, Suite 401-402, Hackensack, NJ 07601

UK office: 57 Shelton Street, Covent Garden, London WC2H 9HE

Library of Congress Cataloging-in-Publication Data
Lipman, Frederick D.
    New methods of financing your business in the United States : a strategic analysis / by Frederick
D. Lipman.
        pages cm
    Includes bibliographical references and index.
    ISBN 978-9814632645
    1. New business enterprises--United States--Finance. 2. Small business--United States--Finance.
3. Business enterprises--United States--Finance. I. Title.
    HG4027.6.L56 2015
    658.15'224--dc23

                                                              2014035529

British Library Cataloguing-in-Publication Data
A catalogue record for this book is available from the British Library.

In-house Editors: Sandhya Venkatesh /Dipasri Sardar

Typeset by Stallion Press
Email: enquiries@stallionpress.com

Printed in Singapore by B & Jo Enterprise Pte Ltd

To my partners at Blank Rome LLP who permit me
to continue to write books.

ACKNOWLEDGMENTS

The author would like to acknowledge the contributions to this book of the following attorneys, librarians, and paralegals at Blank Rome LLP, namely: Yelena M. Barycher, Carol Buckalew, Jennifer J. Daniels, Esq., Jonathan Scott Goldman, Esq., Cheryl Halvorsen, Nicholas C. Harbist, Esq., Abraham J. Kwon, Esq., Christopher A. Lewis, Esq., William H. Roberts, Esq., and John P. Wixted, Esq.

Dr. Jeffry Rubin, my good friend and tennis partner, made an excellent suggestion for marketing securities offerings under SEC Rule 506(c).

I want to acknowledge the work of Barbara Helverson, my Administrative Assistant, who served as the typist and initial editor of this book.

CONTENTS

INTRODUCTION

This book is intended for entrepreneurs (both U.S. and international) who are thinking about growing their business with outside capital from U.S. investors. The U.S. has one of the deepest pools of potential investors of any country. It has been reported that over 9 million U.S. households qualify as so-called "accredited investors" with a net worth of over $1 million (exclusive of primary residence).[1] The U.S. has more than 33 million total investors, both accredited and non-accredited.[2] More than 1 million U.S. households have a net worth between $5 million and $25 million (exclusive of primary residence).[3]

It has been reported that there are over 700,000 so-called "angel investors" in the U.S.[4] The term "angel investors," which, although initially referring to investors in Broadway shows, now refers to high net worth individuals who are willing to invest their own money in ranges of $150,000 to $2 million.[5]

---

[1] http://spectrem.com/Content/Millionaire-Households-Back-to-Pre-Recession-Levels. aspx. According to the U.S. Securities and Exchange Commission ("SEC"), as of 2010, 8.7 million U.S. households, or 7.4% of all U.S. households, qualified as accredited investors based on the net worth standard in the definition of "accredited investor." See analysis presented in SEC Rel. No. 33-9415 (July 10, 2013) [78 FR 44771].

[2] SEC Rel. No. 33-9497 at p. 216.

[3] http://spectrem.com/Content/Millionaire-Households-Back-to-Pre-Recession-Levels. aspx.

[4] T. Prive, "Angel Investors: How The Rich Invest," Forbes.com, March 12, 2013.

[5] *Id.*

REVOLUTION IN RAISING U.S. CAPITAL

In 2012, the U.S. Congress was concerned about the continued high unemployment in the U.S. It was viewed that the federal and state securities laws interfered with raising capital for businesses, both large and small, which would create new jobs. On April 5, 2012, the Jumpstart Our Business Act ("JOBS Act") was enacted.

Part I of this book deals with some of the major provisions of that law and the resulting SEC rules. In Part II of this book, there is an analysis of the decision as to whether or not to grow a business with outside capital, the potential strategies for doing so, and advance planning to raise capital.

The JOBS Act started a revolution in the method of raising capital in the U.S. for businesses, particularly for small- and medium-sized businesses as well as start-ups. The JOBS Act created three new methods of legally raising outside capital from strangers, subject to implementation by the U.S. Securities and Exchange Commission "SEC":

- **Securities Crowdfunding under Section 4(a)(6)**: Effective May 16, 2016, eligible U.S. companies (with their principal office in the U.S.) are permitted to raise from eligible non-accredited, as well as accredited, investors up to $1 million every 12 months by selling to them debt and equity securities under Section 4(a)(6) of the Securities Act of 1933 ("1933 Act"). The marketing must be conducted by a registered funding portal or registered securities broker and other restrictions must be satisfied. U.S. public trading markets in the crowdfunding securities can potentially be developed approximately one year after sale completion.
- **Rule 506(c) Sales to Accredited Investors**: Effective September 23, 2013, SEC Rule 506(c) offerings permit eligible companies (both U.S. and international) to raise unlimited amounts of capital from accredited investors in the U.S. over the Internet and through other public solicitations, subject to verification requirements and other limitations. These offerings, particularly when made over an Internet platform, are also confusingly called "crowdfunding." Even though an offer and sale can be made to more than 9 million U.S. accredited investors, this offering is still considered a non-public offering for purposes of the U.S. Securities Act of 1933 ("1933 Act"), thereby avoiding the large

costs of a traditional U.S. initial public offering (IPO). The rule permits a direct public offering by the company without an underwriter. U.S. public trading markets can potentially be developed in the securities approximately one year after sale completion.

- **Tier 2 of Regulation A:** Effective June 19, 2015, the SEC adopted Tier 1 and Tier 2 of Regulation A. Tier 2 which permits eligible U.S. companies (with their principal office in the U.S.) to raise from eligible non-accredited, as well as accredited, investors, up to $50 million every 12 months, and permits secondary sales by insiders up to $15 million during this same period (subject to a 30% first year limitation), provided the total company and insider sales do not exceed $50 million during this same period. Tier 2 permits a direct public offering by the company without an underwriter. Securities resale is not restricted and therefore U.S. public trading markets can be developed immediately.

International companies that create a U.S. corporation or other entity with its principal office in the U.S. may be able to qualify for both securities crowdfunding and Tier 2 of Regulation A. For international companies wishing to sell securities to U.S. accredited investors under Rule 506(c), there is no requirement to form a U.S. entity or to have its principal office in the U.S.

It is theoretically now possible to simultaneously raise $1 million by securities crowdfunding from eligible non-accredited as well as accredited investors, an unlimited amount from accredited investors under Rule 506(c), and $50 million in a Tier 2 of Regulation A offering from eligible non-accredited as well as accredited investors.[6] In addition, companies can continue to simultaneously raise unlimited funds through non-securities crowdfunding through Internet portals such as Kickstarter.com ("Kickstarter").

These new SEC rules constitute a radical change from past practices and will facilitate raising capital from U.S. investors.

---

[6]This assumes that the requirements for each registration exemption are separately satisfied. See SEC Rel. No. 33-9470, pp. 17–18; see also SEC Rel. No. 33-9497, pp. 56–57. Caution should be exercised since SEC Rule 251(c) under Regulation A by its terms only excludes securities crowdfunding from integration with a Regulation A offering and does not refer to simultaneous Rule 506 offerings.

DEFINITIONS

This book defines "venture capital" broadly to include not only professionally managed private equity funds but also junk bond financing, private placements to angel investors, and high-risk IPOs. This broad definition permits a strategic analysis and comparison of these different growth strategies.

The term "accredited investors" includes various entities as well as individuals who satisfy either of the following tests:

- a natural person whose individual net worth, or joint net worth with that person's spouse, exceeds $1 million. The investor's primary residence is not included in determining their net worth and mortgage indebtedness up to the fair market value of their primary residence is excluded from their liabilities (subject to a minor exception); or
- a natural person who had an individual income in excess of $200,000 in each of the two most recent years, or joint income with that person's spouse in excess of $300,000 in each of those years, and has a reasonable expectation of reaching the same income level in the current year.

The full definition of "accredited investors" is contained in Rule 501 of Regulation D, which is reproduced in Appendix 1 of this book.

ORGANIZATION OF THIS BOOK

This book is organized into two parts: Part I consists of Chapters 1–5 which contain a description of the new funding methods.

Chapter 1 contains a discussion of crowdfunding, including the difference between past crowdfunding and the newly-adopted form of securities crowdfunding.

Chapter 2 analyzes some of the potential methods of marketing a public offering to accredited investors under Rule 506(c), which is considered a private offering by the SEC.

Chapter 3 provides a technical discussion of the requirements to satisfy Rule 506(c), including methods of verifying accredited investor status. Enhanced verification of accredited investor status was the *quid pro quo* for permitting general solicitation of accredited investors under the JOBS Act.

Chapter 4 furnishes a description of Tier 2 of Regulation A which permits companies that cannot qualify for a traditional U.S. IPO to raise up to $50 million every 12 months as well as Tier 1 which is less useful. Tier 2 also permits founders and other shareholders to sell up to $15 million of their own securities every 12 months, provided the total amount sold between the company and the selling shareholders does not exceed $50 million. Tier 1 of Regulation A, which is less useful because of intrusive state regulation, is also covered in this chapter.

Chapter 5 contains a summary of the U.S. financing choices, both new and existing ones. The chapter starts with a brief discussion about U.S. angel investors and professionally managed private equity funds.

Part II consists of Chapters 6–10 which provide strategic guidance to entrepreneurs raising capital.

Chapter 6 analyzes the commonly-used methods of valuing a business. If a business owner intends to sell equity securities, Chapter 6 provides a method of determining how much equity dilution the owner may suffer.

The strategic considerations in raising capital from outside sources are reviewed in Chapter 7. This chapter discusses, among other things, the various forms of debt and equity securities which are used to finance a business, and personal considerations of the owner of the business in determining whether to accept outside capital, including control and family business issues.

Chapter 8 describes the advanced planning steps needed in order to successfully raise outside capital, including the creation of a professional team and other important considerations.

Chapter 9 analyses strategies for increasing the value of a business through so-called "roll-ups" and other acquisitions. Securities offerings are more attractive to investors if the proceeds are used to grow the company through well-structured acquisitions.

Chapter 10 summarizes many of the important issues in negotiating with a professional investor, including subtle methods that a professional investor may use to enhance its equity position.

LEGAL REQUIREMENTS: BEFORE AND AFTER THE JOBS ACT

It is not possible to sell securities in the U.S. without complying with federal and state securities laws in the U.S. These laws typically have two main provisions: (i) a registration provision and (ii) an anti-fraud provision. The cost to register securities under federal and state securities laws can easily exceed $1 million. Unless a company is valuable enough to qualify for a traditional U.S. IPO, the cost of the registration is extremely burdensome. Companies, therefore, look for exemptions from the registration provisions to avoid the large costs in legal, accounting, printing, and other expenses of a registration.

Prior to the JOBS Act, the most prominent registration exemption was contained in Section 4(a)(2) of the 1933 Act, the so-called "private placement" exemption, and this exemption continues after the JOBS Act. Private placements to individual accredited investors were typically conducted pursuant to Rule 506(b) of SEC Regulation D, a so-called "safe harbor" to comply with Section 4(a)(2). If the offering complied with Rule 506(b), it was considered to be automatically exempt from registration under Section 4(a)(2) of the 1933 Act. Rule 506(b), which also continues in effect after the JOBS Act, prohibits general solicitation or general advertising. A private placement under Rule 506(b) requires the filing of a Form D with the SEC, which is publicly available. Private placements to institutional investor were typically conducted under the Section 4(a)(2) registration exemption under the 1933 Act, rather than Rule 506(b), since most institutional investors preferred not to notify the SEC or the public of their offering using Form D.

The problem with the private placement exemption prior to the JOBS Act was that it was difficult to raise U.S. capital, particularly for middle-market and start-up businesses. This was due to the requirement that the company or its investment banker must have a preexisting substantive relationship with the all potential investors and could not use general solicitation or general advertising.[7] This severely limited the number of persons who could qualify as private placement investors.

---

[7]On August 6, 2015, the SEC clarified how an issur of securities can conduct a private placement under Rule 506(b) in a password protected web page, without it being deemed

As previously noted, in 2012, the U.S. Congress was concerned about the continued high unemployment in the U.S. It was viewed that the federal and state securities laws interfered with raising capital for businesses, both large and small, which would create new jobs. On April 5, 2012, the JOBS Act became law.

The U.S. Congress was influenced in passing the JOBS Act by a report entitled "Rebuilding the IPO On-Ramp"[8] which was issued to the U.S. Department of the Treasury. The report noted that, during the past 15 years, the number of "emerging growth companies"[9] having U.S. IPOs had plummeted relative to historical norms. The report stated as follows: "This trend has transcended economic cycles during that period and has hobbled U.S. job creation. In fact, by one estimate, the decline of the U.S. IPO market had cost America as many as 22 million jobs through 2009."[10]

The U.S. Congress heeded this report and adopted within the JOBS Act a provision making it easier and less costly for so-called "emerging growth companies" (companies with less than $1 billion in revenue for their last fiscal year) to have a traditional U.S. IPO. However, the U.S. Congress did not stop there. Instead, the JOBS Act made other significant changes in federal securities laws to facilitate capital growth for all companies. These changes included, but were not limited to, the three changes previously discussed (Section 4(a)(6) securities crowdfunding, Rule 506(c), and Tier 2 of Regulation A) and increasing the number and nature of shareholders which would trigger SEC registration and reporting requirements for a company. The JOBS Act created a new registration exemption to permit securities crowdfunding by adding new Section 4(a)(6)

---

a "general solicitation" or "general advertising," and thereby being subject to the additional requirements imposed by Rule 506(c). See Citizen VC No Action Letter dated August 6, 2015.

[8] Report dated October 20, 2011; See also J. R. Ritter, X. Gao and Z. Zhu, *Where Have all the IPOs Gone?* (August 2013) at 8, available at http://ssrn.com/abstract=1954788 (noting a decrease in the average annual volume of IPOs from 310 during 1980–2000 to 99 during 2001–2011).

[9] For an interesting study of the effect of the JOBS Act on emerging growth companies, see D. Dharmapala and V. Khanna, "The Cost and Benefits of Mandatory Securities Regulation: Evidence from Market Reactions to the JOBS Act of 2012," Center for Economic Studies & Ifo Institute ("CESifo"), May 2014.

[10] See also M. Andreessen, "The IPO is dying," www.vox.com, June 26, 2014

to the 1933 Act and expanded the very limited dollar Regulation A registration exemption contained in Section 3(b) of the 1933 Act to permit what is now called by the SEC Tier 1 and Tier 2 of Regulation A.

An important provision of the JOBS Act required the U.S. SEC to remove the prohibition in Rule 506 against general solicitation and general advertising in private placements provided that all purchasers of the securities were accredited investors and that the issuer of securities "take reasonable steps to verify that purchasers of the securities" were accredited investors. The SEC subsequently did this in adopting a new Rule 506(c) to supplement Rule 506(b). The U.S. Congress presumably believed that the prohibition on general solicitation and general advertising in capital-raising inhibited raising capital by severely limiting the number of potential investors and, therefore, was partly to blame for the continued high unemployment in the U.S.

By eliminating the prohibition on general soliciting and general advertising as a condition for a registration exemption (as provided currently in Rule 506(c)), the JOBS Act effectively permits public offerings of securities to both accredited and non-accredited investors, which are exempt from registration under the 1933 Act so long as the ultimate purchasers are accredited investors, there were reasonable steps to verify that the investors were accredited, and other reasonable requirements are satisfied. Gone is the requirement that there must be a preexisting substantive relationship with the investor, so long as the requirements of current SEC Rule 506(c) are satisfied.

Even though new Rule 506(c) was intended to create jobs in the U.S., there was no requirement in Rule 506(c) that the capital raised be used in the U.S. Indeed, international issuers as well as U.S. issuers are qualified to raise capital under both Rule 506(b) and Rule 506(c).

As a result of new SEC Rule 506(c), which implements the JOBS Act mandate, all businesses, including start-ups, are now permitted to raise capital (both debt and equity) by general solicitation and general advertising, such as through the Internet, social media, e-mail, television, mailings, newspaper advertisements, and billboards.

Tier 2 of Regulation A is also very important to larger middle-market companies, including family-owned businesses, by enabling them to raise significant capital cheaply compared to a traditional U.S. IPO. Tier 2 of

Regulation A rules, adopted by the SEC as mandated by the JOBS Act, substantially increased the dollar amount of securities which could be publicly sold through general advertising every 12 months from $5 million to $50 million. These new SEC rules also increased permitted sales by selling stockholders from a miserly $1.5 million to a healthy $15 million every 12 months (subject to first year limitations), provided the total amount raised by the company and selling stockholders did not exceed $50 million and a first year limitation is satisfied.

The registration provisions of state securities laws in the U.S. greatly inhibited capital necessary for middle-market and start-up companies. All three of the new SEC rules, i.e., securities crowdfunding, Rule 506(c), and Tier 2 of Regulation A, preempted the registration provisions, but not the anti-fraud provisions, of state securities laws.

Each of these three new rules contains a number of complicated exceptions and qualifications which are explained in Chapters 1–4 of this book. These new SEC rules supplement older rules which permit the raising of outside capital that remain in effect and provide alternative methods of raising capital from U.S. investor. The old and new rules are discussed in Chapter 5.

This book was written about the same time as the new SEC rules on Section 4(a)(6) securities crowdfunding and Tier 2 of Regulation A were being adopted. Consequently, this book does not reflect issues which may arise as these new rules are rolled out.[11]

The new Section 4(a)(6) crowdfunding rules mandated by the JOBS Act are probably the most important rule change for start-up companies. We will therefore start with an analysis of the new Section 4(a)(6) securities crowdfunding rules.

---

[11] Moreover, this book does not reflect SEC rules proposed in SEC Rel. 33-9416 dated July 10, 2013, which required advanced filing of Form D for Rule 506(c) offerings and proposed amendments to the content of Form D, among other things. As of the publication of this book, these proposals have not been adopted.

PART I
NEW FINANCING METHODS

CHAPTER 1

CROWDFUNDING

Crowdfunding is a financing technique that uses online social networks linked to a web internet-based platform to raise capital. In this chapter, we will discuss so-called "retail crowdfunding." This involves using social networks to raise capital from the general public either without selling any investment securities or, effective May 16, 2016, by selling investment securities to both non-accredited investors as well as accredited investors pursuant to a registration exemption contained in Section 4(a)(6) of the 1933 Act. In the next chapter, we will discuss crowdfunding as well as other marketing methodologies which permit sales of investment securities solely to accredited investors pursuant to a registration exemption contained in Rule 506(c) under the 1933 Act (so-called "non-retail crowdfunding"). In contrast to retail crowdfunding discussed in this chapter, Rule 506(c) permits unlimited amounts of funds to be raised but limits sales solely to accredited investors.

Effective May 16, 2016, there are now two forms of retail crowdfunding:

- Crowdfunding where the reward to contributors does not include investment securities ("non-securities crowdfunding"), which can raise unlimited amounts of funds and is not subject to the restrictions on securities crowdfunding discussed in this chapter.
- Crowdfunding under Section 4(a)(6) where the reward to contributors includes investment securities ("securities crowdfunding"), which can raise up to $1 million every 12 months and is subject to the restrictions discussed in this chapter.

In this chapter, we will examine two successful non-securities crowd-funding examples in order to better understand how securities crowd-funding will operate in the future. The two examples of non-securities crowdfunding are Pebble Watch, which raised over $10 million, and SCiO, which raised close to $3 million.

The purpose of studying these two examples of non-securities crowd-funding is to make it clear that companies can engage simultaneously in both non-securities crowdfunding and securities crowdfunding under Section 4(a)(6). Therefore, the total fundraising need not be limited to $1 million every 12 months. The significant expense and limitations on securities crowdfunding under Section 4(a)(6), which are explained in this chapter, do not apply to non-securities crowdfunding. Moreover, non-securities crowdfunding avoids potential dilution to the equity ownership of the entrepreneur and can, in certain cases, result in interest by venture capitalists as well as potential buyers for the business. Having a large number of retail equity investors in a business as a result of Section 4(a)(6) crowdfunding, can actually be a negative factor in attracting venture capital firms and other professional investors.

U.S. SECURITIES CROWDFUNDING

Prior to the JOBS Act and the Securities and Exchange Commission's ("SECs") securities crowdfunding rules, investment securities could not be part of the reward for crowdfunding contributors. That has now changed.

SEC rules, effective May 16, 2016, permit eligible issuers to sell up to $1 million[1] in investment securities through crowdfunding under Section 4(a)(6) during any 12-month period, computed as discussed in this chapter. The business must be owned by an entity organized under, and subject to, the laws of a state or territory of the United States or the District of Columbia, among other requirements.

However, there is nothing in the rules to prevent an international company from forming a U.S. company with its principal offices in the U.S. The SEC declined to impose any limitation on the use of crowdfunding proceeds. Therefore, the funds raised through securities crowdfunding

---

[1]SEC Rel. No. 33-9974, p15; The Jobs Act requires that this amount is to be adjusted not less frequently than every five years based on the Consumer Price Index.

could then be used to finance international operations. However, the SEC Staff will likely require that the company's officers, partners or managers primarily direct, control and coordinate the company's activities from the principal office in the U.S.

The transaction must be conducted through an intermediary qualified under Section 4A(a) of the 1933 Act, which is either a registered securities broker ("registered broker") or registered funding portal, and the transaction must be conducted exclusively through the intermediary's "platform." The term "platform" means an Internet website or other similar electronic medium through which a registered broker or a registered funding portal acts as an intermediary in a transaction involving the offer or sale of securities in reliance on the securities crowdfunding exemption. The issuer must also comply with the disclosure requirements hereafter mentioned (described in Section 4A(b) of the 1933 Act) and other applicable provisions of the Section 4(a)(6) securities crowdfunding statutory provisions and rules.

Sales may be made through the intermediary to any investor, whether or not they are an accredited investor. However, the total amount sold to any single investor (including accredited investors) across all issuers (as defined hereafter) in reliance on the Section 4(a)(6) securities crowdfunding exemption (Section 4(a)(6)) during the 12 months preceding the Section 4(a)(6) transaction, including the current sale, must not exceed:

- If either the annual income and net worth of the investor is below $100,000,[3] the total amount sold to that investor may not exceed the greater of $2,000 or 5% of the lesser of the annual income or net worth of that investor; or
- if both the annual income and net worth of the investor are $100,000 or more,[4] the total amount sold to that investor may not exceed 10% of the lesser of the annual income or net worth of that investor, subject to a $100,000 cap.[5]

---

[2]SEC Reg. §227.100; The issuer cannot conduct the offering or a concurrent offering under Section 4(a)(6) using more than one intermediary.

[3] *Id.*

[4]*Id.*

[5]*Id.*

The SEC has provided the following examples of how to compute the investment limit which appiles to the aggregate amount of securities sold to any investor under Section 4(a)(6) within a 12-month period across all issuers relying on Section 4(a)(6).[6]

Table 1.1　Investment Limits

Investor Annual Income	Investor Net Worth	Calculation	Investment Limit
$30,000	$105,000	Greater of $2,000 or 5% of $30,000 ($1,500)	$2,000
$150,000	$80,000	Greater of $2,000 or 5% of $80,000 ($4,000)	$4,000
$150,000	$100,000	10% of $100,000 ($10,000)	$10,000
$200,000	$900,000	10% of $200,000 ($20,000)	$20,000
$1,200,000	$2,000,000	10% of $1,200,000 ($120,000), subject to $100,000 cap	$100,000

A natural person's annual income and net worth may be calculated jointly with the annual income and net worth of the person's spouse.[7] However, when a joint calculation is used, the aggregate investment of the spouses may not exceed the limit that would apply to an individual investor at that income or net worth level. The company is permitted to rely on the intermediary to ensure that investor limitations are not exceeded, provided the issuer does not know that the investor has exceeded those limits or would exceed the investor limits as a result of purchasing the securities.

The term "issuer" includes all entities controlled by or under common control with the company, including their respective predecessors. Therefore, in computing the $1 million limitation, sales by subsidiaries or predecessors of the company will count against that limitation.

The term "securities" includes promissory notes, common stock and preferred stock of corporations and equity interests in limited liability companies, limited partnerships, and other entities. In addition, the term "securities" includes warrants or other rights to purchase stock or other

---

[6]SEC Rel. No. 33-9974, p. 26.

[7]SEC Reg. §227.100. The annual income and net worth of a person is calculated as described in Chapter 3 for sales to accredited investors under Rule 506(c).

equity interests, guarantees, and a variety of other arrangements which may constitute an "investment contract." The U.S. courts have interpreted the term "investment contract" very broadly and, in general, it includes any arrangement in which there is an investment of funds in a project where the profits arise solely or primarily from the efforts of others.

As noted, the SEC rules permit the same company to engage in both securities and non-securities crowdfunding simultaneously and the non-securities crowdfunding does not count toward the $1 million dollar limit. By engaging in both forms of crowdfunding, a company could raise substantially more than $1 million within a 12-month period.

The use of crowdfunding with securities as rewards under Section 4(a)(6) is very new and it may take some time for the funding techniques to be fully developed. Therefore, it is important to understand how crowdfunding worked before the SEC permitted securities to be issued by crowdfunders.

U.S. NON-SECURITIES CROWDFUNDING

Crowdfunding platforms exist in approximately 30 countries throughout the world, with the U.S. having by far the most platforms.[8]

The most successful non-securities crowdfunder was neither Pebble Watch nor SCiO. Ryan Grepper, age 39, raised a whopping $13.28 million from 62,642 backers in mid-2014 for what he called the Coolest Cooler, a new kind of cooler which comes with a built-in blender, waterproof Bluetooth speaker, USB charger and a predicted price tag of $399.[9]

It is not necessary to raise a enormous amount of money through crowdfunding in order to create a valuable business. Palmer Luckey, at age 19, raised $2.4 million from Kickstarter in non-securities crowdfunding in 2012 for his Oculus Rift, a new type of virtual reality headset. Between 2012 and 2013, his entity received private equity financing. On March 25, 2014, Facebook acquired Oculus Rift for $2 billion.[10]

---

[8] http://www.statista.com/statistics/251573/number-of-crowdfunding-platforms-world-wide-by-country/; See also http://thesoholoft.com/global-list-of-crowdfunding-sites/. [Accessed on September 1, 2014]

[9] C. Rouvalis, "The Big Chill," hemispheremagazine.com, February 2015.

[10] S. Kovach, "Facebook Buys Oculus VR For $2 Billion," Business Insider, March 25, 2014, http://www.businessinsider.com/facebook-to-buy-oculus-rift-for-2-billion-2014-3; [Accessed on September 1, 2014] See also, L. Benedictus, "Why Oculus's $2bn Sale to

According to the Massolution, 2015CF Crowdfunding Industry Report ("Report")[11] prior to the adoption of the Section 4(a)(6) crowdfunding rules, crowdfunding was generally lending-based, reward-based, donation-based, lending-based, royalty-based, equity-based (outside the U.S.), and hybrid.[12] The Report states that reward-based crowdfunding is a model where funders receive a "reward," such as a token or a manufactured product sample, and it defines donation-based crowdfunding as a model where funders donate to causes that they want to support, with no expected compensation or return on their investment. Lending-based refers to peer-to-peer lending. According to the 2015 Report, approximately $1.6 billion in financing was raised worldwide through crowdfunding platforms during 2014, with over half of that amount raised in the U.S.

More than a decade before the passage of the JOBS Act in 2012, new companies were raising capital in the U.S. using non-securities crowdfunding, but were unable to issue investment securities as a reward because of U.S. securities laws. Other countries, such as the United Kingdom, were far more advanced in permitting investment securities to be issued through funding portals.[13] The U.S. has now caught up.

Facebook Sparks Fury from Kickstarter Funders," theguardian.com, March 26, 2014; See also, R. Mitchell, "Oculus Rift: From $2.4 million Kickstarter to $2 billion Sale," Joystiq. com; http://www.joystiq.com/2014/03/28/oculus-rift-from-2-4-million-kickstarter-to-2-billion-sale/, March 28, 2014; http://www.theguardian.com/technology/short-cuts/2014/mar/26/oculus-rift-facebook-fury-kickstarter-funders. [Accessed on September 1, 2014]

[11] See Massolution, *2015CF Crowdfunding Industry Report: Market Trends, Composition and Crowdfunding Platforms, available at* http://reports.crowdsourcing.org/index.php?route=product/product&product_id=54 ("Massolution 2015") at 56.

[12] The Massolution Report does not identify which jurisdictions were represented in the survey. For example, France, Italy, Japan, and the U.K. have adopted specialized equity crowdfunding regimes.

[13] The United Kingdom has for some time permitted investment securities to be issued through its crowdfunding platforms. See Crowdfunding Industry Report, Phase 1, December 2013. According to the report, £263 million have been raised for small and medium enterprises in the form of debt or equity as of October 2013, p. 8.

As this book is being written, three of the top non-securities crowd-funding sites are[14]:

- www.kickstarter.com;
- www.indiegogo.com;
- www.gofundme.com.

Prior to the adoption of the SEC securities crowdfunding rules under Section 4(a)(6), the vast majority of U.S. crowdfunding projects sought charitable or artistic donations.[15] The crowdfunding site "GoFundMe" permits funding for personal items such as pleas for tuition assistance, breast augmentation, mastectomies, school trips and pet surgeries.[16] Many sites, such as Kickstarter, also raised capital for businesses, primarily using product preorders (usually with a price discount) and prizes such as T-shirts as a reward for contributors who pledged funds. Hollywood films have been financed through Kickstarter, such as "Veronica Mars" and "Wish I was Here," with the latter movie receiving over $3 million of pledges from over 46,000 backers. However, investment securities could not be part of the reward to contributors prior to the adoption of these new SEC rules.

The following are two examples of successful non-securities crowdfunding, using products as rewards for contributors: Pebble watch and SCiO.

PEBBLE WATCH — U.S. NON-SECURITIES CROWDFUNDING

A successful crowdfunding to date was accomplished by Pebble Technology Corp., currently located in Palo Alto, California, which offered the Pebble watch for sale on Kickstarter. The Pebble watch is a smart watch which connects wirelessly to smartphones and serves as an

---

[14] http://crowdfundingpr.wordpress.com/2013/06/12/crowdfunding-press-center-releases-the-first-global-100-crowdfunding-site-index/. [Accessed on September 1, 2014]

[15] E. Jollick, "The dynamics of crowdfunding: An exploratory study," The Wharton School of the University of Pennsylvania (August 13, 2013).

[16] S. Melamed, "High-Tech Panhandling?," The Philadelphia Inquirer, January 14, 2015, C-1.

on-the-wrist notification center.[17] The founder of the Pebble watch, Eric Migicovsky, initially approached 10 venture capitalists in Silicon Valley, and was rejected by all.[18] He then posted the watch on Kickstarter and reached his funding goal of $100,000 within a few hours.[19] Ultimately, he raised more than $10 million from close to 69,000 backers.[20]

Some features of the Pebble watch, depending on its style, are as follows:

- View notifications from e-mail, SMS, Caller ID, calendar, and your favorite apps on your wrist.
- Download watch faces and apps to suit your style and interests.
- Control music playing on iTunes, Spotify, Pandora, and more.
- Rechargeable battery lasts five to seven days on a single charge.
- Compatible with both Apple and Android devices.

Below are a few rewards offered by Pebble Technology to its contributors:

---

[17] W. M. Cunningham, "The JOBS Act" (Apress, 2012), p. 39.
[18] L. Segall, "$7 Million Pebble Watch Shatters Kickstarter Records," CNN.com, May 2, 2012.
[19] *Id.*
[20] *Id.*

"Pledge: $99 or more":

"EARLY BIRDS" Help us get started! One Jet Black Pebble watch. This Watch will retail for more than $150. Free shipping to USA (add $10 for shipping to Canada, $15 for international shipping).

· · ·

"Pledge: $240 or more":

"TWO PEBBLES" in any color (choose from Arctic White, Cherry Red, Voter's choice, or Jet Black). Free shipping to USA (add $10 for shipping to Canada, $15 for international shipping).

· · ·

"Pledge $1,250 or more":

"CUSTOM WATCHFACE" Let us create a custom watchface precisely to your specifications! Send us your ideas and we will design a watchface just for you. You will also receive five Color Pebble watches so you and your friends can share the fun. Free shipping to USA (add $10 for shipping to Canada. $15 for international shipping).

SCiO EXAMPLE — INTERNATIONAL NON-SECURITIES CROWDFUNDING

A second way to understand non-securities crowdfunding is to examine an international project which raised, before the new SEC rules, close to $3 million from approximately 13,000 backers without offering any debt or equity securities to the backers.

An Israel-based company, Consumer Physics Inc., sold SCiO, a USB-sized sensor that identifies the chemical make-up of food and sends it directly to a smartphone. The company was founded by Dror Sharon and Damian Goldring, who met each other while pursuing degrees in electrical engineering at the Technion — Israel Institute of Technology.

SCiO is a handheld device which scans the molecular fingerprint of a physical matter and immediately provides information about it such as protein, nutrients, and calories in any food. It claims to be able to also measure how ripe a fruit is even without peeling it.

SCiO stated on the Kickstarter website as follows: SCiO "is the world's first affordable molecular sensor that fits in the palm of your hand. SCiO is a tiny spectrometer and allows you to get instant relevant information about the chemical make-up of just about anything around you, sent directly to your smartphone ... Out of the box, when you get your SCiO, you'll be able to analyze food, plants, and medications. For example you can:

- Get nutritional facts about different kinds of food: salad dressings, sauces, fruits, cheeses, and much more.
- See how ripe an Avocado is, through the peel!
- Find out the quality of your cooking oil.
- Know the well-being of your plants.
- Analyze soil or hydroponic solutions.
- Authenticate medications or supplements.
- Upload and tag the spectrum of any material on Earth to our database."

Below is a picture of the SCiO:

In order to induce contributors to pledge money, it is typical to grant certain rewards to pledgors. Prior to the adoption of the SEC's crowdfunding regulations under the JOBS Act, these rewards to contributors were generally related to discounts on sales of the product. The rewards offered by SCiO could not include debt or equity security since the SCiO offering preceded the adoption of the SEC's crowdfunding rules.

SCiO REWARD LEVELS

Below are the rewards offered by SCiO in connection with raising the approximately $3 million on Kickstarter:

Big Thanks	:)	$1
SCiO T-Shirt		$35
Super Early Birds		$149 SOLD OUT
Early Birds		$179 SOLD OUT
Early Adopters		$199 ALL GONE
Makers kit II		$201 ALL GONE
Kickstarter Special & Limited Edition		$299 ALL GONE
Get SCiO		$299
Early Beta Adopters		$399
Early Developers		$399 ALL GONE
Hacker & Researcher Special		$999 ALL GONE
Educational Kit	10X / 1X	$2499
Superstar Backers		$3,000
Partner Support		$10,000 ALL GONE

For example, the award levels below for a pledge of $999–$2,499 and $10,000 or more, respectively, are described as follows:

"Pledge $999–$2,499":

"HACKER & RESEARCH SPECIAL — GET THE DEVELOPER PACKAGE — You will get early access to the ADK and we will send you one of the first prototype SCiO in November 20 you can get started coding and building applications. You will also receive another SCiO when the full batch ships. You get FREE download of any SCiO app we will develop in the next two years."

...

"Pledge $10,000 or more":

"PARTNER WITH US. Let us start a dialogue on how we can form a business relationship. You will be invited to have dinner with the founders in San Francisco (Travel and Accommodations not included). You will be among the first group in the world outside of our team to have access to the SCiO developer's kit. We will seek your feedback to improve our future designs. Of course, you will also receive an SCiO when it is available. Free shipping anywhere in the world. PLEASE NOTE: Subject to Kickstarter's guidelines — this reward DOES NOT offer you any shares of the company."

HOW DOES KICKSTARTER WORK FOR NON-SECURITIES CROWDFUNDING[21]

Kickstarter is a funding platform for creative projects, including films, games, music, art, design, and technology. Even gourmet potato salad raised capital on Kickstarter. The "Veronica Mars" movie project was funded to the tune of $5.7 million. Kickstarter claims that, since its launch on April 28, 2009, over $2 billion has been pledged by 9.7 million people,

---

[21] See generally, D. Steinberg, "The Kickstarter Handbook: Real-Life Crowdfunding Success Stories," Quirk Books (2012); See also C. Huston, "How to Prepare for Crowdfunding," The Wall Street Journal, February 3, 2014.

for funding more than 94,830 creative projects. These projects could not, prior to the adoption of the SEC rules, legally include investment securities as part of the rewards to pledgors.

An entrepreneur must set a funding goal with Kickstarter, i.e., how much money the entrepreneur is actually going to ask for from contributors. With Kickstarter, if the entrepreneur fails to make his or her funding goal, nothing is received from contributors. Therefore, setting too high a funding goal is dangerous. Likewise, setting too low a funding goal might result in a funding slowdown once the goal is reached. However, that is not always the case.

For example, the "Exploding Kittens" game passed its initial funding goal of $10,000 in the first eight minutes of the campaign. It was 1,000% funded in the first hour. "Exploding Kittens" is a card game "where players try to avoid drawing a card in which a cat innocently sets off an explosion by walking across a keyboard and launching a nuclear bomb, or chewing on a grenade."[22]

In order for a contributor to pledge for a project, he or she must click the green "Back This Project" button on any project page. The contributor would then be asked to enter a pledge amount and select a reward tier. For U.S.-based projects, the contributor would go through the Amazon checkout process. For projects launched outside of the U.S., the contributor would checkout through Kickstarter. To complete a pledge toward any project, the contributor would need to have and be logged into a Kickstarter account.

If a project in the U.S. is successfully funded, Kickstarter will apply a 5% fee to the funds raised and Amazon will apply credit card processing fees (about 3–5%). If the funding is not successful, there are no fees. Fees for other countries vary and are contained on the Kickstarter website.

The contributor's pledged amount is only available to the project creator, according to Kickstarter. The pledgor's amount is not publicly displayed.

Project creators will see the contributor's Kickstarter name, the pledge amount, and the reward selected. If the funding succeeds, Kickstarter gives the creator the e-mail address of the contributor.

---

[22] J. Bischoff, "A Card Game About Exploding Kittens Broke a Kickstarter Record," Newsweek.com, February 2, 2015.

Kickstarter sends an e-mail to each contributor when the funding period ends, no matter whether the funding was successful or not.

If a proposed contributor has questions about a project, there is an "Ask a Question" button at the bottom of each project page. This sends the question directly to the project creator. A contributor could, if he or she wishes, make the question public and post a comment on the project. The creator is notified by e-mail when this is done.

The contributor can change his or her reward level, but that does not automatically change the pledge amount. It is technically possible for the contributor to cancel the pledged amount, but that is discouraged.

It is the responsibility of the project creator to fulfill the promises of his or her project. Kickstarter claims that it reviews projects to ensure that they do not violate its rules. However, Kickstarter does not investigate a creator's ability to finish their project.

Sometimes, when a project is overfunded, Kickstarter lets the creator put that money back into the project to create something better for the backers and the company. In other cases, overfunding leads to better margins and the creator may even profit from the project.

Kickstarter provides an FAQ section on its website for entrepreneurs which should be consulted before its use.[23]

It is not yet clear how Kickstarter will operate after the new SEC rules. Stay tuned!

WHAT IS THE EFFECT OF ADDING INVESTMENT SECURITIES TO THE REWARDS?

With the adoption of the SEC crowdfunding rules, businesses can now add higher reward levels and add debt and equity securities to their rewards. For example, the SCiO could now create a $50,000 or more or $100,000 or more contributor level and add debt or equity securities to the rewards. However, in order to do so, Consumer Physics Inc., the owner of SCIO, would have to first create a U.S. entity with its principal office in the U.S. to engage in securities crowdfunding and likely will be required to direct, control and coordinate their activities in the U.S. The debt or

---

[23] www.kickstarters.com. [Accessed on September 1, 2014]

equity securities of the U.S. entity, or its Israeli affiliate, could be issued either alone or in combination with the product rewards.

However, under the SEC crowdfunding rules, no more than $1 million could be raised in any 12-month period from the sale of securities. There would be nothing to prevent the U.S. affiliate of Consumer Physics Inc., the owner of SCiO, from raising, through product pre-orders, more than $1 million in a 12-month period so long as they do not exceed the $1 million limit on securities sales in any rolling 12-month period. Moreover, once the 12-month period had expired, there is nothing to prevent them from again raising $1 million from sales of debt and equity securities in the next 12-month period plus an unlimited amount from preorders of products.

In order to use a platform such as Kickstarter, the platform would have to qualify as a registered broker or a registered funding portal as described in a subsequent section of this chapter.

CROWDFUNDING SITES

There are a variety of crowdfunding sites available on the Internet in addition to Kickstarter. There are sites for musicians, charities, and also separate sites for business owners.

For example, Crowdfunder.com ("Crowdfunder") claims that it is the crowdfunding platform for businesses, with a social network of investors, tech start-ups, small businesses, and social enterprises, which include both financially sustainable/profitable businesses with social impact objectives. Crowdfunder offers a blend of donation-based and investment crowdfunding from individuals and angel investors, and claims to be a leading participant in the development of the JOBS Act. Crowdfunder provides "The Equity Crowdfunding Campaign Success Guide" on its website.[24]

Other crowdfunding sites for businesses include Indiegogo.com and AngelList.com. A search of the Internet for crowdfunding sites that specialize in raising capital under the JOBS Act will reveal many more such sites.

---

[24]www.crowdfunder.com. See also www.startengine.com. [Accessed on September 1, 2014]

In order to serve as a securities crowdfunding intermediary, the site must register with the SEC either as a securities broker or as a funding portal. The JOBS Act requires these intermediaries to, among other things:

- Provide disclosures that the SEC determines appropriate by rule, including regarding the risks of the transaction and investor education materials;
- Ensure that each investor: (1) reviews investor education materials; (2) positively affirms that the investor understands that the investor is risking the loss of the entire investment, and that the investor could bear such a loss; and (3) answers questions that demonstrate that the investor understands the level of risk generally applicable to investments in start-ups, emerging businesses, and small issuers and the risk of illiquidity;
- Take steps to protect the privacy of information collected from investors;
- Take such measures to reduce the risk of fraud with respect to such transactions, as established by the SEC, by rule, including obtaining a background and securities enforcement regulatory history check on each officer, director, and person holding more than 20% of the outstanding equity of every issuer whose securities are offered by such person;
- Make available to investors and the SEC, at least 21 days before any sale, any disclosures provided by the issuer;
- Ensure that all offering proceeds are only provided to the issuer when the aggregate capital raised from all investors is equal to or greater than a target offering amount, and allow all investors to cancel their commitments to invest;
- Make efforts to ensure that no investor in a 12-month period has purchased crowdfunded securities that in the aggregate, from all issuers, exceed the investment limits set forth in Section Title III of the JOBS Act; and
- Any other requirements that the SEC determines are appropriate.[25]

All funding portals must become members of a national securities association that is registered under Section 15A of the Securities Exchange

---

[25] "Jumpstart Our Business Startups Act. Frequently Asked Questions About Crowdfunding Intermediaries," U.S. Securities and Exchange Commission, Division of Trading and Markets, May 7, 2012.

Act of 1934 Act ("1934 Act"), in addition to registering with the SEC. Financial Industry Regulatory Authority ("FINRA") is currently the only national securities association in existence which is registered under Section 15A of the 1934 Act.

To qualify as a funding portal under the JOBS Act, the portal is not permitted to:

- Offer investment advice or make recommendations;
- Solicit purchases, sales, or offers to buy the securities offered or displayed on its platform;
- Compensate employees, agents, or other persons for such solicitation or based on the sale of the securities displayed or referenced on its platform;
- Hold, manage, possess, or otherwise handle investor funds or securities; or
- Engage in any other activities the SEC determines to prohibit in its crowdfunding rulemaking.[26]

Each crowdfunding broker and funding portal is prohibited under the JOBS Act from, among other things:

- Compensating promoters, finders, or lead generators for providing the intermediary with the personal identifying information of any potential investor; or
- Allowing its directors, officers, or partners (or any person occupying a similar status or performing a similar function) to have a financial interest in any issuer using the services of the intermediary.[27]

INELIGIBLE ISSUERS

The Section 4(a)(6) crowdfunding exemption does not apply to transactions involving the offer or sale of securities by any "issuer," as defined below, that:

- Is not organized under, and subject to, the laws of a state or territory of the U.S. or the District of Columbia;

---

[26] *Id.*
[27] *Id.*

- Is subject to the requirement to file reports pursuant to Section 13 or Section 15(d) of the 1934 Act, so-called public companies;
- Is an investment company, as defined in Section 3 of the Investment Company Act of 1940, or is excluded from the definition of investment company by Section 3(b) or Section 3(c) of that Act;
- Is not eligible to offer or sell securities in reliance on the crowdfunding exemption contained in Section 4(a)(6) of the 1933 Act as a result of a disqualification under the so-called "Bad Boy" rule (a substantially similar "Bad Boy" rule is described in Chapter 3);
- Has sold securities in reliance on Section 4(a)(6) of the 1933 Act and has not filed with the SEC and provided to investors, to the extent required, the ongoing annual reports required by this part during the two years immediately preceding the filing of the required SEC Offering Statement; or
- Has no specific business plan or has indicated that its business plan is to engage in a merger or acquisition with an unidentified company or companies.

The term "issuer," as noted, includes all entities controlled by or under common control with the issuer. It also includes any predecessor of the issuer. An entity is controlled by or under common control with the issuer if the issuer possesses, directly or indirectly, the power to direct or cause the direction of the management and policies of the entity, whether through the ownership of voting securities, by contract or otherwise.

HOW DO YOU COMPUTE THE $1 MILLION SECURITIES CROWDFUNDING LIMITATION?

The $1 million aggregate amount limitation for securities crowdfunding under Section 4(a)(6) is computed as follows: First, the issuer includes any amount sold by the issuer in reliance on Section 4(a)(6) during the preceding 12-month period. Second, the issuer would have to add in all amounts sold in reliance on Section 4(a)(6) by entities controlled by the issuer or under common control with the issuer, as well as any amounts sold in reliance on Section 4(a)(6) by any predecessor of the issuer in reliance on crowdfunding during the preceding 12-month period. Third, the issuer would then have to aggregate any amounts computed under the first and second sentences above, with the amount the issuer intends to raise in reliance on the Section 4(a)(6) exemption, and the combined amount could not exceed $1 million.

For example, if the issuer, together with entities controlled by or under common control with the issuer or its predecessor, sold $800,000 in a crowdfunding transaction pursuant to Section 4(a)(6) during the preceding 12 months, the issuer would be required to count that amount toward the $1 million aggregate amount. Thus, the issuer could only offer and sell $200,000 more in reliance on Section 4(a)(6) securities crowdfunding.[28]

An issuer would not be required to include amounts sold in other exempt securities offerings during the preceding 12-month period, such as sales solely to accredited investors under Rule 506(c) discussed in Chapters 2 and 3. However, a company conducting a concurrent exempt offering for which general solicitation is not permitted (such as Rule 506(b)), will need to be satisfied that the purchasers in that offering were not solicited by means of Section 4(a)(6) securities crowefunding.[29] Likewise, the issuer would not need to consider amounts received through methods that do not involve the offer or sale of securities, such as donations it received from a separate non-securities-based crowdfunding effort. Thus, for example, it is possible to raise $5 million in an exempt non-securities crowdfunding and still raise $1 million in Section 4(a)(6) securities crowdfunding.

DISCLOSURE REQUIREMENTS AND ONGOING REPORTING OBLIGATIONS

There are three major disclosure and filing requirements and ongoing reporting obligations for companies wishing to use Section 4(a)(6) securities crowdfunding. All of the filing are made on Form C which is reproduced in Appendix 3 of this book. These documents must be filed on the SEC's EDGAR system, which requires an identification number obtainable by filing Form 1D, as well as:

* Form C — Offering Statements and Amendments. This form, reproduced in Appendix 3, contains the Offering Statement with a long

---

[28] SEC Rel. 33-9470, p. 18.
[29] *Id.*

laundry list of required information and must be filed with the SEC on EDGAR prior to offering or selling securities under the Section 4(a)(6) crowdfunding provisions. This portion of Form C may be created in an optional Q&A format. This form must also be provided to investors, potential investors, and the relevant intermediary, namely the registered broker or the funding portal. The actual information required for this form is contained in Regulation 227.201 of the SEC crowdfunding regulations. The Offering Statement must disclose that the company will file a report with the SEC annually and post the report on its website not later than 120 days after its fiscal year end and also disclose how the company may terminate its reporting obligations in the future. Amendments to the Offering Statement reflecting any material change must also be filed on this form under the titled Form C/A.

- Form C-U (Progress Updates). A company must file with the SEC on EDGAR, provide to investors and to the relevant registered broker or funding portal, and make available to potential investors a Form C: Progress Update (Form C-U) to disclose its progress in meeting the target offering amount no later than five business days after the issuer reaches 50% and 100% of the target offering amount, subject to an exception if the intermediary reports. If the issuer will accept proceeds in excess of the target offering amount, the issuer must file with the SEC on EDGAR, provide to investors and the relevant intermediary, and make available to potential investors, no later than five business days after the offering deadline, a final Form C-U to disclose the total amount of securities sold in the offering.
- Form C-AR: Annual Report. A company that has sold securities in reliance on the crowdfunding regulations must file and post on its website an annual report on this form no later than 120 days after the end of the fiscal year covered by the report. The annual report must include the laundry list of information required by the SEC under its Regulation 227.202(a).

There is another filing on Form C-TR required within five business days from the date the company is no longer required to file reports under the Section 4(a)(6) crowdfunding regulations because any of the following has happened: (a) the company has become a public company required to file reports under Section 13(a) or Section 15(b) of the 1934 Act; or (b) the company has filed, since its most recent sale under Section 4(a)(6), at least one annual report and has fewer than 300 holders of record; or (c) the company has filed, since its most recent sale under Section 4(a)(6), the annual reports for at least the three most recent years and has total assets that do not exceed $10 million; or (d) the company or another party repurchases all of the securities issued in reliance Section 4(a)(6), including any payment in full of debt securities or any complete redemption of redeemable securities; or (e) the issuer liquidates or dissolves its business in accordance with state law.[30]

Subject to the forgoing, the annual reporting obligations continue so long as even one crowdfunding share remains outstanding.

Strategy: Consideration should be given to creating crowdfunding securities which permit the company or another party, through an option or a call right, to repurchase these securities at any time for their fair market value. For example, a venture capitalist might wish the company to effectuate such a repurchase prior to making its investment in order to avoid minority shareholders in the company and the expense of further public disclosures by the company.

COMPANIES WILL NEED A U.S. SECURITIES LAWYER TO ASSIST IT

It is clear that the laundry list of information required in the Form C Offering Statements and Amendments will require the help of a U.S. securities lawyer to prepare. The company must be prepared to answer many questions whose answers are not obvious to the average layperson. Examples of such questions include the following:

- A discussion of the material factors that make an investment in the issuer speculative or risky;
- The terms of the securities being offered and each other class of securities of the issuer, including the number of securities being offered and/or outstanding, whether or not such securities have voting rights, any limitations on such voting rights, how the terms of the securities being

---

[30] SEC Reg. 227.202(b).

offered may be modified and a summary of the differences between such securities and each other class of security of the issuer, and how the rights of the securities being offered may be materially limited, diluted, or qualified by the rights of any other class of security of the issuer;

- How the securities being offered are being valued, and examples of methods for how such securities may be valued by the issuer in the future, including during subsequent corporate actions;
- The risks to purchasers of the securities relating to minority ownership in the issuer and the risks associated with corporate actions including additional issuances of securities, issuer repurchases of securities, a sale of the issuer, or of assets of the issuer or transactions with related parties; and
- A description of any transaction since the beginning of the issuer's last full fiscal year, or any currently proposed transaction, to which the issuer or any entities controlled by or under common control with the issuer was or is to be a party and the amount involved exceeds 5% of the aggregate amount of capital raised by the issuer under the Section 4(a)(6) crowdfunding exemption during the preceding 12-month period, inclusive of the amount the issuer seeks to raise in the current securities crowdfunding offering, in which any of the following persons had or is to have a direct or indirect material interest:

  o Any director or officer of the issuer;
  o Any person who is, as of the most recent practicable date, the beneficial owner of 20% or more of the issuer's outstanding voting equity securities, calculated on the basis of voting power;
  o If the issuer was incorporated or organized within the past three years, any promoter of the issuer; and
  o Any immediate family member of any of the foregoing persons, which means any child, stepchild, parent, stepparent, spouse, sibling, mother-in-law, father-in-law, son-in-law, daughter-in-law, brother-in-law, or sister-in-law of the person, and any persons (other than a tenant or employee) sharing the household of the person.

The term "issuer" is not limited to just the company. As previously noted, the term includes all entities controlled by or under common control with the issuer and any predecessor of the issuer. An entity is controlled by or under common control with the issuer if the issuer possesses, directly or indirectly, the power to direct or cause the direction of the management and policies of the entity, whether through the ownership of voting securities, by contract or otherwise.

COMPANIES WILL NEED AN ACCOUNTANT TO ASSIST IT

One of the items required in the Form C Offering Statements is a description of the financial condition of the issuer. This discussion must include, to the extent material, the issuer's liquidity, capital resources and historical results of operations. For issuers with no prior operating history, the description should include a discussion of financial milestones and operational, liquidity, and other challenges. For issuers with an operating history, the discussion should address whether historical earnings and cash flows are representative of what investors should expect in the future. Issuers must take into account the proceeds of the offering and any other known or pending sources of capital. Issuers must also discuss how the proceeds from the offering will impact the issuer's liquidity, and whether receiving these funds and any other additional funds is necessary to the viability of the business. In addition, issuers must describe the other available sources of capital to the business, such as lines of credit or required contributions by shareholders.

Moreover, if the offering, together with all other Section 4(a)(6) crowdfunding offerings within the preceding 12-month period, have, in the aggregate, target offering amounts of more than $500,000, financial statements of first-time issuers must be reviewed (but are required to be audited for non-first-time issuers) by a public accountant who is independent of the issuer in accordance with the Statements on Standards for Accounting and Review Services Committee of the American Institute of Certified Public Accountants ("AICPA"). If audited financial statements are available or required (i.e., non-first-time issuers), the audit must satisfy auditing standards issued by either the AICPA or the U.S. Public Company Accounting Oversight Board ("PCAOB"). Financial statements must include a balance sheet, income statement, statement of cash flows and statement of changes in owners' equity, and notes to the financial statements prepared in accordance with U.S.

Generally Accepted Accounting Principles (U.S. GAAP). The required financial statements must cover the shorter of the two most recently completed fiscal years or the period since inception.

If the target offering amount is more than $100,000 but not more than $500,000, financial statements must be reviewed by a public accountant who is independent of the issuer, using the Statements on Standards for Accounting and Review Services issued by the Accounting and Review Services Committee of the AICPA.

If the target offering amount is $100,000 or less, specific information must be provided from the federal income tax returns must be provided which were filed by the issuer for the most recently completed year (if any). In addition, and financial statements of the issuer, which must be certified by the principal executive officer of the issuer to be true and complete in all material respects, must be provided.

A complete description of the required financial information is contained in Appendix 3 of this book (Form C and related forms), particularly Question 29.

ESTIMATED COST OF SECTION 4(a)(6) CROWDFUNDING

The SEC has published (Table 1.2), which summarizes its estimate of the cost of complying with its Section 4(a)(6) crowdfunding rules. The author. considers this table as underestimating the cost of compliance and certain commenters to the SEC made similar comments with respect to the estimated cost in the proposing release. As a result, the SEC eliminated the requirement of audit financial statements for first-time issuers relying on Section 4(a)(6). However, in the author's opinion, the costs continue to be underestimated in this table, particularly the legal costs.

The SEC table does not include costs to (1) obtain EDGAR access codes on From ID; (2) prepare and file progress updates on From C-U; and (3) prepare and file Form C-TR to terminate ongoing reporting. For purposes of the above table, the SEC estimated the ranges of fees that an issuer would pay the intermediary assuming the following: (1) the fees

Table 1.2. SEC Cost Estimates

	Offerings of $100,000 or less	Offerings of more than $100,000, but not more than $500,000	Offerings of more than $500,000
Fees paid to the intermediary	$2,500–$7,500	$15,000–$30,000	$37,500–$56,250
Cost per issuer for preparation and filing of Form C for each offering and related compliance costs	$2,500	$2500–$5,000	$5,000–$20,000
Cost per issuer for preparation and filing of annual report for Form C-AR and related compliance costs	$1,667	$1,667–$3,333	$3,333–$13,333
Costs per issuer for review or audit of financial statements	Not required	$1,500–$18,000	$2,500–$30,000 ($1,500–$18,000 for first-time issuers raising more than $500,000 but not more than $1,000,000)

would be calculated as a percentage of the offering amount ranging from 5% to 15% of the total offering amount for offerings of

It is the author's view that a significant portion of the $1 million initially raised under Section 4(a)(6) securities crowdfunding regulations will be spent on commissions to the registered broker or funding portal and the cost of SEC compliance.

The SEC estimates the cost of outside counsel at a rate of $400 an hour, which is substantially below the current rate for an experienced securities lawyer. The total cost of external professionals was estimated in the SEC's final release at only $10,000.[32]

---

[31] SEC Rel. No. 33-9975, p. 415.
[32] *Id.* at 505.

However, the securities crowdfunding regulations permit up to a maximum of $1 million to be raised in any 12-month period. This permits a much greater portion of the proceeds of the second 12-month crowdfunding raise to be retained by the company, even if there are additional costs for an audit. Moreover, there is nothing to prevent the company from also offering product rewards (such as the Pebble Watch and SCiO offering) at the same time as the securities crowdfunding, thereby substantially increasing the total funds raised.

Finally, there is nothing to prevent the company from selling securities in unlimited amounts to accredited investors pursuant to Rule 506(c) (discussed in Chapters 2 and 3), including accredited investors who pledged funds in the product crowdfunding process or who were introduced to them by the crowdfunding intermediary, i.e., the registered broker or funding portal operator. It should be noted that the SEC has specifically stated that offerings under Rule 506(c), as well as other exempt offerings not under the crowdfunding regulations, would not be integrated for purposes of computing the $1 million limitation provided each offering complied with the applicable exemption.[33]

ADVERTISING

An issuer is not permitted to advertise, directly or indirectly, the terms of a Section 4(a)(6) crowdfunding offering. The only exception is for notices that direct investors to the intermediary's platform and contains only certain prescribed information.[34]

PROMOTER COMPENSATION

An issuer is permitted to compensate or commit to compensate, directly or indirectly, any person to promote its Section 4(a)(6) crowdfunding offerings through communication channels provided by an intermediary on the intermediary's platform. However, the issuer must take reasonable steps to ensure that the promoter clearly discloses the receipt, past

---

[33] SEC Rel. No. 33-9974, p. 19.
[34] SEC Regulation 227.204.

or prospective, of such compensation with any such communication, regardless of whether the compensation is specifically for the promotional activities. Except as noted above, an issuer or person acting on its behalf, cannot compensate or commit to compensate, directly or indirectly, any person to promote the issuer's Section 4(a)(6) offering, subject to a limited exception.[35]

RESTRICTIONS ON RESALE: PUBLIC TRADING MARKET

Securities issued pursuant to crowdfunding cannot be transferred by the purchaser during the one-year period beginning on the date of purchase, subject to four exceptions described below. However, after one year, there is nothing to prevent a U.S. public trading market from developing in the crowdfunding security if there is sufficient trading interest. As described more fully in Chapter 4, a securities broker or dealer could after the one-year period become a market-maker in the security after satisfying certain filing and information requirements. This would permit the security could be traded in the U.S. over-the-counter (OTC) market (exclusive of the OTC Bulletin Board), which does not require that the company be an SEC reporting company.

Crowdfunding companies can create markets in their own securities, without a broker-dealer, by matching investors who want to buy with those who wish to sell. These companies could attempt to avoid broker-dealer registration requirements by not taking any compensation for performing this service for their investors and staying within an SEC safe harbor (SEC Rule 3a4-1 under the 1934 Act) as described in Chapter 2 ("Avoiding Broker-Dealer Registration").

The four exceptions that permit a transfer prior to the end of the one-year period are as follows:

- Securities transferred to the issuer of the securities;
- Securities transferred to an accredited investor;

---

[35] SEC Regulation 227.205.

- Securities transferred as part of an offering registered with the SEC; or
- Securities transferred to a member of the family[36] of the purchaser or the equivalent, to a trust controlled by the purchaser, to a trust created for the benefit of a member of the family of the purchaser or the equivalent, or in connection with the death or divorce of the purchaser or other similar circumstance.

EXEMPTION FROM PUBLIC COMPANY REQUIREMENTS

The 1934 Act requires companies with assets exceeding $10 million and a class of securities held of record by either 2,000 persons or 500 non-accredited persons to register the class under Section 12 of that law. This registration is expensive and triggers all sorts of ongoing reporting obligations under the 1934 Act which are even more expensive.

Fortunately, persons holding Section 4(a)(6) crowdfunding securities do not count for purposes of computing the 2,000 persons and 500 non-accredited persons tests. The JOBS Act specifically exempted crowdfunding securities issued in compliance with Section 4(a)(6) of the 1933 Act from these tests, subject to certain conditions. These conditions require that the company be current in filing its ongoing annual reports, have total assets not in excess of $25 million as of the end of its most recently completed fiscal year, and have engaged a transfer agent registered under the 1934 Act to perform the function of a transfer agent with respect to these securities.

For example, this means that a crowdfunding company can have over 100,000 crowdfunding persons as shareholders who each purchased one share for $10, and the company itself could have over $10 million in assets and still be exempt from the expensive registration and reporting requirements applicable to public companies, provided the company satisfies the above conditions.[37]

---

[36]The term *member of the family of the purchaser or the equivalent* includes a child, stepchild, grandchild, parent, stepparent, grandparent, spouse or spousal equivalent, sibling, mother-in-law, father-in-law, son-in-law, daughter-in-law, brother-in-law, or sister-in-law of the purchaser, and includes adoptive relationships.

[37]See Section 303 of the JOBS Act and Section 12(g)(6) of the 1934 Act.

INTERMEDIARIES

The term "intermediaries" refers to registered securities brokers and registered funding portals through which the securities crowdfunding transaction is conducted. As noted, the securities crowdfunding transaction under Section 4(a)(6) must be conducted exclusively through the intermediary's platform.

Intermediaries are subject to very substantial regulations under the securities crowdfunding rules, some of which have been previously discussed. The details of those regulations some of which were mentioned previously, are beyond the scope of this book.

However, as noted, the issuer offering and selling securities under the crowdfunding provisions are entitled to rely on the efforts of the intermediary to ensure that the aggregate amount of securities purchased by an investor will not cause the investor to exceed the investment limits previously described, provided the issuer does not know the investor has exceeded the limits or would exceed the limits with issuer's offering.

An issuer is also not permitted to conduct an offering under the Section 4(a)(6) securities crowdfunding using more than one intermediary (i.e., registered broker or registered funding portal). However, there is nothing to prevent a company from simultaneously conducting a non-securities crowdfunding on Kickstarter and a securities crowdfunding on Crowdfunder.

CROWDFUNDING VERSUS RULE 506(c)

Securities crowdfunding under Section 4(a)(6) is filled with very prescriptive rules and funding limitations, which have been previously described. The major advantage of the Section 4(a)(6) crowdfunding rules is the ability to sell securities to eligible non-accredited investors and the ability to use popular Internet sites, such as Kickstarter (assuming Kickstarter elects to qualify as a registered funding portal), to access both accredited and non-accredited investors.

In contrast, Rule 506(c), discussed in Chapters 2 and 3, has no funding limitation and can be used by international companies without the necessity of creating a U.S. affiliate with its principal office in the U.S. However, securities can only be sold under Rule 506(c) to accredited investors.

As previously noted, a Rule 506(c) offering can be combined with a Section 4(a)(6) securities crowdfunding or a non-securities crowdfunding.

Table 1.3 is a comparison of fundraising under Section 4(a)(6) and Rule 506(c). Issuer liability to investors under Rule 506(c) is generally limited to fraud, whereas a negligence standard[38] applies to crowdfunders thereby making crowdfunders more susceptible to personal liability.

Table 1.3.   Fundraising under Section 4(a)(6) and Rule 506(c)

Qualification or activity	Section 4(a)(6)	Rule 506(c)
Qualified issuers	Only U.S. companies with their principal office in the U.S. which do not fall within the category of ineligible issuers.	Any issuer, whether international or U.S., that is not subject to the "Bad Boys" or "Bad Actors" prohibitions.
Amount that can be raised	Limited to $1 million during any 12-month period.	Unlimited.
Nature of investors	Can be accredited or non-accredited investors.	Only accredited investors.
Amount that each investor can invest	Limited in Amount.	Unlimited.
Manner of sale	Cannot use more than one intermediary and may not advertise terms, except for notices directing investors to the intermediary's platform.	Unlimited and includes any form of public advertising or general solicitation.
Restrictions on issuers	Not available to "Bad Boys" or "Bad Actors," non-U.S. issuers, SEC reporting companies, and investment companies. Cannot compensate any third party to promote crowdfunding unless disclosed.	None except, "Bad Boys" or "Bad Actors" prohibitions.
Restrictions on resale	One-year, with limited exceptions.	One year, with limited exceptions but can be as little as six months if the company is a reporting issuer.

---

[38] SEC Rel. No. 33-9974, p. 339. Section 4A(c)(3) of 1933 Act.

STATE CROWDFUNDING

A number of states within the U.S. have adopted a securities crowdfunding exemption from the registration provisions of their state's securities laws. For example, the State of Colorado adopted the Colorado Crowdfunding Act effective August 5, 2015. The purpose of these exemptions is to encourage companies, which are incorporated in, and doing business almost exclusively within the state,[39] to raise local funds through funding portals which limit offerings to state residents. A total of 29 states, plus the District of Columbia, have adopted these exemptions.

These state crowdfunding statutes are unlikely to be widely used because of the necessity of the company complying with the very narrow intrastate offering exemption from the registration provisions of 1933 Act.[40] The intrastate offering exemption is so restrictive that even a single offer to a non-resident investor will destroy the exemption. Consequently, it is unlikely that these state crowdfunding exemptions will become very popular. However, at least one state, namely Maine, has elected to permit sales pursuant to Rule 504 of Regulation D which is mentioned in Chapter 5 and does not limit solicitation and sales solely to the residents of Maine. At the time this book was written, the SEC had proposed amendments to both the intrastate offering exemption and Rule 504 which would liberalize these rules.

Chapter 2 will discuss the methods of marketing to accredited investors under Rule 506(c), which can be combined with a Section 4(a)(6) crowdfunding.

---

[39] See SEC Rule 147 which is a "safe harbor" for complying with the intrastate offering contained in Section 3(a)(11) of the 1933 Act and is currently proposed to be further liberalized.
[40] *Id.*

CHAPTER 2

MARKETING THE PUBLIC OFFERING UNDER RULE 506(c)

The purpose of this chapter is to discuss two separate issues:

- The business background of Rule 506(c).
- Marketing issues under Rule 506(c).

Chapter 3 will discuss the technical requirements to comply with Rule 506(c).

BUSINESS BACKGROUND

Effective September 23, 2013, the U.S. Securities and Exchange Commission ("SEC") permitted a relatively inexpensive public offering by both U.S. and international companies to raise capital from over 9 million U.S. accredited investors under SEC Rule 506(c). This new method of raising capital is relatively inexpensive because it permits use of crowdfunding as well as other marketing methods to solicit accredited investors with whom the company had no prior relationship. Crowdfunding Internet sites using the Rule 506(c) exemption include EquityNet, Crowdfunder, CircleUp, Wefunder.com, AngelList, EarlyShares and a host of others.

Most people would consider the solicitation of over 9 million accredited investors to be a public offering. However, the U.S. Congress in its wisdom deems this offering as not involving a public offering, and therefore exempted from the extremely expensive requirement to register the offering, so long as sales are made solely to accredited investors and their status as accredited investors is subjected to required verification.

For example, if an individual wanted to start his or her own business or expand an existing business, they could advertise their business on Facebook or Twitter, or purchase a list of accredited investors and solicit them for capital. They can set up a website touting the offering or purchase billboards, taxi signs, sandwich boards, or even send an e-mail to every person on earth without violating U.S. law. However, there are legal limitations on spam e-mail and cold calling to U.S. accredited investors which are discussed in this chapter, and any general solicitation must comply with the anti-fraud provisions of federal and state law.

EXAMPLE NO. 1

On January 9, 2014, a company called FBSciences Holdings, Inc. filed a Form D with the SEC which contemplated an offering under Rule 506(c). Form D, which is discussed in more detail in Chapter 3, is required to be filed within 15 days after the first "sale" of securities under Rule 506(c). (See Chapter 3 for definition of "sale.")

According to its website, FBSciences Holdings, Inc., located in Collierville, Tennessee, is a bioscience company with a global focus on improved crop yield and quality through improved plant health and efficiency. The company's website claims that its researchers have identified, extracted, and refined compounds, derived from natural sources, with unique power to distinctively improve crop health and crop productivity. The Form D indicated that the company had been formed over five years ago, but declined to disclose any financial information as is permitted by Form D.

The filing by FBSciences Holdings, Inc. was one of the earliest filings under Rule 506(c) and permitted the company to make a general solicitation to both accredited and non-accredited investors, provided sales were made only to accredited investors whose status was verified. Its Form D contemplated an offering of debt securities with warrants or other forms of equity options. The minimum investment accepted from any outside investor was $100,000 in debt securities. The total amount raised at the time of filing the Form D was $3.09 million out of a total contemplated offering of $4.59 million. Thus, when the Form D was filed by FBSciences Holdings,

Inc. on January 9, 2014, the company still needed to raise an additional $1.5 million in debt. This offering appears to be a direct public offering by the company, without the use of either a broker-dealer or an Internet portal.

The filing by FBSciences Holdings, Inc. is illustrative of the need by both middle-market and start-up companies to raise capital, both debt and equity, under Rule 506(c). These companies typically do not have the ability to obtain normal bank financing.

EXAMPLE NO. 2

On July 22, 2014, the owner of the Hard Rock Hotel Palm Springs closed on what is touted as the first major "crowdfunding" campaign for a U.S. hotel, having raised within 90 days more than $1.5 million from accredited investors who took an equity stake in the project.[1] The investor offering was actually made pursuant to the Rule 506(c) registration exemption since retail securities crowdfunding under Section 4(a)(6) was not legal in the U.S. on July 22, 2014 and the amount raised would have exceeded the retail securities crowdfunding limits in any event.

The funds were raised from investors through a website limited to accredited investors called "Realty Mogul" located at www.realtymogul. com. Realty Mogul advertises itself as providing "crowdfunding" for real estate and as a "marketplace for accredited investors to pool money online and buy shares of pre-screened real estate investments." Realty Mogul claims that it allows accredited investors to invest in real estate opportunities online through a private, secure website, allowing investors to browse investments, review legal documents and due diligence materials, and sign legal documents securely online. An entity called "Realty Mogul 20 LLC" filed the Form D for the project on June 20, 2014.

A total of 85 investors, with one investor putting up $150,000, invested over the 90-day period an aggregate of $1.5 million in the Hard Rock Hotel Palm Springs, with the minimum investor stake being $10,000. These funds were to be used to make improvements to the Hotel

---

[1] N. Rodriguez, "Calif. Hard Rock Brings in $1.5 M in 1st Equity "Crowdfunding," Law360, July 22, 2014, http://www.law360.com/articles/559681?utm_source=rss&utm_medium=rss&utm_campaign=articles_search. [Accessed on September 1, 2014]

which would include possibly upgrading a spa facility, adding a nightclub, or bringing in new entertainment acts.

The Hard Rock Hotel Palm Springs was one of many real estate projects advertised on the Realty Mogul website. Prior to the adoption of Rule 506(c), such general advertisements would have made the offering illegal under existing Rule 506(b).

To satisfy Rule 506(c), investors registering with Realty Mogul have to provide supporting documentation that proved they were an "accredited investor," including the verification requirement necessary to satisfy this new rule. The equity stakes in the hotel were sold by WealthForge LLC, a securities broker-dealer registered with the SEC.

The adoption by the SEC of Rule 506(c) thus provides both the U.S. and international company with a brand new alternative for publicly raising venture capital from U.S. accredited investors without the necessity of registering the securities under the 1933 Act. It is no longer necessary for the entrepreneur to have a preexisting substantive relationship with his or her investors and both general advertising and general solicitation of investors are now permitted.

MARKETING SECURITIES UNDER RULE 506(c)

Capital may now be publicly solicited under Rule 506(c) through social media from strangers as long as these strangers who do invest are accredited investors and their status is verified as described in Chapter 3. Social media can include not only the Internet but also television, mailings, newspaper advertisements, and billboards. E-mails can be sent to thousands of potential investors whose e-mail addresses are purchased from an Internet provider. A direct offering over the Internet is relatively inexpensive, thereby opening the door for both U.S. and international middle-market and start-up companies to raise capital.

Companies that wish to market their securities under Rule 506(c) have two major choices:

- Internet portals, many of which are sponsored by registered broker-dealers to market their services or, in the case of aceportal.com, in association with the NYSE.
- Direct offerings to accredited investors.

The advantage of using an Internet portal is that the portal usually provides verification services for accredited investors and markets the investment to accredited investors who have signed up for the portal. The disadvantage of the portal is that it may charge for featuring the company on the portal and will take a percentage of the funds raised. In addition, not all portals may be interested in featuring the company, since the broker-dealer sponsoring the portal may not be comfortable with promoting the investment.

Crowdfunding portals, such as Realty Mogul or Kickstarter, permit advertisement of a new project or product widely, and can generate investor interest in the company. This is true even if the crowdfunding does not offer securities to contributors, but only products. For example, the non-securities crowdfunding on Kickstarter by Oculus Rift for virtual reality headsets, mentioned in Chapter 1, may well have helped bring this company to the attention of private equity funds which subsequently financed the company. A company featured on a popular crowdfunding site will also help attract accredited investors to a Rule 506(c) offering.

Some of the Internet portals identify themselves as "crowdfunders" but do not limit themselves to the $1 million fundraising limit within a 12-month period on retail crowdfunding discussed in Chapter 1. Realty Mogul is an example. Many of the Internet portals specialize in investment in a particular industry. For example, HealthFundr.com claims that it allows accredited investors to easily get to know and invest in early- to growth-stage, health, and "medtech" companies. VentureHealth.com states that select physicians and other knowledgeable accredited investors are invited to participate in biomedical financings.

There are also Internet portals for accredited investors which are not limited to a specific industry such as FundersClub, Inc. which claims that it allows accredited investors to become equity holders in FundersClub-managed venture funds — which then fund pre-screened, private companies. ARCAngelFund.com states that it invests in seed- and early-stage companies with high growth potential, in which its members have experience, with investments averaging from $50,000 to $250,000, each, over the life of the investment. Other Internet platforms include: Fundable. com, CircleUp.com, ConfidentCrowd.com, GrowVC.com, to name a few. A more complete list can be found at www.crowdfundinsider.com.

Whether the company is using a funding portal or a direct offering to market its securities, the company will need an offering circular or prospectus to satisfy anti-fraud requirements of securities laws, a subscription agreement, and related legal documents. The offering circular or prospectus is typically reviewed by a U.S. securities lawyer, who also creates the other legal documentation. In addition, if the company elects a direct offering, the company must seek the advice of a U.S. securities attorney as to (a) the methods of verifying that the investors under a Rule 506(c) offering are actually accredited investors and (b) methods by which the company can avoid any requirement to register as a broker-dealer.

The entrepreneur need not limit the offering to solely equity securities of his or her entity. The securities sold may be, or include, promissory notes, possibly with a high yield to make them attractive to investors. The entrepreneur can also have his or her company offer warrants to purchase equity securities in the company, along with the promissory notes, in order to make the offering more attractive. There is no restriction on the type of security which can be offered and sold by the company under Rule 506(c) so long as the company is the issuer of that security.

THE EXCLUSIVITY SYNDROME

There are groups of accredited investors who will not invest in widely-advertised securities offerings and would automatically delete e-mails from strangers or treat them as spam. They prefer to only invest in securities offerings that are limited to selected wealthy individuals. Bernard Madoff, who created the largest Ponzi scheme in history, took advantage of this preference to be part of an exclusive group by initially (but not ultimately) rejecting certain potential investors who requested to invest with him, in order to create an aura of exclusivity.

Therefore, any general solicitation or marketing of securities should be tailored to take advantage of this preference for exclusivity. The exclusivity syndrome was humorously recognized by Groucho Marx, who is quoted, in rejecting membership in an elite private club, as saying "I don't want to belong to any club that will accept me as a member."

TWO MARKET STRATEGIES

There are two marketing strategies that are worth discussing to make a Rule 506(c) offering more attractive:

- to have a Rule 506(b) offering immediately before a Rule 506(c) offering; and
- to couple retail securities crowdfunding simultaneously with a Rule 506(c) offering, which has a lower valuation for the company than the retail securities crowdfunding.

From a strategy viewpoint, it may make sense to attempt to conduct a private offering under Rule 506(b) prior to conducting a public offering under Rule 506(c). The strategy would be to see how much capital could be raised in the Rule 506(b) private offering before commencing a Rule 506(c) offering. As noted, a private offering under Rule 506(b) requires the company or its solicitor to have a preexisting substantive relationship with the offeree and general solicitation or general advertising is prohibited. This clearly limits the number of persons who can be reached in a Rule 506(b) private offering.

However, the Rule 506(b) private offering has at least several significant advantages over a Rule 506(c) offering, to wit:

- The Rule 506(b) private offering creates an aura of exclusivity not present in the public Rule 506(c) offering, which may assist in sales of securities. This would be particularly true if the intention of the company to have a subsequent Rule 506(c) offering was mentioned in the offering circular and the subsequent offering was at a higher valuation.
- The verification of an accredited investor status is much simpler in a Rule 506(b) private offering. There may be potential investors who would not be willing to share personal financial information in a Rule 506(c) offering who would be willing to purchase in a more exclusive and less intrusive Rule 506(b) private offering.
- If the Rule 506(b) private offering is made solely to accredited investors, no offering circular is required to be prepared in order to satisfy the registration exemption under the 1933 Act, although an offering circular may be required to satisfy the anti-fraud provisions of the securities laws.

It is unclear whether a Rule 506(c) offering can commence immediately after the completion of the Rule 506(b) private offering. The SEC Staff has stated that if a company commences an offering under Rule 506(b), the company may determine, *prior to any sales in the Rule 506(b) offering*, to convert the offering into a Rule 506(c) offering, subject to amending the Form D (see discussion in Chapter 3) to indicate the reliance on Rule 506(c).[2]

However, there is no published SEC Staff guidance as to how quickly a Rule 506(c) offering can follow a Rule 506(b) offering which has already resulted in sales. There are a number of law firms that believe that there is no reason there cannot be an immediate Rule 506(c) offering after the conclusion of the private offering under Rule 506(b). In any event, if there are no offers or sales of the same security for a period of six months after the completion of the Rule 506(b) offering, the Rule 506(c) would not be integrated with the prior Rule 506(b) offering.

A second marketing strategy would be to simultaneously engage in retail securities crowdfunding and a Rule 506(c) offering, ignoring Rule 506(b) altogether. These simultaneous offerings are permitted under SEC rules, as previously noted. The retail securities crowdfunding could be structured with lower minimum purchase amounts (e.g., a $1,000 minimum investment amount) than the Rule 506(c) offering (e.g., a $50,000 minimum investment amount).

The higher minimum investment amount in the Rule 506(c) offering could justify a lower valuation for the company than is provided in the retail securities crowdfunding. The valuation differential would, of course, have to be fully disclosed to both sets of investors. The valuation differential provides potential accredited investors in the Rule 506(c) offering with an incentive because of the valuation discount they are receiving.

OTHER MARKETING ISSUES FOR DIRECT OFFERINGS

The legal ability under the new rules to directly market securities to strangers through general advertising does not ensure that capital will, in fact,

---

[2]Compliance and Disclosure Interpretations: Securities Act Rules, Question 260.12, http://www.sec.gov/divisions/corpfin/guidance/securitiesactrules-interps.htm.

be raised by the middle-market or start-up company. That marketing effort still requires a thoughtful and convincing marketing document and will, in many cases, require face-to-face meetings with potential investors.

The key issue under Rule 506(c) is whether the business can attract sufficient capital from accredited investors who are solicited directly by the company or its representative to satisfy the needs of the business.

It was reported that in 2013, there were more than 9 million households in the U.S. that satisfied the net worth standard for accredited investors.[3] The same report stated that 1.24 million of these households had more than $5 million of net worth and 132,000 of these households had a net worth exceeding $25 million.[4] There were in 2013 more than 15 million U.S. households which had a net worth over $500,000, according to that report.

Some have questioned these statistics, which are based upon statistics provided by the Spectrem Group. However, regardless of the accuracy of these figures, it is clear that there are a large number of accredited investors in the U.S. based upon the net worth test. Moreover, the figures stated above may not include all of the investors who satisfy the income test for accredited investors but not the net worth test.

Notwithstanding the large number of potential U.S. accredited investors, there are three significant obstacles that must be overcome in the U.S. in order to directly market these accredited investors under Rule 506(c). These obstacles may suggest that using funding portals, such as Realty Mogul, Crowdfunder or Kickstarter, or registered broker-dealers, are better choices for accessing accredited investors rather than a direct offering by the company.

These obstacles are as follows and they are each described in more detail below:

- Contact information obstacle: The ability to obtain accredited investor contact information.
- E-mail obstacle: The CAN-SPAM Act.
- Telephone obstacle: The Do Not Call Statutes and Registries.

---

[3] "Affluent Market Insights" (2014). Spectrem Group, p. 6.
[4] *Id.*

There is no prohibition on sending unsolicited letters to accredited investors. However, this requires the payment of postage.

The least expensive method of communicating with potential accredited investors is through e-mails. However, the U.S. CAN-SPAM Act, which is described below, must be complied with in connection with any e-mail solicitation.

ACCREDITED INVESTOR CONTACT INFORMATION

Lists of accredited investors are available on various Internet sites. They vary in quality and quantity. One Internet advertiser claims to have over 900,000 accredited investors on a mailing list and e-mail lists of over 200,000 accredited investors. Many of the lists advertised on the Internet contain only phone numbers, but no e-mail information. Some of the accredited investor lists contain 18,000–20,000 names with phone numbers. No one claims to have 9 million accredited investor names.

Those who advertise their possession of e-mail lists of accredited investors will not release the list, but instead will e-mail company's solicitation directly to their full e-mail list.

It is to be hoped that, as Rule 506(c) becomes more popular, additional information about accredited investors will become available. One important source of accredited investors is contributors to crowdfunding by the company. If the company starts to raise capital through crowdfunding, whether or not the rewards include company securities, the company might be able to obtain information about contributors who will also qualify as accredited investors for a subsequent Rule 506(c) offering. The SCiO crowdfunder, discussed in Chapter 1, encouraged contributors who were entitled to product rewards to have further private meetings with the company, presumably to solicit an investment in the company. It would not be surprising if in the future registered crowdfunding portals seek information from contributors about their accredited investor status and provide that information to companies that use their portal.

CAN-SPAM ACT

One method of reaching accredited investors under Rule 506(c) is to purchase an e-mail list of accredited investors and send them a podcast which contains a discussion of the company's business plan. E-mail lists of accredited investors are not easily found, as previously noted. Most accredited investor lists contain only their phone number. Assuming that the company can access e-mail addresses of accredited investors, the e-mails could violate the U.S. CAN-SPAM Act.

The acronym CAN-SPAM derives from the law's full name: **Controlling the Assault of Non-Solicited Pornography and Market Act of 2003**. The CAN-SPAM Act is occasionally referred to as the "You-Can-Spam" Act because the law fails to prohibit many types of e-mail spam, and overrides some anti-spam state laws. Some have claimed that the CAM-SPAM Act has not been vigorously enforced by the Federal Trade Commission ("FTC") given the large percentage of e-mails received in the U.S. that are considered spam.

The CAN-SPAM Act sets the rules for commercial e-mails, establishes requirements for "commercial electronic mail messages," gives recipients the right to have the sender stop e-mailing them, and spells out penalties for violations. A "commercial electronic mail message" is defined by the FTC as "any electronic mail message the primary purpose of which is the commercial advertisement or promotion of a commercial product or service," including e-mail that promotes content on commercial websites. The e-mail to the accredited investor touting an investment in a company could technically be considered a "commercial electronic mail message." However, an argument exists that securities were not intended to be covered as a commercial product or service.

The CAN-SPAM Act does not require e-mailers to obtain permission before sending the first e-mail. The Act merely contains certain requirements which must be satisfied by the e-mailer and the e-mail. According to the FTC, the e-mail solicitation must follow seven main rules in order to comply with the CAN-SPAM Act:

- **Do not use false or misleading header information**: Your "From," "To," "Reply-To," and routing information — including the originating domain name and e-mail address — must be accurate and identify the person or business who initiated the message.
- **Do not use deceptive subject lines**: The subject line must accurately reflect the content of the message.

- **Identify the message as an ad**: The law gives you a lot of leeway in how to do this, but you must disclose clearly and conspicuously that your message is an advertisement.
- **Tell recipients where you are located**: Your message must include your valid physical postal address. This can be your current street address, a post office box you have registered with the U.S. Postal Service, or a private mailbox you have registered with a commercial mail receiving agency established under U.S. Postal Service regulation.
- **Tell recipients how to opt out of receiving future e-mail from you**: Your message must include a clear and conspicuous explanation of how the recipient can opt out of getting e-mail from you in the future. Craft the notice in a way that is easy for an ordinary person to recognize, read, and understand. Creative use of type size, color, and location can improve clarity. Give a return e-mail address or another easy Internet-based way to allow people to communicate their choice to you. You may create a menu to allow a recipient to opt out of certain types of messages, but you must include the option to stop all commercial messages from you. Make sure your spam filter does not block these opt-out requests.
- **Honor opt-out requests promptly**: Any opt-out mechanism you offer must be able to process opt-out requests for at least 30 days after you send your message. You must honor a recipient's opt-out request within 10 business days. You cannot charge a fee, require the recipient to give you any personally identifying information beyond an e-mail address, or make the recipient take any step other than sending a reply e-mail or visit a single page on an Internet website as a condition for honoring an opt-out request. Once people have told you they do not want to receive more messages from you, you cannot sell or transfer their e-mail addresses, even in the form of a mailing list. The only exception is that you may transfer the addressees to a company you have hired to help you comply with the CAN-SPAM Act.
- **Monitor what others are doing on your behalf**: The law makes clear that even if you hire another company to handle your e-mail marketing, you cannot contract away your legal responsibility to comply with the law. Both the company whose product is promoted in the message and the company that actually sends the message may be held legally responsible.

Each separate e-mail sent in violation of the CAN-SPAM Act is subject to penalties of up to $16,000. There is no provision in the CAN-SPAM Act for private rights of action by the recipient of the e-mail.

DO NOT CALL STATUTES, RULES, AND REGISTRIES

Another method of soliciting investments from accredited investors is through telephone solicitations. Federal and state Do Not Call rules and registries present a much more formidable obstacle to telemarketing accredited investors than the CAN-SPAM Act does to e-mails. If an accredited investor places his or her phone number on the national or a state Do Not Call Registry, unsolicited phone calls are prohibited, subject to exceptions. These statutes can be enforced not only by the FTC, the Federal Communications Commission "FCC," or state regulatory authority, but also by the accredited investor who placed his or her name on the Do Not Call list.

The National Do Not Call Registry applies to any plan, program, or campaign to sell goods or services through interstate phone calls. This includes telemarketers who solicit consumers, often on behalf of third-party sellers. It also includes sellers who provide, offer to provide, or arrange to provide goods or services to consumers in exchange for payment. The National Do Not Call Registry does not limit calls by political organizations, charities, or telephone surveyors.

In addition, the National Do Not Call Registry is only for personal phone numbers. Business-to-business calls and faxes are not covered by the National Do Not Call Registry.[5] Therefore, if the company can obtain the business telephone number of the accredited investor, the phone call would not violate the National Do Not Call Registry. However, it is important to check the relevant state Do Not Call statute to determine whether there is a similar exception for business-to-business calls.

A list of state "Do Not Call List" Laws and Regulations is contained at http://donotcallprotection.com/do_not_call_chart.shtml.

Is there any way around these federal and state Do Not Call, statutes, rules, and registries? As noted, calls to business lines of accredited investors are not prohibited by the National Do Not Call Registry, but

---

[5] http://www.consumer.ftc.gov/articles/0108-national-do-not-call-registry.

state laws must be checked for a similar exclusion. To the extent that the National Do Not Call Registry or a state law applies only to those who attempt to sell "goods or services," an argument exists that an investment security is neither a good nor a service. For example, Section 2-105 of the Uniform Commercial Code, which has been adopted in almost all states, excludes from the definition of the word "goods" any investment security, as defined elsewhere in the law. It is not clear that this argument would prevail in any litigation.[6]

If the company decides to start soliciting accredited investors through cold telephone calls, it is best to contact a U.S. attorney who specializes in this area prior to commencing the marketing campaign. The federal and state rules are very complicated and it is easy to violate them.

AVOIDING BROKER-DEALER REGISTRATION

One of the problems in the company directly selling debt or equity securities under Rule 506(c) is that the entrepreneur or his or her employees may have to be registered as broker-dealers by reason of their participation in the sale of securities. Broker-dealer registration requires the taking of a test and subjects the entrepreneur or his or her employees to a variety of rules under the Securities Exchange Act of 1934 ("1934 Act"). The need to register as a broker-dealer can be avoided if the owner and his or her employees carefully follow the safe harbor contained in Rule 3a4-1 of the 1934 Act. The safe harbor requires that the entrepreneur and his or her employees (referred to as an "associated person" of the issuer) meet the requirements of Clause (a)(iii) below of the Rule.

The safe harbor in Clause (a)(iii) of Rule 3a4-1 requires the associated person to do no more than the following activities:

- Preparing any written communication or delivering such communication through the mails or other means that does not involve oral solicitation by the associated person of a potential purchaser; *provided however* that the content of such communication is approved by a partner, officer, or director of the issuer;

---

[6]Another argument, albeit weak, is that the JOBS Act preempted these Do Not Call statutes, rules, and registries.

- Responding to inquiries of a potential purchaser in a communication initiated by the potential purchaser; *provided however* that the content of such responses are limited to information contained in a registration statement filed under the 1933 Act or other offering documents; or
- Performing ministerial and clerical work involved in effecting any transaction.

If the company or its employees cannot safely fit within this safe harbor, it does not necessarily mean that they would have to register as a broker-dealer. It is important, however, to avoid compensating any employees by giving them a percentage of the proceeds from the sale of securities. The SEC takes the position that such transaction-based compensation is a key factor in requiring broker-dealer registration.

RULE 506(c) VERSUS TRADITIONAL IPO

The effect of SEC Rule 506(c) is that middle-market and start-up comapnies now have a new alternative for raising public capital from accredited investors, which is still considered a non-public offering for securities law purposes. Offers may be made under Rule 506(c) to strangers, whether or not accredited investors, so long as sales are made only to accredited investors. A traditional initial public offering (IPO) permits both offers and sales to both accredited and non-accredited investors, whereas under Rule 506(c), sales may be made only to accredited investors.

However, offerings under Rule 506(c) also have significant advantages over a traditional U.S. IPO. As previously noted, a traditional U.S. IPO is only feasible if the company has a post-IPO valuation of at least $200 million, which is a figure needed to interest many institutional buyers. Very few middle-market and start-up companies can qualify for this post-offering valuation. In contrast, there is no minimum post-offering valuation for a Rule 506(c) public offering. Moreover, the over $1 million cost to prepare a traditional IPO registration statement is also unaffordable by many smaller companies.

In addition, there are many more restrictions for raising capital through a traditional IPO than through Rule 506(c). For example, in a traditional IPO, issuers and underwriters cannot make any offers prior to filing a registration statement with the SEC and written offers are prohibited prior to the effective date of the registration statement. After the closing of the traditional IPO, expensive periodic and current reports must be prepared and filed with the SEC.

None of these technical rules apply to the SEC's Rule 506(c) offerings. Both oral and written offers can be made to both accredited and non-accredited investors prior to filing Form D with the SEC pursuant to Rule 506(c). There is no legal requirement for expensive post-offering reports in a Rule 506(c) offering.

The major disadvantage of a Rule 506(c) offering compared to a traditional IPO is the restriction on resale by the investor of the securities. In a traditional IPO, the investor can immediately resell the securities in a liquid market place. Securities sold in a Rule 506(c) offering are considered "restricted securities" and cannot be resold for at least six months. Even after that period, there is no guaranty that a liquid market will develop. Accordingly, Rule 506(c) securities will not be as attractive to investors as traditional IPO securities and will suffer a significant valuation discount unless a public trading market can be developed.

INVESTOR RESALE RIGHTS: PUBLIC TRADING MARKET

Securities sold under Rule 506(c) are considered "restricted securities" for purposes of the resale legal rights of investors under Rule 144 of the 1933 Act. The legal restrictions on investor securities resale depends on whether or not the issuer of the securities has become a "Reporting Issuer" under Rule 144 by either becoming an SEC filer (an expensive proposition) or otherwise provides "adequate public information" (a less expensive alternative) and whether the reselling investor is in a control relationship with issuer (a so-called "affiliate") or is just an ordinary investor. Complying with Rule 144 is considered a "safe harbor" to avoid violating the 1933 Act.

Tables 2.1 and 2.2 explain the legal resale rights of investors, depending on whether the issuer is considered a "Reporting Issuer" or a

Table 2.1. Restricted securities of reporting issuers

Affiliates or person selling on behalf of an affiliate	Non-affiliate (and has not been an affiliate during the prior three months)
During six-month holding period: No resales under Rule 144 permitted.	*During six-month holding period*: No resales under Rule 144 permitted.
After six-month holding period: May resell in accordance with all Rule 144 requirements including: • Current public information; • Volume limitations; • Manner of sale requirements for equity securities; and • Filing of Form 144.	*After six-month holding period but before one year*: Unlimited public resales under public information requirement still applies. *After one-year holding period*: Unlimited public resales under Rule 144 requirements.

Table 2.2. Restricted securities of non-reporting issuers

Affiliate of person selling on behalf of an affiliate	Non-affiliate (and has not been an affiliate during the prior three months)
During six-month holding period: No resales under Rule 144 permitted.	*During six-month holding period*: No resales under Rule 144 permitted.
After six-month holding period: May resell in accordance with all Rule 144 requirements including: • Current public information; • Volume limitations; • Manner of sale requirements for equity securities; and • Filing of Form 144.	*After six-month holding period but before one year*: Unlimited public resales under Rule 144 except that the current public information requirement still applies. *After one-year holding period*: Unlimited public resales under Rule 144 requirements.

"Non-Reporting Issuer" and whether or not the investors are a so-called "affiliate." The term "Reporting Issuer" refers to public companies which file reports with the SEC pursuant to Section 13 or 15(d) of the 1924 Act and companies otherwise providing "adequate public information"; all other companies are considered "Non-reporting Issuers." The term "Affiliate" refers generally to control persons of the company and

"Non-Affiliate" refers generally to persons not in a control position with the company.

PUBLIC TRADING MARKET

The company's ability to sell securities under Rule 506(c) depends in part on the resale rights of the investors. If a liquid market will ultimately develop in the company's securities, which permits its investors to easily resell their securities, the company's Rule 506(c) offering will be much more attractive to potential investors. This is particularly true if the offering consists of equity securities, as opposed to promissory notes or other debt securities.

To create a liquid public trading market in the company's securities, two elements must be present. First, there can be no legal restrictions on securities resale by investors. Tables 2.1 and 2.2 reflect that investors in companies which are "Non-Reporting Issuers" will generally have to wait one year after the completion of a sale under Rule 506(c) before they can freely sell their security, except the wait may only be six months if certain requirements are satisfied.

Second, a broker or dealer must be willing to create a market for the company's securities. The U.S. over-the-counter (OTC) market (exclusive of the OTC Bulletin Board) does not require the company to become a "Reporting Issuer." Broker-dealers will create markets in the U.S. OTC market only if there is some incentive for them to do so, usually because there is significant trading interest in the security. The broker or dealer must file a Form 211[7] with the Financial Industry Regulatory Authority (FINRA) and receive certain information concerning the company in order to become a market-maker. This topic is discussed more fully in Chapter 4.

Some securities issuers, particularly community banks, create markets in their own securities without a broker-dealer by matching investors who want to buy with those who wish to sell. These companies attempt to

---

[7]FINRA Form 211 requires the security to have a CUSIP number. The CUSIP stands for Committee on Uniform Securities Identification Procedures and identifies most securities which are publicly-traded in the U.S. The website for obtaining a CUSIP number is CUSIP.com.

avoid broker-dealer registration requirements by not taking any compensation for performing this service for their investors and staying in the safe harbor (Rule 3a4-1) previously described.

COMBINING INTERNATIONAL WITH U.S. RULE 506(c) OFFERINGS

Many companies may wish to concurrently sell securities both in the U.S. and internationally. The concurrent combination of an international and U.S. Rule 506(c) offering is permissible under SEC rules provided the international offering complies with SEC Regulation S.

SEC Regulation S provides a "safe harbor" for offers and sales of securities outside the U.S. and includes an issuer and a resale safe harbor. Two general conditions apply to both safe harbors: (1) the securities must be sold in an offshore transaction and (2) there can be no "directed selling efforts" in the U.S. SEC Rule 902(c)(1)[8] broadly defines "directed selling efforts" as any activity undertaken for the purpose of, or that could reasonably be expected to have the effect of, conditioning the market in the U.S. for any of the securities offered in reliance on Regulation S. Such prohibited activity includes:

- Sending certain promotional materials to U.S. investors;
- Holding promotional seminars for U.S. investors; and
- Placing an advertisement in a publication "with a general circulation in the U.S." that refers to the offering of securities being made in reliance upon Regulation S.

Therefore, care must be taken to comply with SEC Regulation S in any concurrent U.S. and international offering.

Since compliance with SEC Regulation S is complicated, a company which intends concurrent U.S. and international offerings will need a U.S. securities lawyer to help structure the international portion of the transaction.

A description of the technical requirements to comply with Rule 506(c) is contained in Chapter 3.

---

[8] 17 CFR 230.902(c)(1).

CHAPTER 3

TECHNICAL REQUIREMENTS
TO SATISFY SEC RULE 506(c)

The following is a technical description of each of the requirements to satisfy the registration exemption contained in Rule 506(c). This technical description is followed by a general discussion of the legal background of the JOBS Act:

- **Accredited Investor Requirement:** Offers of securities may be made to both accredited investors and non-accredited investors, but all purchasers of securities must be accredited investors.
- **Verification Requirement:** The company takes reasonable steps to verify that purchasers of its securities are in fact accredited investors.
- **Integration Requirement:** Sales of securities that are made before the commencement or after the completion of the Rule 506(c) offering may be integrated with the Rule 506(c) offering.
- **Limitation on Resale Requirement:** Securities sold under Rule 506(c) cannot be resold without registration under the 1933 Act or an exemption therefrom and reasonable care must be taken by the issuer in this regard.
- **Form D Requirement:** An issuer offering or selling securities in reliance on Rule 506(c) must file with the SEC a notice of sales containing the information required by Form D (reproduced in Appendix 2[1]) for each new offering of securities no later than 15 calendar days after the first "sale" of securities in the offering, unless the end of that period

---

[1] https://www.sec.gov/about/forms/formd.pdf. [Accessed on September 1, 2014]

falls on a Saturday, Sunday, or holiday, in which case, the due date would be the first business day following.

- **"Bad Actor" Disqualification Requirement:** The issuer and affiliated persons may not be disqualified as "bad actors."

Each of these requirements to comply with the registration exemption under Rule 506(c) is discussed subsequently in this chapter. However, complying with these requirements does not exempt the Rule 506(c) offering from the anti-fraud provisions of federal and state securities laws. Thus, it is possible to comply with all of the requirements set forth below and still violate the anti-fraud provisions of federal and state securities laws.

To avoid violating these anti-fraud provisions, the company will need to prepare an offering circular (also called an investor information statement or prospectus) which fairly describes the company's business and the use of proceeds. The offering circular should contain a complete list of risk factors so that the investor is fully apprised of the investment risks.

Any offering circular should be reviewed before its use by a U.S. securities law attorney. In addition, a U.S. securities law attorney should prepare the necessary subscription agreements for execution by investors, assist the company in preparing Form D (described subsequently in this chapter), and advise the company as to compliance with the requirements set forth below. Not all U.S. licensed attorneys are capable of providing securities law advice. Therefore, the company should seek recommendations of a competent U.S. securities law attorney.

ACCREDITED INVESTOR REQUIREMENT

The full definition of accredited investors is contained in Appendix 1. The definition includes both banks and other institutional investors as well as individual investors and their entities. These rules are subject to extensive Compliance and Disclosure Interpretations which are available on the SEC website.

The purpose of this discussion is to identify the attributes of an "accredited investors," in their order of importance in order to identify potential targets for a Rule 506(c) solicitation. These attributes are as follows.

INCOME TEST

A qualified investor includes any natural person who had an individual income in excess of $200,000 in each of the two most recent years or joint income with that person's spouse in excess of $300,000 in each of those years and has a reasonable expectation of reaching the same income level in the current year.

If the investor has not been married for all three years of the income test, the income test must be satisfied without the income of the future spouse during the unmarried period.[2]

Many upper middle-class families in the U.S. satisfy this test, particularly if the husband and wife are both wage owners. These families may not necessarily satisfy the net worth test described below. Therefore, the estimate that there are over nine million U.S. households that satisfy the net worth test means that this 9 million figure significantly understates the total number of U.S. accredited investors. To the extent that these two-income families do not have a net worth of at least $1 million, it is not clear whether they are ripe targets for a general solicitation except for small investment amounts (e.g., $10,000).

NET WORTH TEST

An accredited investor includes any natural person whose individual net worth, or joint net worth with that person's spouse, exceeds $1 million, whether or not they satisfy the income test. However, it is much more difficult to obtain verification of "net worth" than to obtain verification of "income," since both assets and liabilities must be verified.

For purposes of calculating net worth:

- The person's primary residence is not to be included as an asset;
- Indebtedness that is secured by the person's primary residence, up to the estimated fair market value of the primary residence at the time of the sale of securities, is not to be included as a liability (except that if the amount of such indebtedness outstanding at the time of sale of securities exceeds the amount outstanding 60 days before such time,

---

[2]Compliance and Disclosure Interpretations: Securities Act Rules, Question 255.15, http://www.sec.gov/divisions/corpfin/guidance/securitiesactrules-interps.htm. [Accessed on September 1, 2014]

other than as a result of the acquisition of the primary residence, the amount of such excess shall be included as a liability); and

- Indebtedness that is secured by the person's primary residence in excess of the estimated fair market value of the primary residence at the time of the sale of securities shall be included as a liability.

ENTITIES WITH ALL ACCREDITED INVESTORS

Any entity will qualify as an accredited investor if all of the equity owners of the entity are themselves accredited investors. In a questionable SEC Staff interpretation, trust beneficiaries are not considered "equity owners."[3]

RETIREMENT PLANS

Any trust for a retirement plan in which a bank or similar institution is the fiduciary will qualify as an accredited investor.[4] However, suppose the fiduciary of the retirement plan is not a bank or similar institution? If all of the beneficiaries of the retirement plan are themselves accredited investors, the plan itself will qualify as an accredited investor.[5]

Many U.S. investors have self-directed 401(k) plans which are used typically for retirement funding. The term "401(k) plans" refers to a provision of the U.S. Internal Revenue Code which permits the accumulation of retirement capital which is generally free from federal and state income taxes to the extent the capital remains in the plan. If the individual can direct the investment of these 401(k) funds, they are a possible target for general solicitation. Similar retirement plans, such as so-called "Keogh" plans, individual retirement accounts, profit-sharing plans, and similar retirement plans, may also be self-directed.

---

[3] Compliance and Disclosure Interpretations: Securities Act Rules, Question 255.21, http://www.sec.gov/divisions/corpfin/guidance/securitiesactrules-interps.htm. [Accessed on September 1, 2014]

[4] Compliance and Disclosure Interpretations: Securities Act Rules, Question 255.19, http://www.sec.gov/divisions/corpfin/guidance/securitiesactrules-interps.htm. [Accessed on September 1, 2014]

[5] Compliance and Disclosure Interpretations: Securities Act Rules, Question 255.23, http://www.sec.gov/divisions/corpfin/guidance/securitiesactrules-interps.htm. [Accessed on September 1, 2014]

To the extent that the sole beneficial owner of these plans, which are funded in the form of trusts, is an accredited investor under either the income or net worth test, these plans are also a target for a general solicitation. All of the beneficial owners of these trusts must be accredited investors in order for the trust entity to be considered an accredited investor.

Some of these plans (such as 401(k) plans) have been set up by employers and are partially subsidized by the employer. However, these employer-sponsored plans typically are not self-directed and provide very few investment choices. As a result, these plans may not be legally permitted to invest directly in a specific business.

TRUSTS WITH ASSETS IN EXCESS OF $5 MILLION

An accredited investor includes any trust, with total assets in excess of $5 million, not formed for the specific purpose of acquiring the securities offered, whose purchase is directed by a sophisticated person. A "sophisticated person" is a person who, either alone or with his or her purchaser representative, has such knowledge and experience in financial and business matters that they are capable of evaluating the merits and risks of the prospective investment, or the issuer of the securities reasonably believes immediately to making any sale that the purchaser comes within this description. A retirement plan trust with more than $5 million, whose fiduciary is a "sophisticated person," will also qualify as an accredited investor.

Many wealthy families in the U.S. have formed, for estate planning purposes, family trusts, or other types of trusts with substantial assets. If those assets exceed $5 million and the trustee satisfies the sophistication test describe above, that trust is a potential target for a general solicitation.

DIRECTORS, OFFICERS, AND GENERAL PARTNERS

An accredited investor includes any director, executive officer, or general partner of the issuer of the securities being offered or sold, or any director, executive officer, or general partner of a general partner of that issuer.

The SEC Staff has issued an interpretation that an executive officer of a parent of the issuer does not qualify as an accredited investor unless the executive officer of the parent is an executive officer of the subsidiary issuer.[6]

VERIFICATION REQUIREMENT

As previously noted, the verification requirements start once an investor has indicated an intention to enter into a contract of sale which will be legally binding upon the investor. The SEC Staff would likely view the receipt of a check or cash from the investor as a "sale." Therefore, it is important that the verification requirements be satisfied prior to either the execution by the investor of a contract of sale or the receipt of a check or other cash from the investor.

Some companies may choose not to use Rule 506(c) because the determination of whether the steps taken are "reasonable" is based on a facts and circumstances analysis conducted by the company. A company conducting a private placement under current Rule 506(b) does not need to engage in the verification process described below and can rely on its reasonable belief that the purchaser satisfies one or more accredited investor criteria set forth in Rule 501(a). In addition, companies may decide not to use the new Rule 506(c), not only to avoid such verification process but also in order to make private placements to non-accredited investors who meet the sophistication requirements of Rule 506(b).

A significant part of the SEC's adopting release is focused on the analysis that a company must conduct to verify that a purchaser of securities in a Rule 506(c) offering is an accredited investor. *The SEC has specifically stated in the adopting release that a company will not be deemed to have taken reasonable steps to verify accredited investor status if it only required an investor to check a box in a questionnaire or sign a form (which is an acceptable practice now under the current "reasonable belief standard" applicable to offerings under Rule 506(b)), in the absence of other information indicating accredited investor status of the purchaser.* The SEC has embraced a principles-based method of

---

[6]Compliance and Disclosure Interpretations: Securities Act Rules, Question 255.10, http://www.sec.gov/divisions/corpfin/guidance/securitiesactrules-interps.htm. [Accessed on September 1, 2014]

verification and believes that a company should consider the following factors in its analysis:

- The nature of the purchaser and the type of accredited investor that the purchaser claims to be;
- The amount and type of information that the company has about the purchaser; and
- The nature of the offering (e.g., the manner in which the purchaser was solicited to participate in the offering, and the terms of the offering, such as a minimum investment amount).

These factors are interconnected and the SEC stated that "[a]fter consideration of the facts and circumstances of the purchaser and the transaction, the more likely it appears that a purchaser qualifies as an accredited investor, the fewer steps the issuer would have to take to verify the accredited investor status." To illustrate this, the SEC produced the following example: "*if the terms of the offering require a high minimum investment amount and a purchaser is able to meet those terms, then the likelihood of that purchaser satisfying the definition of accredited investor may be sufficiently high such that, absent any facts that indicate that the purchaser is not an accredited investor, it may be reasonable for the issuer to take fewer steps to verify or, in certain cases, no additional steps to verify accredited investor status other than to confirm that the purchaser's cash investment is not being financed by a third party.*"

A company may rely on a third party that has verified a person's status as an accredited investor (assuming the company has a reasonable basis to rely on such third-party verification) or on publicly-available information in filings with a federal, state, or local regulatory body (e.g., proxy statement disclosing the compensation of a purchaser who is a named executive officer of a public company or IRS Form 990 disclosing total assets of a Section 501(c)(3) organization with $5 million in assets).

The means used by the company to solicit purchasers may be relevant in determining the reasonableness of the steps that a company should take to verify accredited investor status. The SEC has pointed out that "[a]n *issuer that solicits new investors through a website accessible to the general public, through a widely disseminated email or social media solicitation, or through a newspaper, will likely be obligated to take greater measures to verify accredited investor status than an issuer that solicits new investors from a database of pre-screened accredited investors created and maintained by a reasonably reliable third party."*

Recognizing the difficulty of determining what steps would be reasonable to verify an accredited investor's status of a natural person and in response to comments, the SEC has provided the following examples of non-exclusive and non-mandatory methods that a company may use to verify that a natural person purchasing its securities in a Rule 506(c) offering is an accredited investor (assuming that the company does not have knowledge that such person is not an accredited investor):

- Reviewing any IRS Form that reports the purchaser's (or with the purchaser's spouse in the case of a person who qualifies as an accredited investor based on joint income with that person's spouse) income for the two most recent years (including, but not limited to, Form W-2, Form 1099, Schedule K-1 to Form 1065, and Form 1040) and obtaining a written representation from the purchaser (or with the spouse) that he or she has a reasonable expectation of reaching the income level necessary to qualify as an accredited investor during the current year;

- Reviewing one or more of the following types of documentation dated within the prior three months and obtaining a written representation from the purchaser (or with the purchaser's spouse in the case of a person who qualifies as an accredited investor based on joint net worth with that person's spouse) that all liabilities necessary to make a determination of net worth have been disclosed:

  o *With respect to assets*: bank statements, brokerage statements, and other statements of securities holdings, certificates of deposit, tax assessments, and appraisal reports issued by independent third parties; and

  o *With respect to liabilities*: a consumer report from at least one of the nationwide consumer reporting agencies; or

- Obtaining a written confirmation from one of the following persons or entities that such person or entity has taken reasonable steps to verify that the purchaser is an accredited investor within the prior three months and has determined that such purchaser is an accredited investor;

o   A registered broker-dealer;
o   An investment adviser registered with the SEC;
o   a licensed attorney who is in good standing under the laws of the jurisdictions in which he or she is admitted to practice law; or
o   a certified public accountant who is duly registered and in good standing under the laws of the place of his or her residence or principal office.

- In regard to any person who purchased securities in a Rule 506(b) offering as an accredited investor prior to the effective date of 506(c) and continues to hold such securities, for the same issuer's Rule 506(c) offering, obtaining a certification by such person at the time of sale that he or she qualifies as an accredited investor.

A word of caution is needed in complying with the verification requirement. Most accredited investors have no desire to provide their personal financial information to a stranger and view all financial information regarding them to be strictly confidential.[7] Therefore, great care must be exercised in seeking to comply with the verification requirement so that the accredited investor does not view the company's request to be inappropriate and offensive.

A simple letter from the company's accountant or broker that the person's net worth meets or exceeds the $1 million level (not including primary residence) is probably the least offensive request the company can make. This might be accompanied by an offer to reimburse the investor for any cost they might incur in obtaining such a letter.

Suppose a company takes reasonable steps to verify that the purchaser was an accredited investor and reasonably believes that to be the case, but after the sale discovers that the investor was not accredited? The SEC Staff has taken the position that, under these circumstances, Rule 506(c) still protects the company.[8]

However, let us assume that all the investors in the Rule 506(c) offering are in fact accredited but the company failed to take reasonable steps to

---

[7] See SEC Rel. 33-9354, p. 17, Note 49.

[8] Compliance and Disclosure Interpretations: Securities Act Rules, Question 260.06, http://www.sec.gov/divisions/corpfin/guidance/securitiesactrules-interps.htm. [Accessed on September 1, 2014]

verify their status before the sale. Under these circumstances, the offering violates the 1933 Act. This is because the verification requirement of Rule 506(c) is separate from and independent of the requirement that all sales be limited to accredited investors.[9]

Suppose the verification of accredited investor status is obtained from a reputable source and turns out to be false. Can the investor then sue the company to receive back his or her money, particularly if the investment turns out poorly? To protect the company from this possibility, the subscription agreement executed by the investor should have the investor warrant and represent that he or she is an accredited investor. The courts have generally been unsympathetic to investors who seek to recover their investments in this situation.[10]

Verification services are now available for accredited investors on the Internet. These include www.accreditedinvestorsolutions.com and www.earlyshares.com, among others.

The Securities Industry and Financial Markets Association have issued guidance on June 23, 2014 for registered broker-dealers and investment advisors as to methods of verifying accredited investor status.[11]

INTEGRATION REQUIREMENT

Sales of securities that are made before the commencement or after the completion of the Rule 506(c) offering may be integrated with the Rule

---

[9]Compliance and Disclosure Interpretations: Securities Act Rules, Question 260.07, http://www.sec.gov/divisions/corpfin/guidance/securitiesactrules-interps.htm. [Accessed on September 1, 2014]

[10]See, e.g., Wright v. Nat'l Warranty Co., 953 F.2d 256 (6th Cir. 1991) (rejecting the plaintiffs' argument that Rule 505 was unavailable because the plaintiffs "specifically warranted and represented in the subscription agreement ... that they were accredited investors"); Goodwin Properties, LLC v. Acadia Group, Inc., No. 01-49-P-C, 2001 U.S. Dist. LEXIS 9975 (D. Me. 2001) (noting that the plaintiffs "provided the defendants with reason to believe that they were accredited investors as defined by 17 C.F.R. Section 230.501(a)" and stating that therefore "[t]hey cannot now disavow those representations in order to support their claims against the defendants"); F. L. Roth Revocable Trust v. UBS Painewebber Inc., 323 F. Supp. 2d 1279 I (S.D. Fla. 2004) (stating that the plaintiffs "cannot disavow their representations that they were accredited investors" and concluding that there was no material dispute that the offering complied with Regulation D).

[11]SIFMA Guidance on Rule 506(c) Verification, June 23, 2014, http://www.sifma.org/issues/item.aspx?id=8589949595. [Accessed on September 1, 2014]

506(c) offering. Thus, if a non-accredited investor were sold securities shortly before or shortly after the completion of the Rule 506(c) offering, that fact could disqualify the offering. However, sales to non-accredited investors under the retail securities crowdfunding exemption of Section 4(a)(6) of the 1933 Act (whether or not simultaneously) are not integrated and arguably so are sales under Regulation A (see Chapter 4).

In addition to these exceptions, offers and sales to non-accredited investors that are made more than six months before the start of the Rule 506(c) offering or are made more than six months after completion of a Rule 506(c) offering will not be considered part of that Rule 506(c) offering, so long as during those six-month periods, there are no offers or sales of securities by or for the issuer that are of the same or a similar class as those offered or sold under Rule 506(c), other than those offers or sales of securities under an employee benefit plan.[12]

LIMITATION ON RESALE REQUIREMENT

Securities sold under Rule 506(c) cannot be resold without registration under the 1933 Act or an exemption therefrom. The issuer must exercise reasonable care to assure that the purchasers of the securities are not underwriters within the meaning of Section 2(a)(11) of the 1933 Act, which reasonable care may be demonstrated by the following:

- Reasonable inquiry to determine if the purchaser is acquiring the securities for himself or for other persons;
- Written disclosure to each purchaser prior to sale that the securities have not been registered under the 1933 Act and, therefore, cannot be resold unless they are registered under the 1933 Act or unless an exemption from registration is available; and
- Placement of a legend on the certificate or other document that evidences the securities stating that the securities have not been registered under the 1933 Act and setting forth or referring to the restrictions on transferability and sale of the securities.

---

[12]The term "employee benefit plan" is defined in Rule 405 under the 1933 Act (17 CFR 230.405).

FORM D REQUIREMENT

Form D (reproduced in Appendix 2)[13] is required to be filed with the SEC within 15 days[14] after the first sale of securities sold to an accredited investor. For this purpose, the date of first sale is the date on which the first investor is irrevocably contractually committed to invest, which, depending on the terms and conditions of the contract, could be the date on which the issuer receives the investor's subscription agreement or check. If the date on which a Form D is required to be filed falls on a Saturday, Sunday, or holiday, the due date is the first business day following.

Many companies think that a "sale" of securities has not occurred until a check or cash has been received. The rule is clear that the 15 days starts when the investor is "irrevocably contractually committed," regardless of when the check or cash is received from the investor.[15]

State securities laws generally require the filing up of Form D in any state where the sale is made, plus a filing fee and a consent to service of process. Some states may require the filing even before the sale is made.

If the company fails to file a Form D and becomes subject to any order, judgment, or decree of any court of competent jurisdiction enjoining the company from failure to comply with the Form D filing requirements, the company would not be eligible thereafter for a Rule 506 offering. The same is true if any of the company's predecessors or affiliates have been similarly enjoined. The SEC is authorized, upon a showing of good cause, to restore the exemption.

"BAD ACTOR" DISQUALIFICATION REQUIREMENT

The Dodd–Frank Act directed the SEC to adopt rules disqualifying an issuer from reliance on the Rule 506 exemption if that issuer committed securities

---

[13]Changes to Form D have been proposed in SEC Rel. No. 33-9416, which has not been adopted as of October 1, 2014. [Accessed on September 1, 2014]

[14]*Id.* This SEC proposal would require the filing "no later than 15 calendar days prior to the first use of general solicitation or general advertising for such offering," and add other disclosure requirements to Form D. [Accessed on September 1, 2014]

[15]Compliance and Disclosure Interpretations: Securities Act Rules, Question 257.02, http://www.sec.gov/divisions/corpfin/guidance/securitiesactrules-interps.htm. [Accessed on September 1, 2014]

fraud or various other violations of financial regulatory and anti-fraud laws. The SEC's retail securities crowdfunding rules and the SEC's Tiers 1 and 2 of Regulation A rules also contain disqualification provisions that are sometimes referred to as "Bad Boy" provisions and are very similar to the ones below.

Under new Rule 506(d), effective September 23, 2013, an issuer will not be able to rely on the Rule 506 exemption, including Rule 506(c), if certain "covered persons" have been subject to one or more disqualifying events, such as a conviction for securities fraud. Individuals and entities that are "covered persons" include:

- The issuer;
- A predecessor of the issuer;
- Affiliated issuers, unless the event occurred prior to the commencement of the affiliation, and the affiliated issuer is not under the issuer's control and is not "under common control with the issuer by a third party that was in control of the affiliated entity at the time of such events";
- Beneficial owners of 20% or more of the issuer's voting equity securities (calculated on the basis of voting power);
- An issuer's directors, executive officers, and other officers, as well as general partners and managing members, who participate in the offering; and
- Any person who has received or will receive direct or indirect compensation for solicitation of purchasers in connection with a securities offering.

If any of the following events has occurred to any of the individuals or entities designated above, the "Bad Boy" disqualification is applicable:

- **Criminal Convictions:** Has been convicted, within 10 years before such sale (or five years, in the case of issuers, their predecessors, and affiliated issuers), of any felony or misdemeanor:
   - In connection with the purchase or sale of any security;
   - Involving the making of any false filing with the SEC; or
   - Arising out of the conduct of the business of an underwriter, broker, dealer, municipal securities dealer, investment advisor, or paid solicitor of purchasers of securities.

- **Court Injunctions and Restraining Orders:** Is subject to any order, judgment, or decree of any court of competent jurisdiction, entered within five years before such sale, that, at the time of such sale, restrains or enjoins such person from engaging or continuing to engage in any conduct or practice:

  - In connection with the purchase or sale of any security;
  - Involving the making of any false filing with the SEC; or
  - Arising out of the conduct of the business of an underwriter, broker, dealer, municipal securities dealer, investment adviser or paid solicitor of purchasers of securities.

- **Final Orders of Regulators:** Is subject to a final order of a state securities commission (or an agency or officer of a state performing like functions); a state authority that supervises or examines banks, savings associations or credit unions; a state insurance commission (or an agency or officer of a state performing like functions); an appropriate federal banking agency; the U.S. Commodity Futures Trading Commission; or the National Credit Union Administration that:

  - At the time of such sale, bars the person from:

    - Association with an entity regulated by such commission, authority, agency, or officer;
    - Engaging in the business of securities, insurance, or banking; or
    - Engaging in savings association or credit union activities; or

  - Constitutes a final order based on a violation of any law or regulation that prohibits fraudulent, manipulative or deceptive conduct entered within the 10-year period before such sale.

- **SEC Disciplinary Orders**: Is subject to an order of the SEC entered pursuant to Section 15(b) or 15B(c) of the Exchange Act or Section 203(e) or (f) of the Investment Advisors Act of 1940 that, at the time of such sale:

  - Suspends or revokes such person's registration as a broker, dealer, municipal securities dealer, or investment adviser;
  - Places limitations on the activities, functions, or operations of such person; or

- ○ Bars such person from being associated with any entity or from participating in the offering of any penny stock.

- **SEC Cease-and-Desist Orders:** Is subject to any order of the SEC entered within five years before such sale that, at the time of such sale, orders the person to cease and desist from committing or causing a violation or future violation of:

  - ○ Any scienter-based anti-fraud provision of the federal securities laws; or
  - ○ Section 5 of the 1933 Act.

- **Suspension or Expulsion from SRO Membership or Association with an SRO Member:** Is suspended or expelled from membership in, or suspended or barred from association with a member of, a registered national securities exchange or a registered national or affiliated securities association for any act or omission to act constituting conduct inconsistent with just and equitable principles of trade.

- **SEC Stop Orders:** Has filed (as a registrant or an issuer), or was or was not named as an underwriter in, any registration statement or Regulation A offering statement filed with the SEC that, within five years before such sale, was the subject of a refusal order, stop order, or order suspending the Regulation A exemption, or is, at the time of such sale, the subject of an investigation or proceeding to determine whether a stop order or suspension order should be issued.

- **U.S. Postal Service False Representation Orders:** Is subject to a United States Postal Service false representation order entered within five years before such sale, or is, at the time of such sale, subject to a temporary restraining order or preliminary injunction with respect to conduct alleged by the U.S. Postal Service to constitute a scheme or device for obtaining money or property through the mail by means of false representation.

Any disqualifying events that occurred *prior* to the effectiveness of the new rules will not prevent an issuer from relying on Rule 506, though they will be subject to mandatory disclosure requirements. For disqualifying events occurring *after* the effectiveness of the new rules, an issuer may nevertheless rely on Rule 506 if the SEC determines upon a showing of good cause that denial of an exemption is not necessary under the circumstances, the court or regulator that issued the disqualifying order advises the SEC in writing that the exemption should not be denied, or the issuer can demonstrate that it did not know and, in the exercise of reasonable care, could not have known that a disqualifying event existed.

STATE SECURITIES LAWS

Securities issued in compliance with Rule 506(c) are exempt from the registration provisions of securities laws of various states of the U.S. However, the 1933 Act preserves the state's anti-fraud authority, its right to impose fees, and its right to receive a notice of the offering, together with a consent to service of process. Therefore, it is important to understand the provisions of the securities laws of the specific states where either an offer or a sale is made to an actual or potential investor.[16]

Almost all states require the filing of the Form D with them, plus a fee, if there is a sale in the state and some states require the filing even before the sale. Therefore, it is important to check the state securities laws of the states in which a sale is made. New York State requires a filing in addition to the Form D.

Chapter 4 of this book describes a new method of having a U.S. initial public offering (IPO) which is substantially less expensive and much more flexible than a traditional U.S. IPO and permits sales of securities to non-accredited as well as accredited investors. It is called an exempt offering under enhanced Regulation A.

---

[16]Compliance and Disclosure Interpretations: Securities Act Rules, Question 260.03, http://www.sec.gov/divisions/corpfin/guidance/securitiesactrules-interps.htm. [Accessed on September 1, 2014]

CHAPTER 4

ENHANCED REGULATION A

Tier 1 and Tier 2 of Regulation A became effective June 19, 2015 and permit up to $20 million (Tier 1) and up to $50 million (Tier 2) to be raised every 12 months. They should be considered an alternative to a Rule 506(c) offering if any of the following circumstances are true:

- Potential investors want to be able to immediately resell their securities (Rule 506(c) requires at least a six-month holding period), or are unwilling to provide the verification of accredited investor status required by Rule 506(c) (Regulation A permits reasonable reliance on accredited investor representations);
- Shareholders or other equity holders in the company are interested in selling their personal equity in the company in a secondary offering (not permitted in a Rule 506(c) offering); or
- The capital raising goals of the company cannot be achieved without including sales to qualified non-accredited investors as well as accredited investors (Rule 506(c) does not permit sales to non-accredited investors).

Because of the higher cost of an enhanced Regulation A offering, Rules 506(b) or 506(c) should always be the first choice for raising capital for the company. Even though these rules do not permit secondary sales, there is no prohibition on using the proceeds of these offerings to repay debt used to repurchase securities from existing security holders, provided that intention is properly disclosed. However, securities sold under Rule 506(b) or Rule 506(c) cannot be immediately resold; in contrast, securities sold under enhanced Regulation A can be immediately resold by non-controlling purchasers, thereby permitting a public trading market to immediately develop.

Enhanced Regulation A can be helpful to family-owned businesses and other private companies where there is a need for additional equity capital which can be used to buy-out a family member or other major shareholder as well as a need for additional capital to grow the business. An enhanced Regulation A offering can be viewed as a possible alternative to selling the business or accepting institutional private equity which contains restrictions on the business. More importantly, the possible development of a public trading market immediately after the enhanced Regulation A offering will likely increase the valuation of the business above the valuation which might be offered by a private equity firm.

Prior to the adoption of these new tiers of Regulation A, companies could only raise up to $5 million every 12 months and selling stockholders could only sell up to $1.5 million of securities during this period. These paltry dollar limitations, coupled with the expense of complying with Regulation A, made it generally undesirable. Moreover, prior to the JOBS Act, Regulation A was hardly used because of the necessity of also complying with the registration provisions of state securities laws in those states in which there was an offer or a sale of the security. According to the Securities and Exchange Commission (SEC), from 2009 through 2012, 87 issuers filed Regulation A offering statements and only 19 offering statements were qualified by the SEC, or an average of approximately five qualified offering statements per year.

That has now changed with the SEC adoption of Tier 1 and Tier 2 of Regulation A made possible by the JOBS Act. Under Tier 2 of Regulation A, which is the more useful of the two tiers, the following apply:

- Eligible companies may sell up to $50 million worth of securities (equity, debt, convertible securities, warrants, or guarantees of such securities) during any 12-month period (the 12-month period to be measured before the start of and during the offering period) pursuant to an exempt Regulation A offering. Securities can be sold for either cash or other consideration.
- Up to 30% of the aggregate offering price of the company's first year offering pursuant to Regulation A can be a secondary offering by

security holders. For example, if the aggregate offering price of all securities of the company qualified in the first Regulation A offering is $50 million, existing security holders can sell up to $15 million in that offering. This 30% first year limitation also applies to a subsequent Regulation A qualified within one year of the qualification date of the first offering, but does not apply to Regulation A offerings qualified thereafter.

- Subsequent to the 30% first year limitation, selling security holders who are not control persons (i.e., non-affiliates) of the company can sell up to $50 million of securities every 12 months, and control persons can sell up to $15 million of securities every 12 months. This contrasts with Section 4(a)(6) crowdfunding and Rule 506(b) and 506(c) offerings which do not permit secondary offerings or sales.
- Securities sold in the Regulation A offering are freely resalable by the purchaser, unless the purchaser is an issuer, underwriter, or a dealer, in effect non-controlling purchasers (non-affiliates) can freely resell the purchased securities.
- The registration provisions of states securities laws, which in the past deterred Regulation A offerings, are preempted.

Tier 1 of Regulation A is limited to $20 million (versus $50 million for Tier 2) during any 12-month period (measured as above), with secondary sales subject to the same 30% first year limitation applicable to Tier 2. Thereafter, Tier 1 permits up to $20 million of sales by non-control persons every 12 months and up to $6 million of sales by control persons every 12 months. Unfortunately, Tier 1 does not preempt the registration provisions of state securities law and this is a major drawback. The major advantage of Tier 1 is that it permits the use of unaudited financial statements (Tier 2 requires audited financial statements complying with detailed SEC accounting requirements), requires less disclosure, does not limit the amount a non-accredited investor can invest, and (in contrast to Tier 2) does not require ongoing reporting obligations.[1]

---

[1] After state regulatory review of a Tier 1 offering, the states may require additional disclosures and even imposing ongoing reporting obligations, particularly in states which have merit review.

The following chart contrasts the other material differences between Tier 1 and Tier 2:

	Tier 1 Versus Tier 2	
	Tier 1	Tier 2
Disclosure of annual compensation of three highest paid executive officers or directors for last completed fiscal year	May be disclosed as a group and not individually	Must be disclosed individually
Threshold disclosure for material transactions with management or other insiders	$50,000	Lesser of $120,000 or 1% of average assets
Limitation on amount a non-accredited investor can invest assuming securities are not listed on a national securities exchange upon qualification	None	Natural Persons: greater of 10% of annual income or net worth (as adjusted); Entities: greater of 10% of such entity's revenue or net assets for most recently completed fiscal year end
Financial statement requirements	(a) May be unaudited and need not comply with SEC Regulation S-X. However, if audited financial statements are prepared for another purpose and meet certain conditions, they must be supplied. (b) Current balance sheet, income statement for two years, as well as any interim period. (c) Auditor, if any, need not be registered with PCAOB and must satisfy independence standards of either AICPA or SEC Regulation S-X.	(a) Must be audited, in accordance with either U.S. Generally Accepted Auditing Standards or standards of the U.S. Public Company Accounting Oversight Board, and comply with Article 8 of SEC Regulation S-X relating to smaller reporting companies . (b) Current balance sheet, income statement for two years, as well as any interim period. (c) Auditor need not be registered with PCAOB, but must be independent under SEC Regulation S-X.

(*Continued*)

Tier 1 Versus Tier 2		
	Tier 1	Tier 2
State registration preempted as to offers or sales of securities	No preemption as to offers or sales of securities, assuming security is not offered or sold on registered national securities exchange.	Yes, preempted as to both offers and sales
Ability to sell non-voting or partial voting stock	May be a problem in merit review states.	Permissible
Resale restrictions	Non-controlling security holders are not subject to any resale restrictions. Controlling security holders are subject to Rule 144 resale limitations.	Same
Periodic reporting obligations subsequent to initial qualification	No, company need only file an exit report after termination of the offering.	Yes, including (among others) annual reports, semi-annual reports, and current event reports. The company may suspend its reporting obligations after completing reporting for the fiscal year in which the offering statement was qualified, if there are fewer than 300 record holders and offers and sales are not continuing pursuant to Tier 2.

The drawback of states securities registration review, in addition to SEC review, will likely deter the use of Tier 1 except for very local offerings, or situations in which the company cannot comply with Tier 2 accounting rules. Indeed, the merit review states (such as Pennsylvania) could require impounding of offering proceeds, lock-in or escrows of promotional shares, restrictions on insider loans and advances, restrictions on unequal voting rights, limitations on underwriter compensation and expenses, etc. as a condition of state registration. Moreover, that condition could apply to the entire offering regardless of which state in which it is offered or sold.[2] Therefore, the rest of this chapter will be solely devoted to Tier 2.

The mere legal ability to sell under Tier 2 of Regulation A does not mean that companies will be successful in raising capital. A successful Tier 2 of Regulation A offering requires significant advanced planning as to how the securities will be marketed and the methods of maintaining a liquid public market for these securities.

One of the keys to successful marketing is to be able to provide some assurance to investors that a liquid public market in these securities will develop after the completion of the offering. This issue is discussed below.

COMPARISON TO TRADITIONAL U.S. IPOS

Tier 2 of Regulation A legally permits a public sale of a substantial dollar amount of securities by both the company and its founder or other selling shareholder. Very few private companies qualify for a traditional U.S. initial public offering (IPO) because their market capitalization would not exceed the minimum $250 million post-IPO valuation needed to interest institutional investors. However, these same companies with much lower valuations may now be able to qualify for a public offering under Tier 2.

---

[2] The North American Securities Administrators Association ("NASAA"), an organization of state securities regulators, has implemented a multi-state coordinated review program for Regulation A offerings. http://www.nasaa.org/industry-resources/corporation-finance/coordinated-review/regulation-a-offerings/ The goal of the program is to reduce state law and compliance obligations of Regulation A companies. However, as noted by the SEC, a company which elects to offer or sell Tier 1 securities in any merit review state may be required to comply with the NASAA Statement of Policy to the offering as a whole, which includes the restrictive provisions recited above. SEC Rel. No. 33-9741 at p. 223, March 25, 2015. Moreover, filing fees (which also apply to Tier 2 offerings) must be submitted to individual states and the coordinated review process will take "a minimum of 30 days." An illustrated timeline for NASAA's multi-state coordinated review program is available at: http://www.nasaa.org/wp-content/uploads/2015/03/Coordinated-Review-Chart.pdf.

The SEC believes that this enhanced Regulation A can be used even by companies that can easily qualify for a traditional U.S. IPO. The SEC stated:

> The increased maximum offering size could make Regulation A more attractive not only to start-up medium-sized companies, but also to larger or more mature companies that are in less need of capital than business start-ups... For instance, an issuer that floats 20% of its shares at $50 million would be valued at $200 million following the issuance. For this issuer, secondary market liquidity may facilitate subsequent offerings by founders, employees, affiliates, and other pre-issuance shareholders who are seeking a partial or full exit of their holding. It is not clear whether existing OTC markets would be able to supply the liquidity necessary for large issuers.[3]

It is not clear that a company which otherwise can qualify for a traditional U.S. IPO would be willing to have its securities traded on the U.S. over-the-counter (OTC) market (exclusive of the OTC Bulletin Board) in order to lessen the cost of compliance. However, there are some large private companies that might use this enhanced Regulation A as a stepping stone to a traditional U.S. IPO.

SELLING STOCKHOLDER SALES

Selling stockholders of a company can now sell up to $15 million of securities every 12 months as measured in the manner described above. The SEC noted in the following passage the benefits of this liberalization for secondary sales in Tier 2 of Regulation A:

> Permitting these secondary sales provides exit options for company founders, employees, and institutional investors, such as private equity or venture capital investors, which can have a positive effect on capital formation. For instance, because these investors consider available exit options before participating in a new venture, permitting secondary sales increases the incentives to make the original investment. Allowing these exits could also facilitate an optimal re-allocation of human capital. In particular,

---

[3] SEC Rel. 33-9497. at p. 228.

entrepreneurs and venture capitalists have valuable talents and allowing them to exit may free their attention for new projects and business ventures, and allow them to make investments not otherwise possible. In turn, their exits facilitate new investment opportunities for investors with different skills and risk preferences, and potentially a more appropriate investor base for an issuer.[4]

This provision is very important to private companies, including family businesses. There are many private companies, including family businesses, in which there are some shareholders who need liquidity and the company does not want to provide that liquidity since the company needs the capital for its future growth.

Tier 2 of Regulation A permits the sale to the public of non-voting stock while retaining a higher voting class of stock for family members or other non-selling existing shareholders. Prior to a Tier 2 offering, the company could be recapitalized with a Class A non-voting common stock and a Class B voting common stock. The non-selling shareholders could retain the Class B voting common stock and the company could sell the non-voting Class A common stock in the Tier 2 of Regulation A offering. Those existing shareholders who wished to sell could receive Class A non-voting common stock in the recapitalization instead of the Class B voting common stock. Thereafter, the company could sell $35 million of Class A non-voting common stock in the Tier 2 of Regulation A first year offering and the selling shareholders could sell $15 million of the same Class A non-voting common stock in the same offering.

This provision permits family-owned companies to retain family control for future generations of family members while at the same time raising the necessary capital to expand and grow the business. It also provides a market for family members who are no longer interested in retaining their ownership and want liquidity.

The $15 million limitation on selling security holders applies to each 12-month period as measured above, but is subject to the 30% first year limitation. For example, the retiring founder of a private company could theoretically sell up to $60 million worth of securities of the company in

---

[4]*Id.* at, p. 229.

the U.S. OTC market (exclusive of the OTC Bulletin Board) over an approximately four-year period under Tier 2 of Regulation A.

WHAT SECURITIES SALES COUNT TOWARD THE $50 MILLION AND $15 MILLION TESTS?

In computing the dollar limitations for Tier 2 of Regulation A offerings, crowdfunding securities sold pursuant to Section 4(a)(6) of the 1933 Act, even if offered and sold simultaneously, do not count against the dollar limitations. The SEC release makes it clear that other exempt offerings, such as a simultaneous Rule 506(c) offering, will not be integrated to reduce the dollar limitations so long as each offering complies with the applicable exemption requirements.[5] Unfortunately, SEC Reg. Section 230.251(c) does not clearly state this intention and therefore there is uncertainty on this issue.

If convertible securities or warrants are being offered under Regulation A and such securities are convertible, exercisable, or exchangeable within one year of the Regulation A qualification or at the discretion of the company, the underlying securities must also be qualified and the aggregate offering price must include the actual or maximum estimated conversion, exercise, or exchange price of such securities. Consideration should be given to not having warrants or other exercisable or convertible securities in the Regulation A offering unless they are only exercisable or convertible one year or more after the qualification date.

TESTING THE WATERS

A traditional U.S. IPO generally does not permit pre-filing conversations with investors to determine if there is an interest in the offering. This is

---

[5]See SEC Rel. No. 33-9741, pp. 53–54. For example, the Rule 506(c) offering could not advertise the Regulation A offering without complying with the Regulation A advertising rules. Likewise, in a simultaneous Rule 506(b) offering, the company "will have to conclude that purchasers … were not solicited by means of the offering made in reliance on Regulation A" and that the company had a preexisting substantive relationship with such investors.

called "gun-jumping" or "conditioning the market" and is generally prohibited by the SEC. There is an exception in the JOBS Act for "emerging growth companies" (generally companies with less than $1 billion in annual gross revenues) that permits them to engage before filing in oral or written communications with qualified institutional buyers or institutions that are accredited investors, but not other potential investors. Even that narrow exception does not apply to IPOs of companies with annual gross revenues of $1 billion or more.

In contrast, the enhanced Regulation A permits the company (regardless of the amount of its revenues) to "test the waters" with any potential investor to determine if there is investor interest before launching the Regulation A offering. There is no limitation in Tier 2 which requires the conversation to be with a potential investor who is a qualified institutional buyer or an institution which is an accredited investor. Thus, the "testing the waters" provision is much broader than those applicable to an "emerging growth company."[6]

A simple business plan could be utilized for marketing investors by a potential Tier 2 company, rather than an expensive prospectus, which is required for the traditional U.S. IPO (subject to the limited exception for an "emerging growth company").

The requirements for "testing the waters" are contained in SEC Regulation Section 230.255. Under this regulation, any time before either the submission or public filing of the Regulation A Offering Statement (see Appendix 4), an issuer or any person authorized to act on its behalf may communicate orally or in writing to determine whether there is any interest in the contemplated securities offering. The written communication may include "a means by which a person may indicate to the issuer that such person is interested in a potential offering." Of course, no money can be paid, or unconditional commitment made, by the potential investor until after both the filing and qualification by the SEC of the Offering Statement. Certain disclosures must also be made by the company to potential investors.

---

[6]It should be noted that Rule 506(c) offerings also permit companies to "test the waters."

After the public filing of the Offering Statement with the SEC but before its qualification, "testing the waters" may continue so long as the Preliminary Offering Circular, which is Part II of the Form 1-A (see Appendix 4), is provided, or the potential investor is given a URL, where that document was filed, and other disclosures are provided to the potential investor.

In a Tier 1 offering, whether "testing the waters" is permitted depends upon state law.

DIRECT PUBLIC OFFERINGS

A direct public offering is an offering directly by a company without the involvement of an underwriter. The SEC contemplates that an eligible company could raise capital in a Tier 2 offering without involving an underwriter.[7] However, the company would have to comply with delivering a Preliminary Offering Circular to prospective investors at least 48 hours in advance of the sale, if such a circular was used during the "testing the waters" period. In addition, the company would have to limit the activities of its internal personnel who are engaged in the offering process so as to qualify for an exemption from broker-dealer registration under Rule 3a4-1 under the 1934 Act (see Chapter 2 "Avoiding Broker-Dealer Registration"). Finally, the company would have to make arrangements for a public trading market after the offering (see "Public Trading Market" in this chapter) to avoid a lack of liquidity discount.

Tier 2 permits both direct public offerings by the company as well as underwritten ones to be continuous, subject to certain qualifications. The major qualification is that the offering by the company commences within two calendar days after the Tier 2 qualification date and that, at the time of the Offering Statement is qualified, the amount of securities to be sold is reasonably expected to be offered and sold within two years after the qualification date.[8]

---

[7]SEC Rel. No. 33-9497, p. 71, Note 198.
[8]See SEC Reg. 230.251(d)(3) for the full rule.

COST SAVINGS

Companies can spend significantly less to comply with the Tier 2 of Regulation A offering, compared to a traditional U.S. IPO. In a traditional U.S. IPO on a Form S-1 Registration Statement, the company would normally need three (3) years of audited financial statements (except for emerging growth companies, see Chapter 5) and must file a very expensive registration statement, which includes a prospectus, and then wait in line hoping that the U.S. IPO market will not close. If the U.S. IPO market closes during this waiting period, these costs may never be recovered.

The Offering Circular under Tier 2 of Regulation A (Part II of Form 1-A) will be less expensive to prepare than the prospectus included in a Form S-1 Registration Statement used for the traditional U.S. IPO. The SEC has attempted to simplify the requirements for the Offering Circular, as compared to a traditional U.S. IPO prospectus. However, the cost is still significant.

The Offering Circular under this enhanced Regulation A offering needs only two (2) years of audited financial statements and these audited financial statements do not require an auditing firm which is registered with the Public Company Accounting Oversight Board ("PCAOB"). This means that smaller accounting firms can be used, which tend to be less expensive. However, the financial statements must still comply with PCAOB standards.

The cost savings continue even after the offering is completed, as compared to the traditional U.S. IPO. So long as the securities are not registered under Section 12 of the 1934 Act, there is no need to comply with the proxy rules, or to file Forms 3, 4 or 5 or beneficial owners reports, under the 1934 Act. There is no requirement to file quarterly reports. With minor exceptions, only semi-annual and annual reports, and current event reports, are required under Tier 2 of Regulation A and these reports are somewhat less detailed than the traditional filings under Sections 13 and 15 of the 1934 Act. However, the ongoing cost of these post-offering reports is not insignificant to a smaller company.

It may well be possible to suspend reporting requirements after the fiscal year in which the offering was qualified and completed (see "Post-Offering Reporting Requirements" in this chapter).

WHAT ARE THE DISADVANTAGES?

The following are some of the major disadvantages of a Tier 2 Regulation A offering (assuming the securities are not listed on a national securities exchange upon qualification):

- There is a limit to the amount of securities a non-accredited individual investor can purchase in a Tier 2 offering to no more than 10% of the greater of the investor's annual income and net worth (as adjusted), with other limitations on non-accredited entity investors. Thus, if the non-accredited individual investor's annual income is $40,000 and the investor's net worth is $500,000 (as adjusted), the investor can purchase $50,000 worth of securities. Pursuant to the net worth adjustments, the individual investor's primary residence is not included in determining net worth and mortgage indebtedness up to the fair market value of the investor's primary residence is excluded from liabilities (see Rule 501 in Appendix 1). Unlike a Rule 506(c) offering, the company can rely upon the investor's representation that he or she is qualified, unless the company knew the representation was untrue. An underwriter in a firm commitment offering, or a participating broker-dealer involved in stabilization with respect to the Regulation A offering, would not be subject to these limitations. Likewise, the non-accredited investor limitations do not apply to securities that will be listed on a registered national securities exchange upon qualification of the Regulation A.
- There is no assurance that a public market in the securities will develop after the completion of the Regulation A offering or that a liquid market will develop. However, this risk can in part be ameliorated by making advance arrangements with a broker or dealer to make a market in the securities after the offering (see "Public Trading Market" in this chapter).
- As noted previously, the company will, after the Tier 2 of Regulation A offering, be required to file certain reports with the SEC, including annual, semi-annual and current reports, and this will significantly increase the cost to the company. Although these reports are less onerous than the SEC reports required in a traditional U.S. IPO, they may

require the hiring of additional personnel to prepare and file the reports, the imposition of other internal controls that are applicable to public companies, and additional legal and auditing costs. However, the ongoing Regulation A reporting can be suspended (except for the first year) once the company has less than 300 persons (1,200 for a bank or bank holding company) who are holders of record, provided that there are no ongoing offers or sales of securities of that class of securities made pursuant to Tier 2 and further provided the company has filed all reports due pursuant to Regulation A for the shorter of (i) the period since the company became subject to reporting or (ii) its most recent three fiscal years and any current period. Many companies should be able to avoid the cost of these ongoing reports by taking advantage of this cost-saving provision. Mechanisms can be inserted into the Tier 2 offering terms which would provide reasonable assurance that the company can take advantage of this provision.

- Once the company has total assets exceeding $10 million and a class of equity securities held by record by either (a) 2,000 persons or (b) 500 persons who are not accredited investors, the class of equity securities must be registered under Section 12 of the 1934 Act and the same SEC reports must be filed as those which are required of other public companies. The SEC noted that 2,000 and 500 persons of record limits do not include shares held by beneficial owners at a brokerage firm. Also, persons holding crowdfunding securities sold pursuant to Section 4(a)(6) of the 1933 Act do not count toward these limits.

ELIGIBLE COMPANIES

To be eligible for Regulation A (whether Tier 1 or 2), the issuer of the securities must satisfy the following requirements:

(1) Is an entity organized under the laws of the United States or Canada, or any state, Province, Territory or possession thereof, or the District of Columbia, with its principal place of business in the United States or Canada;

(2) Is not subject to the reporting requirements of the 1934 Act immediately before the offering;

(3) Is not a development stage company that either has no specific business plan or purpose, or has indicated that its business plan is to merge with an unidentified company or companies;

(4) Is not an investment company registered or required to be registered under the Investment Company Act of 1940 or a business development company as defined in that law;

(5) Is not issuing fractional undivided interests in oil or gas rights, or a similar interest in other mineral rights;

(6) Is not, and has not been, subject to any order of the SEC entered pursuant to Section 12(j) of the 1934 Act (relating to suspending or revoking the registration of a security) within five years before the filing of the offering statement;

(7) Has filed with the SEC all the reports it was required to file, if any, pursuant to SEC Reg. Section 230.257 (relating to reports required to be filed after a prior Regulation A offering) during the two years before the filing of the offering statement (or for such shorter period that the issuer was required to file such reports); and

(8) Is not disqualified under the Bad Boy Provisions, which are substantially similar to those described in Chapter 3.

ARE INTERNATIONAL COMPANIES ELIGIBLE?

International companies are not, *per se*, eligible under Regulation A. However, there is nothing to prevent an international company from forming a U.S. or Canadian issuer, having its principal place of business in the U.S. or Canada. The U.S. or Canadian issuer would then exchange its stock for stock or other equity of the international company with the result that the international company became a subsidiary of the U.S. or Canadian issuer.

The SEC considered, but did not adopt, a provision limiting the use of proceeds obtained from Regulation A offerings solely to the U.S. or Canada.[9] Therefore, it would appear that the proceeds obtained by the U.S. or Canadian issuer parent from the Regulation A offering can be used without restriction as to its usage.

---

[9]SEC Rel. No. 33-9497, p. 28

The SEC Staff has stated that a company has its "principal place of business" if its officers, partners, or managers primarily direct, control and coordinate the issuer's activities from the United States or Canada.[10]

PUBLIC TRADING MARKET

Whether the Tier 2 offering is made directly by the company or through an underwriter (on either a firm commitment or best efforts basis), it is important to assure potential investors that there will be a public trading market for the securities immediately after completion of the offering. Securities sold in an exempted Regulation A offering (whether Tier 1 or 2) are immediately resalable by the ordinary investor without restriction. This contrasts with the approximately six months to one-year restriction for securities sold through retail securities crowdfunding or Rule 506(c) for companies that are Non-Reporting Issuers (i.e., companies that do not file reports under Sections 13 or 15(d) of the 1934 Act).

Middle-market or smaller companies raising capital through a Tier 2 offering may not wish to subject themselves to the full cost of being a public company and would prefer instead to enjoy the lower cost of filing the post-offering reports for Tier 2 described in this chapter. This is particularly true in view of the potential for suspending such post-offering reporting obligations (see "Post-Offering Reporting Requirements" in this chapter) which would eliminate this cost completely so long as there were less than 300 shareholders of record and certain conditions were satisfied. However, if the securities sold in the Tier 2 offering are listed for trading on any U.S. securities exchange (e.g., NYSE, Nasdaq, etc.) or on the OTC Bulletin Board, the listing agreements require the same expensive reports that all Reporting Issuers (i.e., public companies) file with the SEC.

To avoid these costs, Tier 2 companies, as well as companies engaged in retail securities crowdfunding under Section 4(a)(6) of the 1933 Act or sales to accredited investors pursuant to Rule 506(c), may wish to have their securities traded on the U.S. OTC market(exclusive of the OTC Bulletin Board which requires reports under the 1934 Act). This quotation medium does not require the company to become a

---

[10]SEC Compliance and Disclosure Interpretations, Question 182.03 (June 23, 2015).

reporting issuer under the 1934 Act. Moreover, this quotation medium publicly displays sale prices for equity securities on Yahoo! Finance, which is a website available to Internet users. Thus, the company and its shareholders obtain many of the benefits of being public without its attendant costs.

In order for a broker or dealer to make a market in the securities of a Tier 2 company (or of a retail securities crowdfunding company or a Rule 506(c) company, once the resale restrictions lapse) in the U.S. OTC market, the broker-dealer must file Form 211 with Financial Industry Regulatory Authority (FINRA) and have certain "reasonably current" information about the company required by SEC Rule 15c2-11 under the 1934 Act. The information must be received by the broker or dealer before publishing or submitting any quotation for the security in any quotation medium, which term would include the U.S. OTC market (exclusive of the OTC Bulletin Board).

The following is the information required to be received by the broker or dealer under SEC Rule 15c2-11 before the broker or dealer can publish or submit any quotation for the security to the U.S. OTC market:

- the exact name of the issuer and its predecessor (if any);
- the addresses of its principal executive offices;
- the state of incorporation, if it is a corporation;
- the exact title and class of the security;
- the par or stated value of the security;
- the number of shares or total amount of the securities outstanding as of the end of the issuer's most recent fiscal year;
- the name and address of the transfer agent;
- the nature of the issuer's business;
- the nature of products or services offered;
- the nature and extent of the issuer's facilities;
- the name of the chief executive officer and members of the board of directors;
- the issuer's most recent balance sheet and profit and loss and retained earnings statements, which statements must be less than six months old if the balance sheet is six or more months old. This will require quarterly financial statements even though only semi-annual financial statements are needed to be filed with the SEC;

- similar financial information for such part of the two preceding fiscal years as the issuer or its predecessor has been in existence;
- whether the broker or dealer or any associated person is affiliated, directly or indirectly, with the issuer;
- whether the quotation is being published or submitted on behalf of any other broker or dealer, and, if so, the name of such broker or dealer;
- whether the quotation is being submitted or published directly or indirectly on behalf of the issuer, or any director, officer, or any person, directly or indirectly the beneficial owner of more than 10% of the outstanding units or shares of any equity security of the issuer, and, if so, the name of such person, and the basis for any exemption under the federal securities laws for any sales of such securities on behalf of such person;
- andvarious filings by the company with the SEC or other government agencies.

To avoid being required to register equity securities under Section 12 of the 1934 Act, and thereby subjecting the company and its insiders to SEC reporting obligations under the 1934 Act, companies that have their securities traded in the U.S. OTC market must be careful to avoid having more than 500 non-accredited shareholders of record or more than 2,000 total shareholders of record, assuming the company has total assets exceeding $10 million. Moreover, even if these shareholders of record limitations are exceeded, registration under Section 12 may not be required for a Tier 2 company if (i) the company is required to file ongoing reports under Regulation A, (ii) is current in its filings, (iii) has engaged a registered transfer agent with respect to its securities issued in the Tier 2 offering and (iv) had a public float of less than $75 million as of the last day of its most recently completed semi-annual period or, in the absence of a public float, had annual revenues of less than $50 million as of its most recently completed fiscal year. The JOBS Act and SEC Rule 12g-6 under the 1934 Act eliminated retail securities crowdfunding under Section 4(a)(6) of the 1933 Act from counting toward these limitations. There is a higher shareholder threshold for banks and bank holding companies.

LIABILITY CONSIDERATIONS

Tier 2 Regulation A offerings are exempt from registration under Section 5 of the 1933 Act and are not subject to the draconian liability provisions of Section 11 of the 1933 Act. The legal liability is basically the same as a private placement under Section 12(a)(2) of the 1933 Act. According to the SEC, liability is limited only to persons offering or selling securities and not those assisting sellers.[11] The SEC specifically stated in its Release that accountants, attorneys, other experts, and placement agents are not included in Section 12(a)(2), and the SEC anticipates that they may not "demand as much compensation for bearing the legal risks associated with participation in Regulation A offerings as they would for offerings subject to Section 11 liability."[12]

FORM 1-A

Form 1-A, which is reproduced in Appendix 4, contains the prescribed Regulation A Offering Statement to be filed with the SEC. The Offering Circular is Part II of the Offering Statement. That form requires, among other things, certain information about the issuer and the offering, including the issuer's contact information; use of proceeds from the offering; price or method for calculating the price of the securities being offered; business and business plan; property; financial condition and results of operations; directors, officers, significant employees, and certain beneficial owners; material agreements and contracts; and past securities sales. The company would also be required to provide information on the material factors that make an investment in the issuer speculative or risky; dilution; the plan of distribution for the offering; executive and director compensation; conflicts of interest and related party transaction; and financial statements.

As noted, Tier 2 financial statements are required to be audited for a two-year period. This is in contrast to Tier 1 of Regulation A financial

---

[11] *Id*, at 62.
[12] *Id*. at p. 237.

statements, which are not required to be audited unless the company has obtained them for other purposes. As previously noted, Tier 2 financial statements must comply with all rules of the PCAOB. However, the auditor need not be registered with the PCAOB.

POST-OFFERING REPORTING REQUIREMENTS

After the completion of the Tier 2 offering, the new rules require certain post-filing reports to be filed with the SEC. However, unlike a traditional IPO, the company is not subject to the proxy rules, short-swing profit rules or beneficial reporting rules of the 1934 Act (among other provisions), thereby somewhat reducing the ongoing compliance costs.

The required post-offering reports include the following, among others:

* An annual report on Form 1-K. (This is similar to Form 10-K but much lighter in requirements.)
* A semi-annual report on Form 1-SA.
* A current event reporting on Form 1-U. (This is similar to the Form 8-K but lighter in requirements.)
* If reporting to the SEC stops being required, a Form 1-Z must be filed.

The duty to file these reports is, as previously noted, automatically suspended with respect to any class of securities held of record by less than 300 persons immediately upon the filing of the Form 1-Z if the company has filed all reports before that date (or, if shorter, the most recent three fiscal years and the current fiscal year) and offers and sales are not continuing pursuant to Tier 2.[13] However, reporting cannot be suspended in the fiscal year in which the Offering Statement was qualified by the SEC or any other fiscal year in which offers or sales are being made in reliance on Tier 2.

Many shareholders elect to have their securities held in so-called "street name" by their brokerage firm. In computing the number of persons whose securities are "held of record" (for purposes of the 300 person

---

[13] See SEC Rule 257(d)(2).

test), only the brokerage firm would normally be counted as a "person," regardless of the number of beneficial owners represented by that brokerage firm. Thus, it is possible that ongoing SEC reporting obligations may be able to be suspended for the fiscal year immediately following the completion of the offering.

Once a duty to file reports is suspended, OTC trading in the securities can, nevertheless, continue, provided the broker or dealer making a market possesses the very limited information required under SEC Rule 15c2-11, described under "Public Trading Market" in this chapter.

Chapter 5 contains a summary of both the existing methods of raising capital from U.S. investors, including the three new methods discussed in prior chapters. The chapter begins with a description of two classifications of types of U.S. investors.

CHAPTER 5

SUMMARY OF U.S. FINANCING SOURCES AND CHOICES

The purpose of this chapter is as follows:

- To briefly describe two primary sources of U.S. capital for private businesses, namely angel investors and private equity funds.
- To explain why a traditional U.S. initial public offering (IPO), which includes the cost of a registration under the 1933 Act, is not practical for most companies.
- To summarize, in table form, both the existing and three new methods previously described of legally accessing U.S. capital by using exemptions from the registration provisions of the 1933 Act.

The primary sources for funding in the U.S. for pre-public businesses are angel investors and professionally managed private equity funds.

ANGEL INVESTORS

Start-up capital for many businesses in the U.S. is many times provided by so-called "angel investors," i.e., high net-worth individuals who are willing to invest in developing companies.[1]

---

[1] See generally, W. Kerr, J. Lerner and A. Schoar, "The Consequences of Entrepreneurial Finance: A Regression Discontinuity Analysis" (Working Paper 10-086), Harvard Business School (2010). This paper supports the position that angel-funded startups have a higher survivor rate.

Apple Inc. got its first round of outside capital from an angel. In 1977, an early Intel executive and shareholder invested $91,000 into Apple and guaranteed another $250,000 in credit lines. At the time of the Apple IPO in 1980, the angel was allegedly worth $154 million.

Angel capital fills the gap between "friends and family" who provide seed financing, and professionally managed private equity funds. Angel money is sometimes called "3F money," for friends, family, and fools. Angel investors currently like startups operating in the following industries: Internet (37.4%), healthcare (23.5%), mobile and telecom (10.4%), energy and utilities (4.3%), electronics (4.3%), consumer products and services (3.5%), and other industries (16.5%).[2]

It is not unusual for successful entrepreneurs who have already exited (i.e., enjoyed the fruits of an IPO or sale) and are looking to do it again with another promising entrepreneur to become angels.

Angels vary widely in personality, methodology, and goals.

On one end of the spectrum is the very unsophisticated investor who likes a particular entrepreneur or business and views their investment no different than gambling in a casino. These investors, sometimes called "recreational investors," like the idea of being identified with a particular company. They enjoy bragging about the investment to their friends at their county club or on a golf course. They typically purchase either common stock or high yield notes (either convertible or with warrants) and do not impose restrictions on the entrepreneur. These recreational investors are sufficiently wealthy so that the loss of the entire investment would not remotely affect them any more than a gambling loss.

The other end of the angel investor spectrum is the sophisticated angel who views the investment as a business. While not necessarily as sophisticated and knowledgeable as the managers of a private equity fund, these investors do a significant amount of due diligence and invest only in businesses they fully understand.

These sophisticated angels tend to purchase preferred stock (or preferred interests in a limited liability company) or convertible notes, and never common stock (or common interests), so as to always be senior to the entrepreneur who holds common stock (or interests). Entrepreneurs

---

[2]T. Prive, "Angel Investors: How The Rich Invest," Forbes.com, March 12, 2013.

should expect significant operating restrictions in any agreement with the sophisticated angel, who thinks and talks like a private equity fund manager.

Many angel investors operate in groups. According to the Angel Capital Association, there are over 330 groups in the U.S. and Canada that are active within the startup community.[3] The leader of the group is sometimes humorously called the archangel. The archangel for the recreational investor is typically the first to invest his or her money, with the remaining group member following on his or her heels. The archangel for sophisticated investors typically arranges for the due diligence for the group and negotiates all of the business terms. It is not unusual for these investors to refuse to invest in any business if no member of the group has any investment experience in that business.

Angel investors typically will invest in a private offering under Rule 506(b) or in an offering complying with Section 4(a)(2) of the 1933 Act. Some angel investors may refuse to invest in a Rule 506(c) offering because of the necessity of revealing personal financial information.

Accredited investor platforms on the Internet are beginning to compete with established angel investor groups. Some of the angel investor platforms were identified in Chapter 2.

PROFESSIONALLY MANAGED PRIVATE EQUITY FUNDS

Most people know that such major companies as Facebook, Google, Microsoft, Genentech, Intel, Digital Equipment Corporation, Federal Express, Compaq, and Sun Microsystems were financed with private equity funds that are professionally managed. However, venture capital, in the sense of private risk capital, has existed in every society in one form or another. For example, in ancient Rome, Marcus Licinius Crossus, reportedly the richest man in Julius Ceasar's Rome, financed many private enterprises.

According to the National Venture Capital Association, in 2013, there was close to $193 billion under professional management by 874 different

---

[3] *Id.*

venture capital firms.[4] In 2013, venture capital firms made investments in 3,382 companies of which 2,360 were in the information technology business.[5] Only 3% of the 2013 investments were made in "seed-stage" companies and 34% were in "early-stage" companies.[6]

Professionally managed venture capital provides a growing company not only with money but also expertise and contacts that may be helpful to the company. The same expertise can also be supplied by angel investors, particularly those who have had experience in the same industry.

Very few businesses qualify for financing under the rigorous standards of the private equity fund. If the business does qualify under these rigorous standards, the entrepreneur should read Chapter 10 of this book entitled "Negotiating With a Professional Investor."

Private equity firms will typically not invest in any securities offering structured to comply with Rule 506's "safe harbor" or the rest of Securities and Exchange Commission (SEC) Regulation D because of the public disclosures required by Form D. Instead, these firms will usually rely on the private placement exemption contained in Section 4(a)(2) of the 1933 Act.

TRADITIONAL U.S. IPOs

Debt and equity securities can be offered and sold by registering them in an IPO under the 1933 Act. There are two major problems with traditional U.S. IPOs. First, middle-market and smaller companies can incur out-of-pocket expenses of $1 million or more for even a small offering of $50 million of the company's securities. If, as a private company, the owner did not have audited financial statements from a large accounting firm which meet SEC and Public Company Accounting Oversight Board ("PCAOB") requirements, the IPO accounting bill can substantially balloon the $1 million figure.

The JOBS Act reduced the period for which financial statements needed to be audited from three years to two years for an IPO of an

---

[4] *2014 National Venture Capital Association Yearbook*, p. 9.
[5] *Id.* p. 12.
[6] *Id.* p. 13.

"emerging growth company" (generally companies with revenues less than $1 billion), and made other beneficial changes designed to reduce costs. Notwithstanding these beneficial changes, Twitter, Inc., which qualified as an emerging growth company, nevertheless paid an accounting bill of $1.9 million and legal fees in expenses of $2 million in its November 2013 IPO. Twitter's total out-of-pocket expenses exceeded $5 million.

If the traditional IPO offering is complicated or there is significant corporate restructuring involved, the owner's costs can also skyrocket. The approximately $16 billion Facebook IPO in May 2012 had out-of-pocket costs exceeding $7 million (excluding underwriters' discounts). The approximately $900 million IPO of Hyatt Hotels Corporation in November 2009 cost close to $8 million (excluding underwriters' discounts). Although the average IPO out-of-pocket costs are substantially lower, it is not unusual to incur out-of-pocket costs exceeding $1 million. If the IPO is cancelled at the last minute, the owner is liable for substantial expenses. However, it is typical to discount professional fees and printing costs in the event of a failed IPO.

The second major problem of a traditional U.S. IPO is that most middle-market and smaller companies are not valuable enough to attract many institutional investors. As previously noted, most institutional investors will not consider investing in an IPO with a post-IPO market capitalization of less than $200 million.

ALTERNATIVES TO A TRADITIONAL U.S. IPO

These major disadvantages of a traditional U.S. IPO cause many companies to consider alternatives that do not involve the registration of securities under the 1933 Act. The major exemptions from the requirement to register debt and equity securities under the 1933 Act are as follows:

- Private placements under Section 4(a)(2) of the 1933 Act, which may include angel investors as well as institutional investors, such as professionally managed venture capital firms.
- Rule 506 of Regulation D which contains a so-called "safe harbor" for complying with registration exemptions contained in Section 4(a)(2) of

the 1933 Act. Offerings under Rule 506(b) prohibit general advertising and require a preexisting relationship with the investor. Offerings under new Rule 506(c), created pursuant to the JOBS Act, and discussed in Chapters 2 and 3 of this book, permit general advertising and do not require a preexisting relationship with the investor.

- Crowdfunding securities offerings qualified under Section 4(a)(6) of the 1933 Act which exemption was created by the JOBS Act and is described in Chapter 1 of this book.
- Offerings under Section 3(b) of the 1933 Act which includes both a Regulation A Tier 1 and a Tier 2 offering exemption described in Table 5.1 as well as offerings under Rules 504 and 505 of Regulation D. The new Regulation A Tier 1 and Tier 2 exemption is described in Chapter 4 of this book.
- Section 3(a)(11) of the 1933 Act, the so-called "intrastate offering exemption."

COMPARISON OF DIFFERENT CAPITAL RAISING CHOICES

Table 5.1 attempts to summarize both the new and existing major choices for selling debt and equity securities to U.S. investors. The table excludes bank loans which typically are not considered debt securities. The reference in the table to "State Securities Law Preemption" refers to whether or not a particular capital raising choice has to also comply with the registration provisions of securities laws of states within the U.S. The three new methods of financing U.S. businesses that have been created by the JOBS Act are shown with an asterisk.

OFFERINGS TO NON-U.S. INVESTORS

Both U.S. and international companies can offer and sell securities to non-U.S. investors outside the U.S. These offerings should comply with the "safe harbor" contained in SEC Regulation S, which is discussed in Chapter 2.

In order to raise capital by selling equity securities of the company, it is necessary to value that company. Chapter 6 will discuss different methods of valuing a company.

Table 5.1. Comparison of Different Capital Raising Choices

Type of offering	Offering limit[7]	Solicitation	Issuer and investor requirements	Resale restrictions[8]	State securities law preemption
Intrastate Offering Section 3(a)(11)	None	Limited to persons resident within a state of which the issuer is a resident	All issuers and investors must be resident in state	Restricted[8]	No
Private Placement Section 4(a)(2)	None	No general solicitation and preexisting relationship required	All investors must meet sophistication and access to information test	Restricted securities	No
Tier 1 of Regulation A	$20 million with $6 million limit on secondary sales by affiliates and 30% first year limitation on secondary sales.	"Testing the waters" permitted before and after filing; general solicitation permitted after qualification	U.S. or Canadian issuers, subject to exclusions contained in Chapter 4 of this book	Freely saleable, except for affiliates	No
*Tier 2 of Regulation A	$50 million with $15 million limit on secondary sales and identical 30% first year limitation.	"Testing the waters" permitted before and after filing; general solicitation permitted after qualification	U.S. or Canadian issuers, subject to exclusions contained in Chapter 4 of this book	Freely saleable, except for affiliates	Preempted

(Continued)

[7] Aggregate offering limit on securities sold within a 12-month period.

[8] Resale restrictions are determined by state securities laws, which typically restrict in-state resales for a one-year period and by the federal intrastate offering exemption which requires that the securities "come to rest" within the state. See also SEC Rule 147(e) which limits resale to residents of the state during the period of the offering and for a period of nine months from the date of the last sale within the state.

Table 5.1   (*Continued*)

Type of offering	Offering limit[a]	Solicitation	Issuer and investor requirements	Resale restrictions	State securities law preemption
Rule 504 of Regulation D	$1 million	General solicitation permitted in some cases[9]	Excludes reporting companies, investment companies, blank-check companies, and "Bad Boys" or "Bad Actors."	Restricted[10]	No
Rule 505 of Regulation D	$5 million	No general solicitation	Excludes investment companies and "Bad Boys" or "Bad Actors." Unlimited accredited investors and 35 non-accredited investors	Restricted securities	No
Rule 506(b) of Regulation D	None	No general solicitation permitted and preexisting relationship required[11]	Unlimited accredited investors and up to 35 non-accredited investors. Limitations on non-accredited investors[12]	Restricted securities	Preempted
*Rule 506(c) of Regulation D	None	General solicitation permitted	All purchasers must be accredited investors, and verification is required	Restricted securities	Preempted
*Crowdfunding under Section 4(a)(6)	Limited to $1 million during any 12-month period	General solicitation permitted	U.S. issuers only, with exclusions discussed in Chapter 1 in this book. Severe limitations on amounts invested by a single investor	One year, with limited exceptions	Preempted

[9] No general solicitation or advertising is permitted unless the offering is registered in a state requiring the use of a substantive disclosure document or sold under state exemption for sales to accredited investors with general solicitation.

[10] Restricted unless registered in a state requiring use of a substantive disclosure document or sold under state exemption for sale to accredited investors.

[11] No general solicitation or advertising is permitted under Rule 506(b). General solicitation and general advertising are permitted under Rule 506(c), provided all purchasers are accredited investors and the issuer takes reasonable steps to verify accredited investor status.

[12] Under Rule 506(b), offerings may involve an unlimited number of accredited investors and up to 35 non-accredited investors who satisfy knowledge and experience tests. Under Rule 506(c), all purchasers must be accredited investors.

PART II
STRATEGIC CONSIDERATIONS

CHAPTER 6

VALUING A BUSINESS

If the owner of a company wishes to sell equity securities in the company pursuant to crowdfunding, Rule 506 or Tiers 1 and 2 of Regulation A, a valuation will initially have to be established for the business both before and after it receives the injection of equity capital. This valuation is necessary in order to determine what percentage of the business should be acquired by the investors in its equity securities.

The value of a business before it receives an injection of equity is called its "pre-money" value and the value after the injection is the "post-money" value. The pre- and post-money values determine how much equity a business has to relinquish to outside investors. For example, if the pre-money value of a business is $20 million and outside investors are injecting $5 million of equity capital into it, the outside investors should receive rights to 20% of its equity. This is computed as follows:

$$\frac{\$5\,\text{million}}{\$20\,\text{million} + \$5\,\text{million}} = \frac{1}{5} = 20\%$$

The numerator of the fraction is the outside equity capital injection and the denominator is the sum of (a) the pre-money value plus (b) the amount of the outside equity capital injection.

VALUATION METHODOLOGIES

The following are some of the more common methods of valuing a business:

- Discounted Cash Flow.

- Earnings before interest, taxes, depreciation, and amortization (EBITDA) Method, which is typically used for middle-market companies rather than start-up companies.
- Comparable Company Method.
- Comparable Transaction Method.
- Asset Accumulation Method.

Most professional investors compute the post-money value of the business at the projected exit date, and discount that figure to the present, before deciding the equity capital percentage they will require of a business. Thus, in the above example, the venture capitalist may compute a present post-money value of $25 million for a business by discounting a projected exit date value of $100 million back to $25 million; therefore, its $5 million investment justifies a 20% equity interest. Using the post-money valuation permits the venture capitalist to factor into the valuation the effect of the $5 million capital injection on the future projections of a business.

Most sophisticated venture capitalists compute the post-money valuation of a business by using a discounted cash flow method of valuation (described in the Section "Discounted Cash Flow Method"). The valuation is designed to permit the venture capitalist to achieve its so-called "hurdle rate," i.e., the minimum yearly investment return that the venture capitalist expects before considering an investment.

For example, if the hurdle rate of the venture capitalist is 35% per annum, the post-money valuation will reflect the likely valuation when the exit occurs (e.g., in five years), discounted by a *minimum* of 35% per annum. The discounting rate will probably significantly exceed the 35% hurdle rate to reflect the risk that the exit valuation will not be achieved. A seed-stage business may have a 100% per year discount rate.

The exit valuation may be based upon a sale or an initial public offering (IPO) valuation, or some combination. Thus, the venture capitalist's valuation analysis begins with a comparison with analogies to other companies in an industry that has been sold or gone public. Once appropriate analyses are obtained, the discount rates are applied to reflect the expected hurdle rate and the risk that a business will never reach the exit objectives.

Tip: The greater the time until the exit date, the greater the total discount for determining the present value of a business. If an owner of a business can reasonably accelerate the exit date in his or her projections, he or she can generally achieve a higher present valuation for the business and, therefore less equity dilution. The only exception is if by postponing the exit date, the owner of the business can increase the valuation by a significant amount greater than the yearly discount rate.

Because of the difficulty in valuing a business, particularly a start-up business, under any methodology, many professional investors will postpone the determination of that valuation until a subsequent round of financing and then use the valuation in the next round, less an agreed discount factor. Thus, a first-round investor might wait until a valuation is established in a second or later round of financing and reduce that valuation by the agreed discount factor. For example, if the second round of financing is based upon a $10 million pre-money valuation, the first-round investors could, by an agreement with the owner, receive a 40% discount from that valuation by reason of the additional risk which they were assuming in financing the first round. Under this example, the first-round investors would compute the pre-money valuation at $6 million.

DISCOUNTED CASH FLOW METHOD

The discounted cash flow method of valuation is typically used for both early-stage business with no earnings as well as late-stage businesses as a method of double-checking the valuation obtained through other valuation methods discussed in this chapter.

Under this method of valuation, the owner of a business looks at future cash flows projected from the operations and discounts them in accordance with time and risk factors. The higher the risk, the higher the discount factor.

The discounted cash flow method begins with a projection of revenues and operating profit. These projected financial results are then adjusted for non-recurring and non-operating items of income and expense, and are reduced by taxes. The projected operating profit estimates after taxes are then further adjusted by adding back depreciation/amortization and deducting net investments in working capital and capital expenditures.

At the end of a given period, typically 5 or 10 years, a "terminal" or "residual" value is calculated for the business. This "terminal" or "residual" value is then combined with the discount and flows to produce an overall valuation for the business. The "terminal" or "residual" value used by venture capitalists is the exit valuation. As noted, the exit valuation will be based on analogous companies which have been sold or are publicly traded.

The net equity value of the business, including the residual value, is then determined by deducting the market value of interest-bearing debt and adding the market value of non-operating assets which remain in the business. An example of this calculation is contained in Table 6.1.

Table 6.1.   Discount Cash Flow Method

Discounted cash flow valuation (in multiples of 1,000)

	Year 1	Year 2	Year 3	Year 4	Year 5	Terminal value
Revenues	$30,000	$45,000	$50,000	$55,000	$62,000	—
EBIT	3,264	3,825	4,322	4,884	5,519	—
Income taxes (cash basis)	1,110	1,301	1,469	1,661	1,876	—
Net operating income	2,154	2,524	2,853	3,223	3,643	$30,358
Cash flow adjustments						
Plus: Depreciation	1,392	1,800	2,034	2,298	2,597	—
Less: Net change in working capital	(405)	(731)	(168)	(204)	(244)	—
Capital expenditures	(1,966)	(3,675)	(4,161)	(4,398)	(4,697)	—
Free cash flows	1,175	(82)	558	919	1,299	—
Net present value at 12.0%	1,049	(65)	397	584	737	17,226
			Total corporate value			$19,928
			Less: Market value of debt			$12,528
			Shareholder value			$7,400

Obviously, a cash flow of 10 years from today is not worth the same amount to the investor as a current cash flow. Thus, the formula tends to give little current value to cash flows which are too far in the future.

DISCOUNT FACTOR

The discount factor applicable to the cash flows is arrived at by using various formulas, one of which is the Capital Asset Pricing Model. The Capital Asset Pricing Model sets the discount rate at the weighted average cost of equity and debt capital.

The Capital Asset Pricing Model estimates the future cost of a company's equity through a multi-factor equation and then determines the after-tax expected future costs of the company's debt. The final step is to compute the weighted average cost of capital, which is the weighted average cost of both equity and debt.

The weighted average cost of equity is computed by using the following equation: $re = rf + B (rm - rf)$, which can be defined as follows:

re = expected future cost of equity;

rf = risk free rate of return; and

B = the beta factor, which is a measurement of market risk with the figure 1 equaling a normative risk. One court has defined the beta factor as "the non-diversified risk associated with the economy as a whole as it affects this firm."

rm = the market risk premium for this particular business.

The "rm" factor, together with the beta factor in the equation, has the effect of discounting the future cash flows by the risk of their non-occurrence. The greater the risk of the projected cash flow not occurring, the higher the expected future cost of equity.

The historical financial results of a business are only relevant to this discounted cash flow method to the extent that they give credence to the projections of future cash flow.

THE EBITDA METHOD

One of the most common methods of valuation for middle-market businesses is the so-called EBITDA method. This involves the determination of the company's accounting earnings before interest, taxes, depreciation, and amortization (EBITDA), and multiplication of the EBITDA, as adjusted by the relevant multiplier to obtain an enterprise valuation.

The following is an example of the EBITDA method:

Example	
Revenues	$10,000,000
Cost of sales	(8,000,000)
Gross profit	2,000,000
General and administrative costs	(500,000)
Depreciation	(100,000)
Amortization	(50,000)
Interest expense	(250,000)
Total expenses	(900,000)
Net income before taxes	1,100,000
Income taxes (40%)	(440,000)
Net income after taxes	$660,000
Calculation of EBITDA	
Net income after taxes	$660,000
Interest	250,000
Income taxes	440,000
Depreciation	100,000
Amortization	50,000
EBITDA	$1,500,000

EBITDA is then adjusted to remove expenses and revenue that will no longer be continued after the investment. These adjustments can be quite substantial for a closely held family business.

Most privately-held businesses are operated to minimize income taxes. As a result, excessive compensation and perquisites may be provided to the owner and his or her family in order to reduce taxes. The excessive compensation and perquisites are really forms of disguised dividends.

The true cost of replacing the owner and his or her family with a high-level executive usually results in a substantial addition to the EBITDA.

Some investors will subtract from the adjusted EBITDA any required yearly capital expenditures.

MULTIPLIERS

The adjusted EBITDA is then multiplied by a multiplier to obtain an overall valuation for the business (also called "enterprise value"). The multiplier typically ranges from four to seven times adjusted EBITDA. However, the multiplier has gone below four and substantially above seven, depending upon whether it is a buyer's market or a seller's market for the sale of businesses.

Multipliers of 10 or more are not unheard of for companies with strong market niches.

The multipliers are derived from comparable company valuations, including the multipliers applicable to public companies in the same industry. For example, if a public company in the same industry has a total market valuation (based on its stock price) of 10 times its EBITDA, this multiplier could be the starting point in determining the appropriate multiplier. This multiplier would then be discounted by the fact that the private company was smaller and had less market dominance.

Many business owners incorrectly assume that the multipliers applicable to larger companies in the industry apply to their smaller company. The multipliers for less dominant companies in an industry are significantly smaller than for dominant companies.

A further discount to the multiplier may be applied to reflect the lack of liquidity of the stock in the hands of the investor (that is, if no public market exists for the stock).

GENERAL

If the company has long-term debt, the overall valuation of the business will be reduced by the market value of this debt (including the current portion of long-term debt). The market value can be greater or less than the principal amount of the debt. For example, long-term debt that bears an interest rate below current interest rates for comparable maturities will have a market value less than its principal amount.

The overall valuation of the company obtained by multiplying the adjusted EBITDA by the applicable multiplier is called the "enterprise value." If the company has no long-term debt, then this figure is the valuation of the business.

COMPARABLE COMPANY METHOD OF VALUATION

The comparable company method of valuation typically involves comparing a company to the market capitalization and multiples of certain financial criteria (such as net income, projected net income, earnings before interest and taxes, earnings before depreciation, amortization, interest and taxes, revenues, and book value) of comparable public companies. Market capitalization refers to the public trading price of the stock multiplied by the number of outstanding shares. Thus, if a comparable public company had a public trading price of $20.00 per share and there were 2 million shares outstanding, the overall market capitalization of that comparable public company would be $40 million.

The market capitalization method of valuation contains a number of defects. The trading price of shares of a public company does not normally reflect any control premium unless the company is expected to be sold shortly. Consequently, the public trading price may significantly understate the overall value of the comparable public company in a sale situation where a control premium is paid for the shares.

In addition, it is difficult to compare a publicly-held company with a privately-held company. Shares of public companies typically trade at a price which reflects the liquidity available to shareholders, which liquidity is not available to shareholders of a privately-held company. As a result, privately-held companies tend to sell at a discount compared to comparable publicly-held companies. The problems with using market capitalization comparisons do not necessarily mean that this method of valuation is defective, since multiples of other financial criteria are also compared to the public company, such as the EBITDA multiple, in using the comparable company method of valuation.

COMPARABLE TRANSACTION METHOD
OF VALUATION

Where information is available on the sale of comparable companies (whether public or private), this information is very valuable in assessing the value of a company. However, great care must be taken in using this information, since every company is unique and there may be significant differences between the owner's company and the so-called "comparable company."

One of the major problems with this method is the lack of sufficient information to be able to judge how "comparable" another company is to yours. For example, a company may have one customer which accounts for 15% of its sales — a negative factor. The company may not be able to determine if the so-called comparable company had this same negative factor. Therefore, information on the sale price of the comparable company may be difficult to assess and should be taken with a grain of salt.

ASSET ACCUMULATION METHOD

This method involves accumulating the going concern value of each of the specific assets of a business. This includes off-balance sheet assets, such as customer lists, product market identification, value of the trained workforce, etc., in addition to the balance sheet assets. In computing going concern value, three standard appraisal methods are utilized:

- Cost approach.
- Income approach.
- Market approach.

The replacement cost of certain off-balance sheet intangible assets may be utilized to value them on the theory that a buyer could have to pay replacement costs to duplicate these assets. For example, if a buyer were to start the business from scratch, the buyer would have to incur costs until a trained management team and work force could be assembled. These costs could be considered to be the value of the management team and work force. A similar value could be applied to value the company's other intangible assets.

The value of the balance sheet and off-balance sheet assets is then combined to calculate the total value of the entire business.

OTHER VALUATION FORMULAS

There are a myriad of other valuation formulas used today.

If the business is asset-intensive, some have suggested that the business value is equal to its "hard-assets" plus goodwill. "Hard-assets" refer to the total fair market value (which can be replacement costs) of the fixed assets and equipment, leasehold improvements, accounts receivable, and inventory. The entrepreneur's "goodwill" is the company's discretionary cash for one year, i.e., the amount of cash received as salary and dividends.

None of these formulas, or the many others currently in use, are universally applied. What is important is that the owner of the business understands the particular valuation formula most likely to be applied to the business.

MINIMUM VALUE FORMULAS

The minimum value of a business is the higher of value (a) its value to service acquisition debt or (b) its liquidation value.

ACQUISITION DEBT VALUE
(LEVERAGE BUYOUT ANALYSIS)

If the business produces positive cash flow before interest, taxes, and depreciation amortization (EBITDA), that cash flow can service (i.e., pay interest and principal) a certain amount of acquisition debt. The amount of acquisition debt that can be so serviced is the minimum value for the business.

For example, assume that the excess cash flow of a business (EBITDA) is $500,000 per year, and that, based upon current interest rates, that $500,000 is sufficient to pay the interest and principal due on $3 million of bank debt which matures over a five-year loan term (exclusive of the balloon principal payment in the fifth year which can be refinanced). The minimum value of a business would be $3 million.

There is a limit to the amount of debt senior lenders will provide for a given business without an equity component. Therefore, once that debt limit is reached, the cash flow must be sufficiently high enough to be able to attract equity investors.

In this sense, an entrepreneur can determine the minimum value of the business using a leveraged buyout analysis.

LIQUIDATION VALUE

Some businesses are only worth the liquidation value of their assets. Liquidation value refers to the price which would be received in an orderly liquidation, and not in a fire sale. These businesses are typically not producing positive cash flow and do not have prospects of doing so.

SPECIFIC FACTORS WHICH AFFECT VALUATION

There can be specific favorable and unfavorable factors to a business which increase or decrease its valuation. Some examples are provided in Table 6.2.

Table 6.2. Examples of Factor Increasing or Decreasing Valuation

Factors increasing valuation	Factors decreasing valuation
• Strong customer relationships at all levels.	• Weak customer relationships and frequent turnover.
• Proprietary products or services.	• Lack of proprietary products or services.
• No single customer accounts for more than 5% of revenues or profits.	• A single customer accounts for over 15% of revenues or profits.
• Strong management team (important mainly to financial buyers).	• A weak management team (so-called "one-man show" syndrome).
• Excellent employee turnover and relations.	• Poor employee turnover and relations.
• Consistent revenue and earnings trends.	• Inconsistent revenue and earnings trends.
• Plant and equipment in good repair.	• Plant or equipment has been neglected and requires significant repairs.

An entrepreneur must analyze the strengths and weaknesses of the business and be prepared to point out the strengths and acknowledge the weaknesses, which the investor will probably discover in its due diligence prices.

One method of increasing the value of the business is to use the investment proceeds to accomplish an industry roll-up or other industry acquisition. This is discussed in Chapter 9.

The two most important issues to an entrepreneur are (1) to obtain the highest valuation for his or her business and (2) to keep control of the business after the investment.

Chapter 7 discusses, among other issues, various strategic issues in deciding to accept outside capital, including the importance of retaining control.

CHAPTER 7

STRATEGIC CONSIDERATIONS

The purpose of this chapter is to examine some of the strategic issues for an entrepreneur to consider before accepting outside venture capital. We begin with the definition of venture capital.

WHAT IS VENTURE CAPITAL?

There is no universally-accepted definition of "venture capital." Everyone agrees that a first-round financing of a start-up software firm by a professionally managed private equity firm is a "venture capital" transaction. Not everyone agrees, however, that "bridge" financing to an initial public offering (IPO) of a late-stage company qualifies as "venture capital" or that a $100 million high-yield note (junk bond) financing for a well-established family business qualifies.

This book uses a broad definition of "venture capital" (also called "outside capital") to refer to any form of high-risk investing. This includes the following:

- A seed capital financing by an angel investor.
- A crowdfunding offering of a start-up business.
- A private offering under Rule 506(b) to accredited investors with whom the company or its solicitor have a preexisting substantive relationship.
- An offering under Rule 506(c) over the Internet or with other forms of general solicitation and advertising.
- A fifth-round financing by a professionally managed private equity firm.
- A high-yield debt offering of a late-stage company to finance its business plan.

- A private placement of convertible preferred stock sold by an investment banker, which serves as a bridge to a traditional U.S. IPO.
- A bank loan that is sufficiently risky to justify the issuance of warrants or options to purchase equity securities of the borrower.
- A traditional U.S. IPO underwritten by a third tier underwriter who raises $25 million.
- An IPO of a biotech company with immaterial amounts of revenues or profits.

DECISION TO GROW WITH OUTSIDE CAPITAL

The decision to grow a business with outside capital is a difficult one for most entrepreneurs and involves weighing personal and business objectives.

Venture capital can take any of the following forms, among others:

- High-yield notes (so-called "junk bonds").
- Convertible notes or notes with warrants.
- Convertible preferred stock in a corporation or preferred interests in a limited liability company.
- Common stock in a corporation or common equity interests in a limited liability company.

The prejudice against outside capital is natural for established businesses. No one wants a partner. This is especially true if the entrepreneur has started and grown the business with his or her own capital or the capital of family and friends. In addition, suppliers of outside capital generally impose restrictions on the business. Some require veto over certain major decisions, board of directors' participation, and limitations on compensation.

Despite these disadvantages, accepting outside capital can still make good sense. Although it is natural to want to own 100% of the business, it may be wiser to own a smaller proportion of a much larger business. This is particularly true if the entrepreneur wishes ultimately to have a traditional U.S. IPO or sell the business at an attractive price.

If the business has a good cash flow, junk bonds may offer a method of obtaining outside capital without diluting the equity ownership.

PUBLICLY-TRADED COMPANIES VERSUS PRIVATE COMPANIES

An "illiquidity discount" is generally applied to the value of the stock of a privately-held company. This illiquidity discount can reduce the value of the stock of a private company by 33⅓% or more compared to the stock of an identical publicly-traded company.

As a general rule, if an entrepreneur is raising capital, the faster he or she can be in a position to offer stock to outside investors that can be publicly traded, the smaller will be his or her personal equity dilution. Both Rule 506(c) offerings and Tier 2 of Regulation A offerings can avoid a major illiquidity discount if the investors are assured that a liquid, public trading market will develop after completion of the offering.

FACTORS TO BE CONSIDERED

The following factors will bear on the entrepreneur's decision to accept outside capital:

- Personal exit strategy.
- The ability and willingness to make the business attractive to sources of outside capital.
- The ability and willingness to accommodate the "hassle" of due diligence by potential investors, capital raising, and the subsequent growth of the business.
- The competitive situation in the entrepreneur's industry.
- The entrepreneur's age.
- The entrepreneur's health.

EXIT STRATEGY

Any outside investor in the business will typically want an exit strategy. There are four main exit strategies:

- Selling the business.
- A traditional U.S. IPO.
- Having the company buy back the investment.
- A secondary offering under Tier 2 of Regulation A.

The time frame for these exit strategies varies with the nature of the investors and their personal goals. Private equity firms and sophisticated accredited investors typically have exit strategies which vary from 3 to 10 years. Most prefer an exit at five years at the latest. However, smaller or less sophisticated accredited investors in a Rule 506(c) offering will not necessarily impose any exit strategy.

Investors in a $1 million crowdfunding offering or a Tier 2 of Regulation A offering will not necessarily impose any exit strategy. Crowdfunding investors may have too small of a financial investment in the business to bother imposing an exit strategy. Investors in a Tier 2 of Regulation A offering will typically not impose an exit strategy on the company if they believe that a public trading market will develop after completion of the offering, since that public market provides them with liquidity.

If an entrepreneur's personal exit strategy does not coincide with the exit strategy of his or her outside investors, the businessperson should think twice before taking outside capital. For example, if the businessperson has no desire to sell the company and he or she does not wish to go public (either traditionally or through Tier 2 of Regulation A) in five years, but his or her investor wants an exit in five years, the businessperson has no choice but to buy back the equity. Yet, the company may not have the funds to afford to buy back the equity in five years and the businessperson may be forced to sell the business prematurely.

If the owner of a family-owned business wants to give the business solely to his or her children, who will pay for his or her retirement with company funds, the owner is not a good candidate for outside capital. One possible exception would be if the owner or his or her children have an exit strategy which would accommodate an outside investor. See "Family Business Strategies."

Some professionally managed private equity firms require a so-called "drag-along" clause in their legal documents, particularly in early-stage investments. This clause requires a businessperson to sell the company if the investor wants to sell. Obviously, if the businessperson has no desire to sell the company, he or she should avoid these venture capitalists.

It is not necessary to sell the company to accommodate the exit objectives of outside investors. Going public, either traditionally or under

Tier 2 of Regulation A, is a perfectly acceptable exit strategy if the businessperson can sell equity publicly. Going public permits the company to raise public funds at attractive prices, creates liquidity for outside investors, and may permit the businessperson to continue to control the company after the public offering.

EXAMPLE

At age 50, an entrepreneur is the owner of a family business started by his or her grandfather. The entrepreneur would like to leave the business to his or her children, one of whom already works in the business. However, the business, which is a niche publishing business, is not doing well. Competition from Amazon and larger print publishers, who have greater capital resources and better distribution channels, is seriously hurting its sales and profitability. Outside capital is needed to grow the publishing business, but there is a limit on what the banks will finance. The businessperson does not want to sell the business in five years and he or she has no desire to go public unless absolutely forced to do so. Therefore, the strategy in attracting outside equity capital is to agree to buy back the investment after five years with internally-generated profits combined (if necessary) with other outside capital which might be obtained at that time. If the businessperson is unable to buy back the investment in five years, his or her fallback is to sell the family business or go public. However, the businessperson should recognize that the public offering fallback is questionable since (1) there might not be an attractive public market in five years and (2) the business might not be sufficiently appealing to attract an underwriter.

ANALYSIS

This businessperson has decided on the best from among many bad choices. Doing nothing means further erosion of the business. Yet, seeking outside equity capital creates the risk that the business cannot buy back the investment in five years and that going public will not work, thereby resulting in the sale of the business at what may be an unattractive price. Even if the going public strategy does work, the entrepreneur risks losing family control of the business.

PERSONAL GOALS

If a businessperson is tired of working so hard and wants to cut back or spend more time with family, he or she should think twice before accepting outside capital. Investors are looking for someone to score a "home run" with their money. A tired executive is unlikely to accomplish that objective.

Of course, if the second-in-command can handle the job almost as well as the entrepreneur, such entrepreneur might kick himself or herself up to Chairman of the Board of the company and let the second-in-command run the show. This permits the entrepreneur to slow down while at the same time permitting the business to raise outside capital.

Some businesspersons find it very difficult to delegate. If that describes the entrepreneur, it is unlikely that the "kick yourself upstairs" strategy will really work.

COMPETITION

If the business must have outside capital to stay competitive, the entrepreneur may have no choice but to seek outside capital. Many industries today are going through so-called "roll-ups" or acquisitions within the industry. These roll-ups are resulting in either large private companies well financed by private equity fund sponsors, or large public companies which are well capitalized, and each is willing to purchase a dominant market share. The entrepreneur may be unable to effectively compete with these companies without outside capital to grow the business.

AGE AND HEALTH

The businessperson's age or health may adversely affect his or her ability to raise outside capital. Passive investors want management in place who will facilitate their exit strategy. If the entrepreneur is 85 years old or in poor health (regardless of age), his or her ability to attract outside investors will be seriously impaired unless the second-in-command is an impressive individual capable of leading the company.

It used to be the case that an entrepreneur could also be too young to attract outside investors. That is no longer true. Very young entrepreneurs can attract venture capital if their product falls into certain categories, such as computer games, social media, and software or related technology. The 19-year old entrepreneur, named Palmer Luckey, who raised $2.4 million on Kickstarter and then sold his company to Facebook at age 21 for $2 billion, disproves that an entrepreneur can be too young. See Chapter 1 for that story.

POSTPONE OUTSIDE CAPITAL AS LONG AS POSSIBLE

The discount rates on seed-stage venture capital runs 80% or more per annum compounded. One seed-stage professionally managed private equity firm has announced a discount rate of 100% per annum. That means that the investment must project to produce a return of 100% per year, compounded, on each $1 million investment in the company until the exit date, i.e., a sale or a public offering. Thus, if the exit date is five years after the investment and the investment is $1 million, the investor expects to receive $32 million upon a sale or an IPO (i.e., $1 million compounded at 100% per year).

On the other hand, the discount rate on second-stage companies can be as low as 20–35% per annum.

> **Moral**: The longer an entrepreneur waits to seek outside capital, the less equity dilution he or she suffers.

DO NOT WAIT TOO LONG

There are some entrepreneurs who wait too long before seeking outside capital. They are so concerned with retaining 100% of the equity in and control of their business that they miss non-recurring market opportunities to grow their business. For example, if a significant strategic merger becomes available in the industry, it may be advisable to seize that opportunity even if the entrepreneur has to dilute the equity ownership earlier than desired.

The moral is that an entrepreneur should weigh equity dilution against the market opportunity available to grow the business.

KEEPING CONTROL OF THE BUSINESS

In general, whoever controls the majority of the members of the board of directors of a corporation controls the corporation under state corporate laws in the U.S. The discussion below may or may not be applicable to a limited liability company or similar entity.

The board of directors of a corporation, and not the shareholders, control all of the following major decisions:

Decision: Hire or fire officers or other employees.
Who Decides: Solely board of directors, not shareholders.

Decision: Incur debt.
Who Decides: Solely board of directors, not shareholders.

Decision: Enter into new line of business within "purpose" clause of charter.
Who Decides: Solely board of directors, not shareholders.

Decision: Purchase assets.
Who Decides: Solely board of directors, not shareholders.

Decision: Issue more common or preferred stock without exceeding authorized number of such shares in charter.
Who Decides: Solely board of directors, not shareholders.

Decision: Sale of some assets but not substantially all assets.
Who Decides: Solely board of directors, not shareholders.

Decision: Register shares under securities laws.
Who Decides: Solely board of directors, not shareholders.

Decisions on which shareholders must vote under state corporate laws generally include only the following:

- Charter amendment.
- Merger, consolidation, or sale of substantially all assets.
- Dissolution or division.
- Election and removal of directors (unless staggered terms).

The following are decisions which generally only the board of directors can initiate and must have prior board approval regardless of the wishes of the shareholders:

- Mergers, consolidations, or sale of substantially all assets.
- In some cases (particularly public companies), charter amendments, dissolutions, and divisions.

Thus, until the directors are replaced by the shareholders, the board of directors is in control. Even the replacement of directors by shareholders can be significantly delayed if the terms of the directors are staggered.

CONTROL PREMIUMS

Under most state laws of the U.S., a controlling shareholder of a corporation is entitled to a premium from the sale of a controlling block of stock and need not share that premium with other shareholders. However, it is illegal to sell corporate office or management control by itself (that is, accompanied by no stock or insufficient stock to carry voting control) or to sell to a looter or to appropriate a corporate asset to the personal benefit of a control person.

According to Section 5.16 of the American Law Institute's *Principles of Corporate Governance: Analysis and Recommendations* (*1994*):

a controlling shareholder ... has the same right to dispose of voting equity securities as ... any other shareholder, including the right to dispose of those securities for a price that is not made proportionally available to other shareholders, but the controlling shareholder does not satisfy the duty of fair dealing to the other shareholders if:

(a) The controlling shareholder does not make disclosure concerning the transaction ... to other shareholders with whom the controlling shareholder deals in connection with the transaction; or

(b) It is apparent from the circumstances that the purchaser is likely to violate the duty of fair dealing ... in such a way as to obtain a significant financial benefit for the purchaser or an associate....

As a *Comment* to Section 5.16 states:

Judicial decisions generally have allowed controlling shareholders to sell their shares at a premium above the market price existing prior to the disclosure of the transaction without having required either that the premium be shared with other shareholders or that the transaction be restructured so that all shareholders could participate on the same terms. See, e.g., *Zetlin v. Hanson Holdings, Inc. 48 N.Y.2d 684, 421 N.Y.S.2d 877, 397 N.E.2d 387 (1979); Clagget v. Hutchinson, 583 F.2d 1259 (4th Cir.1978); Yerke v. Batman, 376 N.E.2d 1211 (Ind.App.1978); Ritchie v. McGrath, 1 Kan.App.2d 481, 571 P.2d 17 (1977)*. Section 5.16 follows these decisions and rejects the competing equal opportunity rule, which would require a premium to be initially offered to or later shared by all shareholders on a *pro rata* basis.

A control premium typically generates a lawsuit in the U.S. However, assuming a properly structured transaction, most of these lawsuits will be lost by the plaintiff. The threat of such a lawsuit, even though without merit, has caused some companies to avoid control premiums.

TAG-ALONG CLAUSES

Most sophisticated investors will insist upon a so-called "tag-along" clause to make certain that they share in any control premium. The clause permits the investor to "tag along" on any sale of stock by the entrepreneur and requires the investor to receive the same price per share, thus insuring a proportionate sharing of any control premium.

FAMILY-OWNED BUSINESSES

It has been estimated that close to 90% of all businesses in the world are family-owned. By their very nature, family-owned businesses do not wish to have non-family members as equity owners of the business.

However, as the family business grows, particularly through various generations, it is inevitable that some of the children and grandchildren will not want to participate in the business. At some point, it may be necessary to buy out the interests of these non-participating family members. Multi-generational family businesses typically try to supply some liquidity to non-family participants in order to preserve family harmony. In addition, some multi-generational family businesses may provide loans to family members for educational purposes, to purchase a home or for certain emergencies. All of these family liquidity needs can drain the family-owned business of capital.

The family-owned business may not be able to compete with larger rivals because of the lack of capital. It is difficult for a family-owned business to compete with a publicly-owned company which has access to unlimited amounts of capital or a private company sponsored by a large private equity fund. The family-owned business may not, because of the lack of capital, be able to acquire smaller companies in their industry through acquisitions even though the acquisition price may be very favorable. Such favorably-priced acquisitions can be made easily by larger and better financed competitors.

Some large family-owned businesses have decided to go public in order to obtain the necessary liquidity to grow their business. Family control is maintained by selling to the public either non-voting stock or low-voting stock.

Tier 2 of Regulation A provides an alternative to a traditional U.S. IPO for the family-owned business. The family-owned business can raise up to $50 million every 12 months and up to $15 million of securities can be sold in a secondary offering by family members during this same period, provided the combination of the primary and secondary offerings does not exceed $50 million during this time period.

One academic study has found that family firms constituted over 35% of the Standard and Poor's 500 and that founding families on average owned almost 18% of their equity.[1] To identify a "family firm," the academic study used equity ownership on the part of the founding family or the presence of family members on the board of directors. A more recent study has confirmed these initial findings.[2]

Table 7.1 shows only a few examples of major public companies which are considered to be family affiliated or family influenced public companies:

Table 7.1.   Examples of Family Affiliated or Family Influenced Public Companies

Name of Company	Name of Family
Wal-Mart Stores, Inc.	Walton
Ford Motor Company	Ford
Hyatt Hotels Corporation	Pritzker
Comcast Corporation	Roberts
News Corporation	Murdoch

Academic research has shown that major, publicly traded family-controlled businesses actually outperform other types of businesses.[3] One

---

[1] R. C. Anderson and D. M. Reeb (2003). "Founding-Family Ownership and Firm Performance: Evidence from the S&P 500," *Journal of Finance*, 58(3), pp. 1301, 1302; J. Lee (2006). "Family Firm Performance: Further Evidence," *Family Business Review*, XIX(2), 2006, p. 103.

[2] B. Villalonga and R. Amit (2006). "How Do Family Ownership, Control, and Management Affect Firm Value," *Journal of Financial Economics*, 80, p. 385.

[3] R. Laporta, F. Lopez-de-Silanes and A. Shleifer (1999). "Corporate Ownership Around the World," *Journal of Finance*, 54, pp. 471–517; D. Miller and I. LeBreton-Miller (2006). "Family Governance and Firm Performance: Agency, Stewardship, and Capabilities," *Family Business Review*, XIX(1), March, p. 73.

study[4] has concluded that the most successful family-controlled large public companies have one or more of the following characteristics:

- The family's voting control was accompanied by significant family ownership.
- There was a strong family CEO without complete voting control who was accountable to independent directors.
- Multiple family members serve as managers.
- The family intends to keep the business for generations.

Chapter 8 will describe important steps which must be taken by a private company in advance of seeking outside capital.

---

[4]D. Miller and I. LeBreton-Miller (2006). "Family Governance and Firm Performance: Agency, Stewardship, and Capabilities," *Family Business Review*, XIX(1), March, p. 73.

CHAPTER 8

ADVANCED PLANNING TO RAISE CAPITAL

The following are the seven most important steps to take prior to seeking outside capital:

- Hire an outstanding professional team.
- Create a business plan.
- Understand the thinking of the proposed capital sources.
- Strengthen the management and board of directors.
- Create protection against competition.
- Unless the business is a start-up, obtain audited or auditable financial statements.
- Eliminate deal-killers.

HIRE AN OUTSTANDING PROFESSIONAL TEAM

The company's professional team should consist of an experienced securities lawyer, an accountant, and a financial advisor.

SECURITIES LAWYER

The company's lawyer should ideally have the following three attributes:

- Contacts in the capital sources which the entrepreneur expects to tap.
- Prior experience in negotiating and structuring deals with those capital sources.
- Securities law expertise.

The company's lawyer should have direct experience in the capital raising process that the entrepreneur proposes. For example, if the entrepreneur will be seeking funds from the professionally managed venture fund community, the lawyer should ideally have contacts in that community, prior experience in negotiating and structuring deals with professionally managed ventures capital funds and securities law expertise.

Likewise, if the entrepreneur proposes to tap the angel community, the lawyer should ideally be able to introduce such entrepreneur to possible angels as well as have prior experience in an angel offering, and have securities law expertise.

If the proposed lawyer has securities law expertise, but no contacts, keep looking. The lawyer can be very valuable in introducing the entrepreneur to proposed capital sources. If the entrepreneur chooses an attorney who has no contacts with capital sources, such entrepreneur is short-changing himself or herself.

The entrepreneur should be able to find a securities lawyer in the major corporate law firms in his or her community who have all of these attributes described.

ACCOUNTANT

The company's accounting firm is an important part of the company's professional team if it is a later-stage business. The audited financial statement of a later-stage business will be important to the company's capital source. The greater the prestige of the accounting firm, the greater will be the comfort of the company's capital sources.

If the entrepreneur is planning a traditional U.S. initial public offering (IPO), most underwriters will usually require an accounting firm with a national or international reputation.

If a businessperson is in the seed or start-up stages, his or her historical financial statements are less important to his or her capital source. Therefore, the accountant is not as important a player. Nonetheless, using a prestigious accounting firm may be helpful in lending credibility to the company and enlarging the potential sources of capital available for referral to the company. A strong regional accounting firm may also be a good choice for introduction to angels and other capital sources.

The use of a prestigious law firm and accounting firm can be helpful in increasing the entrepreneur's credibility with potential capital sources. It helps demonstrate his or her commitment to use professionals who can stay with the company through an IPO or a sale.

FINANCIAL ADVISOR

If neither the entrepreneur nor the chief financial officer (assuming there is one) have prior experience in raising capital, it is wise to hire a financial advisor. The financial advisor serves in three roles:

- Assists in preparing a business plan.
- Opens doors to potential capital sources.
- Negotiates the terms and conditions with capital sources.

Great care must be taken in selecting a financial advisor. The entrepreneur needs a person who has hands-on prior experience in negotiating with likely capital sources. Check the references of the financial advisor carefully both directly and through the company's securities lawyer and accountant. The businessperson needs to talk to other entrepreneurs who are alleged to be prior "satisfied" customers of the potential financial advisor.

Some financial advisors will operate on a complete or partial contingent fee, i.e., their fee will depend upon the monies actually raised. The contingent fee arrangement is usually not considered a problem if the capital source is a single-venture fund. However, if the capital source involves a private placement to numerous "accredited investors," a partial or complete contingent fee raises a question as to whether the financial advisor is required to be registered as a "broker-dealer" or "agent" under federal and state securities law. Since many financial advisors are not properly registered, a contingent fee raises a question as to the legality of the entrepreneur's offering. Although this area of the law is very murky (and kept so by the Securities and Exchange Commission (SEC)), it is best to avoid a contingent fee arrangement in a retail angel offering.

DEVELOP A BUSINESS PLAN

Prior to the selection of a capital source, the entrepreneur should have prepared a business plan. The business plan is essential to raising capital for all but very late-stage companies.

Most entrepreneurs need outside professional help to put together an appealing business plan. If the businessperson has never sought outside capital previously, he or she is well advised not to attempt this task alone. Even if the entrepreneur has a good chief financial officer or controller, if they have no prior experience raising outside capital from the company's intended sources, the entrepreneur will probably not be able to prepare a winning business plan.

There are many outside consultants and professionals who purport to be experts in preparing business plans. However, the entrepreneur must carefully check their qualifications. If they have never successfully raised capital from similar capital sources, look elsewhere.

Even if the entrepreneur uses an experienced outside consultant, his or her own ideas and input are critical to a winning business plan. Professionally managed venture capitalists easily spot "canned" business plans.

Particular care should be used in preparing the short "Executive Summary" of the company's business plan. Many venture capitalists stop reading business plans if the first page or two of the Executive Summary does not appeal to them.

The company's outside consultant or professional should also be used to advise the entrepreneur how to deal with a professionally managed venture capitalist or other capital source. An initial mistake in the first meeting may result in no second meeting.

Business plans many times contain statements and projections that may create issues under the anti-fraud provisions of federal and state securities laws. Therefore, it is wise to require investors to sign subscription agreements in which they warrant and represent that they are relying solely on the offering or disclosure document in making their investment decision and not on the business plan.

A well-drafted subscription agreement will require the investor to indemnify the company and its control persons if such warranty or representation were false. Such indemnification agreements have been upheld by the courts and serve as shields against investor lawsuits based upon alleged material misstatements or material omissions contained in the business plan.

UNDERSTAND THE THINKING OF THE ENTREPRENEUR'S CAPITAL SOURCES

No businessperson would consider trying to negotiate a major sale of the company's goods or services without fully understanding the customers' needs. Yet, many entrepreneurs have no hesitancy in talking to capital sources without fully understanding the source's goals and objectives. Treat capital sources as if they were important customers of the business and study them as if the company were making a major sale to them.

If the businessperson's likely capital source is a professionally managed venture capital fund, he or she should study the types of investments in which the fund has engaged before completing the company's business plan. The entrepreneur should obtain at least the following information concerning the professionally managed venture capital fund:

- Preferred industries and geographic location.
- Would an investment in the company exhaust the remaining uninvested funds (the last investment of a fund may have an advantage since the fund manager may not want to start their next fund until their prior fund is fully invested).
- What is the typical "hurdle rate" of the fund (i.e., the average rate of return they expect on their investment and on companies at its stage of development).
- What stage of business development does the fund prefer for investment (why waste the entrepreneur's time on a fund with later-stage preferences, if he or she needs seed capital).

The entrepreneur also needs to know what U.S. IPOs or sales have happened in the company industry recently and what was the multiple of projected income used by the underwriter in computing the public offering price or sales price. This is important to know in order to convince the venture capital fund of the proper valuation of the business, after applying discounts to reflect the earlier stage of the business. Demonstrating knowledge of recent U.S. IPOs or sales is important in order to impress potential investors with the owner's sophistication.

STRENGTHEN THE COMPANY'S MANAGEMENT AND BOARD OF DIRECTORS

The quality of management is the single most important factor to capital sources, in particular, professionally managed venture funds. Arthur Rock, the dean of the venture capitalists, stated in the *Harvard Business Review* (November–December, 1987):

> As a venture capitalist, I am often asked for my views on why some entre-preneurs succeed and others fail. Obviously, there are no cut-and-dried answers to that question. Still, a few general observations about how I evaluate new businesses should shed some light on what I think it takes to make an entrepreneurial venture thrive and grow.
>
> Over the past 30 years, I estimate that I looked at an average of one business plan per day, or about 300 a year, in addition to the large numbers of phone calls and business plans that simply are not appropriate. Of the 300 likely plans, I may invest in only one or two a year; and even among those carefully chosen few, I'd say that a good half fail to perform up to expectations. The problem with those companies (and with the ventures I choose *not* to take part in) is rarely one of strategy. Good ideas and good products are a dime a dozen. Good execution and good management — in a word, good *people* — are rare.
>
> To put it another way, strategy is easy, but tactics — the day-to-day and month-to-month decisions required to manage a business — are hard. That is why I generally pay more attention to the people who prepare a business plan than to the proposal itself.

CREATE PROTECTIONS AGAINST COMPETITION

One of the key characteristics that are appealing to capital sources is the protection the company has against competitors. Protections that are based solely from the cheapest price for the company's goods or services are not normally considered as important as patent, trade secrets, and similar kinds of intellectual property protections. Therefore, the entrepreneur must be prepared to answer the question as to how the business will fare against its competitors, actual or proposed, and what barriers exist against competitors.

It is wise to review the business operation with a patent lawyer to determine if there is anything the entrepreneur does which is patentable. If there is arguably some patent protection available, he or she should try to file his or her patent applications before seeking outside capital.

OBTAIN AUDITED OR AUDITABLE FINANCIAL STATEMENTS

Unless the company is in the seed or start-up stage, most investors will want the comfort of having audited financial statements for at least the most recently completed fiscal year. If the entrepreneur is seeking bridge financing into a traditional U.S. IPO, he or she will want to demonstrate to investors that the company can qualify for a traditional U.S. IPO by satisfying the SEC's requirements for audited financial statements. A traditional U.S. IPO will generally require three years of audited financial statements (two years in the case of emerging growth companies, see Chapter 5). If the company's IPO is planned for more than one year after the bridge financing, the company can include, as its third year, the period after the bridge financing and, under such circumstances, the company will only need two years of audited financial statements.

An audited financial statement provides the investor with a greater assurance of the company's financial results. In addition, professionally managed venture capitalists are happier if the entrepreneur uses a prestigious international auditing firm to perform the audits, since their own audits are usually performed by these firms.

If the entrepreneur normally uses a good regional accounting firm, there is probably no necessity to change auditors on the eve of the financing.

Even if the company does not have an audited financial statement, the company should at least obtain an auditable financial statement for the three years prior to the proposed financing. An auditable financial statement permits the company to complete the audit retroactively at the time of the financing.

ELIMINATE DEAL-KILLERS

The entrepreneur must eliminate all "deal-killers" before seeking outside capital. Once the businessperson has made a decision to seek financing, he or she should immediately examine the business, with the help of a corporate attorney, to determine whether the company has deal-killers or other impediments to a financing.

The following are typical examples of deal-killers if the resulting contingent liability is large in relation to the value of the business:

- Illegal or improper payments to customers or suppliers or their employees.
- Environmental liabilities.
- Litigation liabilities.
- Tax liabilities resulting from misclassification of employees as independent contractors.
- Unfunded pension obligations and multiemployer pension plan liabilities.
- Product warranty obligations of unreasonable scope or length.

Once the company has completed the advance planning steps, the company decide which capital sources and forms of investment should be pursued. These choices have previously been discussed in this book.

Chapter 9 provides the entrepreneur with an overview of a roll-up strategy which will make the business attractive to outside investors and significantly increase the value of his or her business.

CHAPTER 9

ROLL-UPS AND ACQUISITIONS

OVERVIEW

The value of the business will determine the amount of equity dilution that must be suffered by the owner in connection with issuing new equity securities. This was discussed in Chapter 6.

One method of increasing the value of a business is to engage in a roll-up which is financed with outside capital. A "roll-up" is a consolidation of a previously-fragmented industry. The purpose of the consolidation is to create economies of scale. In some cases, professional management is installed.

Companies that engage in roll-ups are today typically referred to as consolidators. However, we will use the older term "roll-ups" in this chapter.

Roll-ups come in three flavors:

- Roll-ups before a traditional U.S. initial public offering (IPO) or possibly a Tier 2 of Regulation A offering ("Tier 2 Offering").
- Roll-ups after a traditional U.S. IPO or possibly a Tier 2 offering.
- Roll-ups simultaneously with a traditional U.S. IPO or possibly a Tier 2 offering.

The third category, also known as "poof" roll-ups, involves the merger or other consolidation of a group of companies in the same industry that will be funded with the proceeds from an IPO or a Tier 2 offering. If the IPO or a Tier 2 offering occurs, the transactions are closed, and "poof" we have a public company. The advent of the "poof" roll-up started as a 1990s phenomenon but it has continued into the 21st century.

For example, in 2013, there were a number of roll-ups in the real estate investment trusts (REITs) industry, particularly non-listed REITs into REITs listed on the New York Stock Exchange (NYSE). In 2009, there were roll-ups of registered investment advisors by United Capital Financial Partners LLC.

StoneMor Partners L.P. (STON, NYSE) is a consolidator of the death-care industry. During the 11 years ended October 2015, StoneMor has acquired 173 cemeteries and 97 funeral homes (net of dispositions).

Examples of "poof" roll-ups are provided in Table 9.1 which date back to the 1990s:

Table 9.1.   Examples of "Poof" Roll-ups

Company	Line of business	Companies acquired	Offering (millions)
UniCapital	Equipment leasing	12	$532
United Auto Group	Auto dealerships	7	187.5
Advanced Communications	Local exchange carrier	6	128.8
Group MAC	HVAC, plumbing	13	105.0
Integrated Electrical	Electrical contracting	15	91.0
Dispatch Management	Point-to-point delivery	41	79.5
Comfort Systems USA	HVAC services	12	79.3
Condor Technology	IT services	8	76.7
Medical Management	Physician management	5	66.0
USA Floral	Distribution of flowers	8	65.0
Metals USA	Processor of metals	9	59.0
Group 1 Automobile	Auto dealerships	30	57.6
Quanta	Electrical contracting	4	45.0
Compass International	Outsourced services	5	43.0
ImageMax	Document management	11	37.2

American business has a long history of entrepreneurs and financiers consolidating previously-fragmented industries. For example, in the 1980s, large public companies emerged from previously-fragmented industries as diverse as solid waste disposal, funeral services, and video rentals. Companies that emerged from this earlier phase of consolidation include: Paging Network Inc. (paging systems); WMX Technologies Inc. (formerly Waste Management, Inc.) and USA Waste Services, Inc. (solid waste disposal); Service Corporation International (funeral services); and Blockbuster Entertainment Corporation (video rentals).

The roll-up phenomenon is not recent. Approximately, 100 years ago, John D. Rockefeller did something similar when he founded Standard Oil.

THE STRATEGY OF ROLL-UPS

A roll-up is a method of increasing the valuation of a business by combining it with other businesses in the same industry. A roll-up is designed to increase the valuation of a business by:

* permitting a business to grow large enough to qualify for a traditional U.S. IPO, thereby achieving higher public company valuations;
* creating cost-saving efficiencies which further increases a company's combined income and further enhances the traditional U.S. IPO valuation; and
* increasing market penetration.

Roll-ups permit greater market penetration particularly in industries in which customers have multiple locations and prefer their suppliers to have the ability to service those multiple locations. Roll-ups of customers tend to beget roll-ups of their suppliers, since the consolidated customers tend to have central purchasing and prefer dealing with single suppliers who can service multiple facilities.

Roll-ups can also be useful even in industries selling to retail customers or to business customers who do not have multiple locations. All other things being equal, these customers prefer dealing with larger well-capitalized suppliers that will stand behind their product or service. Suppliers which are publicly-traded companies with national operations have greater prestige, which may assist them in marketing customers.

PRIVATE COMPANY ROLL-UPS

A publicly-traded company can effectuate a roll-up either using cash or its own marketable stock, or some combination of the two.

However, it is difficult for a private company to effectuate a roll-up without cash. It is hard to induce someone to sell their business in exchange for stock of a privately-held company, which provides no liquidity to the seller. Even if the privately-held buyer agrees to repurchase its stock after five years if there is no traditional U.S. IPO (or even a Tier 2 offering) or sale, there is a risk that the privately-held company may not be able to afford the repurchase after five years.

Since cash is typically required to effectuate private company roll-ups, it is not unusual for private companies to seek out professionally managed private equity funds to supply the necessary capital. Private equity funds, in turn, are attracted to the roll-up strategy since it may afford an excellent growth strategy if the roll-up is successful, with an exit of either a sale, a traditional U.S. IPO, or possibly a Tier 2 offering in the future.

Some privately-held companies are able to effectuate their roll-up strategy using internally-generated funds and normal bank financing. However, the minimum traditional U.S. IPO offering size requirements make it difficult, without seeking outside capital, for most privately-held companies to ramp up their size sufficiently to qualify for a higher-tier IPO underwriter.

Technically, a "poof" roll-up can be effectuated without a substantial amount of outside capital, since the mergers are completed with the cash proceeds from the IPO. However, a "poof" roll-up will typically require more than several million dollars to cover the legal, accounting, and printing costs of these complicated transactions. Therefore, it is not unusual in these roll-ups to have a promoter fund these transaction costs and for the promoter to either be reimbursed for these costs from the IPO or to receive an equity percentage of the consolidated company to compensate the promoter for the risk, or some combination of cash and stock. It is not yet clear to what extent a promoter would finance the cost of a Tier 2 offering.

MEETING TRADITIONAL U.S. IPO SIZE REQUIREMENTS

Small to medium-sized privately-held businesses tend to have a valuation of four to seven times earnings before interest, taxes, depreciation, and amortization (EBITDA) (less debt). The inability of these businesses to qualify for a traditional U.S. IPO, which requires at least a $200 million post-IPO valuation, or even a Tier 2 offering, prevents them from achieving public company valuations, which can run 10 or more times EBITDA.

COST EFFICIENCIES

A well-structured roll-up permits cost savings for the combined enterprise. The cost-savings efficiency results from:

- reducing back office staff;
- increasing purchasing power;
- advertising efficiencies;
- eliminating duplicate locations;
- eliminating duplicate car and truck fleets;
- efficiencies in purchasing insurance, employee benefits, and administrative expenses; and
- eliminating duplicate executives.

The reduction in the administrative back office staff is usually the primary cost-saving efficiency in a roll-up. It is usually not necessary to grow the back office staff in the exact same proportion as an increase in sales or revenues. As a result, the company's net income should rise after the IPO or a Tier 2 offering from these cost savings alone.

THE MULTIPLIER EFFECT

A well-structured roll-up into a traditional U.S. IPO or a Tier 2 offering increases the company's valuation disproportionately to the actual revenue and income growth. Thus, for example, if the company was worth five times EBITDA before the roll-up, it could be worth 10 or more times EBITDA in an IPO or a Tier 2 offering. This is true even though the combined income of the rolled-up companies has increased only slightly after the roll-up. The higher public company valuation versus the lower privately-held company valuation plays the major role in this phenomenon.

In addition, the actual EBITDA should be disproportionately higher than the percentage increase in the pre-roll-up revenues as a result of the company's cost savings. These cost savings are then multiplied by the higher IPO or a Tier 2 offering valuation to increase the company's valuation.

The combined effect of the higher public companies' valuation plus the increased earnings due to cost savings can have a dramatic overall effect on the post-roll-up valuations, way out of proportion to what can actually been achieved in the roll-up. This disproportionate or multiplier effect is what is driving the roll-up phenomenon.

SUPPOSE A BUSINESSPERSON JUST WANTS TO SELL THE BUSINESS?

Many businesspersons do not want the hassle of an IPO or a Tier 2 offering. They just want to sell their business at a higher valuation than it currently enjoys.

The roll-up strategy is an equally valuable strategy for those who wish only to sell their businesses. By building up their business through roll-up acquisitions, the business can be made extremely attractive to buyers who are interested in a traditional U.S. IPO or a Tier 2 offering roll-ups. This is particularly true if the business is large enough to permit the buyer to qualify for traditional U.S. IPO or a Tier 2 offering or to accelerate the IPO or a Tier 2 offering of the buyer.

If the company is large enough to permit the buyer to qualify for a traditional U.S. IPO or a Tier 2 offering or to accelerate the buyer's IPO or Tier 2 offering, the entrepreneur should be able to achieve a higher valuation when he or she sells to that buyer. This is because the acquisition of the business permits the buyer a higher multiple of EBITDA for the buyer's business through an IPO or a Tier 2 offering and increases the buyer's post closing EBITDA through cost savings.

Growing the business through a roll-up also permits the entrepreneur access to a larger group of potential buyers. Today, there are a large number of financial buyers who are attempting their own roll-ups as a strategy. They are looking for a "platform" company to achieve an industry roll-up. Once they acquire a platform company, they enlarge the platform company through acquisitions.

However, most financial buyers are typically not interested in businesses that are worth less than $10–$20 million. By rolling-up the business to increase its value to over $20 million, the entrepreneur may be able to attract these financial buyers by becoming either their platform company or accelerating the IPO or a Tier 2 offering of their existing platform company.

Increasing the valuation also facilitates the sale of the company through an auction. In general, auctions produce the highest sale prices (see my book *Valuing Your Business*). These auctions are typically conducted by an investment banker. To interest top-tier investment bankers, the business should typically be worth between at least $100 million. However, there are a number of smaller investment bankers who will handle auctions of companies worth $20–$100 million.

SIMULTANEOUS OR "POOF" ROLL-UPS

There are many roll-up promoters who may be interested in financing so-called simultaneous or "poof" roll-ups and obtaining 10–25% of the total IPO shares as consideration. The earliest of these promoters were Jonathan Ledecky and Notre Capital Ventures, II (Houston, Texas), but numerous other promoters have joined the business, including private equity funds.

Mr. Ledecky created one of the earliest and largest roll-ups in U.S. Office Products Co. and has since created three more, including USA Floral Products, Inc., a flower distributor. Steven Harter, Chairman of Notre Capital Ventures II, has completed a number of "poof" roll-ups including Coach USA, Inc., a roll-up in the motor coach industry, Comfort Systems, USA, Inc., which consolidated the HVAC services industry, and Home USA, Inc., a consolidator of mobile home retailers.

These promoters typically interest a number of companies in the same industry into combining at the same time that an IPO occurs. If the IPO occurs, the merger closes and "poof" there is a public company.

These promoters will typically offer each of the combining companies a combination of cash and stock in the public company. The rates vary with transactions and each promoter. The stock of the publicly-held company is not liquid and typically cannot be sold until at least six months and, in some cases, a longer time period or until certain performance goals are satisfied by the publicly-held company.

The percentage of stock and cash received by each of the rolled-up companies is usually negotiable, depending upon the promoter. It is not unheard of to have as much as 70% or more of the consideration payable in cash.

A chief executive officer from outside the combining companies will typically be hired to run the combined publicly-held company.

Poof roll-ups have not recently occurred and are primarily a 1990s phenomenon. However, in the world of IPOs and corporate finance, older trends tend to reappear and, in the right circumstances, so will poof IPOs.

PROTECT ONESELF FROM UNSUCCESSFUL ACQUISITIONS

A significant percentage of all acquisitions are unsuccessful. A study by a New York University professor has indicated that 65% fail. Roll-ups are not exempted from the risk of failure.

In some cases, the failure is the result of bad timing, changes in the marketplace, bad luck, or other unforeseeable events. In other cases, the failure was foreseeable.

As a general rule, the best acquisitions are made by one of two methods:

- Buying a small division of a very large company.
- Buying a business in bankruptcy or on the verge of bankruptcy.

A small division of a very large company is typically sold by large company personnel who have no motivation other than to prevent an accounting loss on the sale. As a result, a sale of assets at the book value of the assets, with no goodwill, is quite feasible. The book value of the assets may be substantially less than their real economic value.

Troubled company acquisitions are very difficult and complicated to complete, but can prove to be the best values. The key is to have an experienced bankruptcy attorney who can protect the entrepreneur from unwanted liabilities and claims.

COMMON MISTAKES IN ROLL-UPS AND OTHER ACQUISITIONS

There is general agreement that the most common reason that roll-ups fail is because of the lack of an experienced management team to operate the combined companies, particularly in roll-ups after the IPO has been completed. However, many mistakes occur in the roll-up process prior to the IPO.

The following are a few of the most common mistakes made in roll-ups and other acquisitions, which are within the control of the acquiring entity.

Common Mistake No. 1: Failing to perform sufficient due diligence on the roll-up or acquisition target.

This is the most common cause of foreseeable failure. If an entrepreneur does not regularly make acquisitions, he or she will need to assemble a sophisticated due diligence team to be certain that he or she is not overpaying for the target. There is no such thing as overdoing the due diligence.

The most common mistake in performing due diligence is the failure to understand the needs of the target's customers and their existing relations with the target's employees. At a minimum, the top five customers should be called upon and visited personally by representatives of the buyer.

Existing personal relationships with the target's key employees must be explored thoroughly with the customers. If such relationships exist, these key employees must be given positive incentives to remain with the buyer and negative incentives from leaving the buyer (e.g., a covenant not to compete or at least not solicit customers).

To the extent possible, the seller's motivations for selling should be understood. Many sellers decide to exit when they foresee problems ahead for the business.

Common Mistake No. 2: Rolling-up or acquiring a company whose financial statements will not satisfy the SEC, resulting in the postponement of the IPO or a Tier 2 offering.

As previously noted, in order to go public, a company will normally need audited financial statements for two or three full fiscal years prior to a traditional U.S. IPO filing or two years for a Tier 2 offering filing. If the company's acquisition target does not have audited financial statements for the required three- or two-year period, the company will have to hold up the IPO or Tier 2 offering until he or she can obtain such audits. It is not always possible to obtain such audits retroactively, particularly if the acquisition target maintains inadequate records or primarily sells from inventory.

Therefore, the company's auditors must be brought into the acquisition process at an early stage to make certain that the target's financial statements can satisfy SEC requirements. If the target acquisition's financial statements cannot pass muster, the company may be required to postpone the IPO or the Tier 2 offering for a many as two to three years, unless the target acquisition falls below certain materiality thresholds established by the SEC.

Common Mistake No. 3: Relying too heavily on the target's audited financial statements.

When the target provides audited financial statements to the buyer, there is a tendency to have these reviewed by the buyer's accountants and to rely upon that review to detect any issues that would affect the valuation of the target's business. The more prestigious the auditing firm for the target, the greater is the tendency of the buyer to rely upon them.

There are three problems with such reliance:

- In many states, the target's auditor has no liability whatsoever to the buyer if the target's financial statements are in error, unless the target's auditors have specifically authorized the buyer to so rely.
- Generally accepted accounting principles are extremely elastic and it is not possible to ferret out all of the actual accounting principles and practices just by reviewing the target's audited financial statement; instead, a thorough review by the buyer's own auditor is essential.

- The auditor for the target's financial statements is generally entitled to rely upon the target's management's representation letter to the auditor; therefore, even if the entrepreneur purchases the stock of the target, the target's outside auditor can defend the buyer's lawsuit by claiming that they were misled by the fraud of the target's management.

Common Mistake No. 4: Obtaining an inadequate escrow or holdback (e.g., notes) of the purchase price.

Possession of an escrow or hold-back of the purchase price places the buyer in the driver's seat. If the buyer has a post-closing claim, the buyer can just refuse to pay the escrow or hold-back amount.

Many sophisticated acquirers refuse to pay the target or its shareholders more cash than the book value of the target's net assets. The balance of the purchase price consists of non-negotiable notes. If the buyer has post-closing claims against the target or its shareholders, these notes can be offset by the claim amount.

If the escrow or hold-back is non-existent or is inadequate, collecting on claims against the target or its shareholders can be extremely expensive, time-consuming, and frustrating. In some cases, after the target or its shareholders pay their taxes on your purchase price and their own attorney's fees, there can be very little left for the buyer to collect even if they win their lawsuit. An arbitration provision in the purchase contract can sometimes be helpful in this regard by reducing litigation discovery expenses and avoiding the cost and delay of endless appeals. To be fully effective, the arbitration provision should prevent or severely limit pre-arbitration discovery and make the arbitrator's award non-appealable to the extent possible.

Common Mistake No. 5: If a company is the buyer in a roll-up, the entrepreneur should avoid paying the same earnings multiplier that the buyer expects to receive in a traditional U.S. IPO or a Tier 2 offering for significantly smaller companies in the industry.

For example, if a buyer expects to receive a multiplier of nine times the company's next 12-month earnings projection in an IPO or a Tier 2 offering, a much smaller company in the roll-up should be priced at a reasonable discount from this multiplier, e.g., six times. Otherwise, the company's only leverage from the consolidation results from the costs savings and efficiencies it can achieve. In some situations, it is not possible to realize these savings and efficiencies, at least initially. As a result, the company's post-IPO or a Tier 2 offering earnings may be flat, resulting in the marketplace punishing the company's post-IPO or a Tier 2 offering trading price.

A major source of private capital for roll-ups comes from private equity funds and other professional investors. The next and final chapter (Chapter 10) discusses negotiating a private equity investment with these professional investors and how to avoid traps.

CHAPTER 10

NEGOTIATING WITH A PROFESSIONAL INVESTOR

Despite popular belief to the contrary, owners of businesses can negotiate with a professionally managed venture capital fund or a sophisticated angel investor. How much the owner can negotiate will depend upon his or her bargaining strength.

Bargaining strength is directly related to what other strategic alternatives the owner has and partly to the professional investor (hereafter also called "investor" or "venture capitalist"). If the owner waits to obtain venture capital until his or her situation is desperate, he or she will have almost no bargaining power. To enhance the owner's bargaining power with the venture capitalist, the entrepreneur should attempt to attract as many other investors as possible to his or her company. However, that strategy may not be effective if the venture capitalists decide to cooperate with each other rather than compete.

A better strategy is to have angel investors waiting in the wings or to obtain a letter of intent from the underwriter for a traditional U.S. initial public offering (IPO) or a Tier 2 offering.

The entrepreneur needs to package his or her business in the most attractive manner. The owner must obtain professional help to assist in the negotiations. As noted in Chapter 8, the professional help should consist of an attorney and a financial advisor who are experienced in venture capital investments. If the owner has personal venture capital experience, he or she may be able to dispense with the financial advisor.

TEN MAJOR ISSUES IN NEGOTIATING VENTURE CAPITAL INVESTMENT

The following is an outline of 10 major issues in negotiating with a professional investor, such as a private equity fund or a sophisticated angel investor:

Valuation

- How much is the business worth? The greater its value, the less equity dilution suffered by the owner for the same amount of investment.

Funding of Investment

- Is all of the investment paid at closing, or is the investment paid over time?

Control of Board of Directors

- Who elects the majority of board members?
- If officers are board members, who controls their compensation (i.e., composition of Board Compensation Committee)?

Form of Investment

- Preferred stock or equity, common stock or equity, and/or notes (convertible or not) and/or warrants.

If Investment is in Preferred Stock or Equity

- What is the dividend rate and when does it commence?
- What are the liquidation rights?
- What are the conversion rights (do accrued but unpaid dividends also convert)?
- Is preferred stock or equity participating or not?
- What are the voting rights for directors and on other shareholder issues?

- What special protections (e.g., veto rights) are given to preferred stock or equity over corporate actions?
- What redemption rights are given to holder of preferred stock or equity and to company?
- Anti-dilution protections — full ratchet, weighted average (how determined?), and other protective clauses.

Management Incentives and Disincentives

- Incentives: Stock options and other incentive plans.
- Disincentives: Forfeiture of stock if terminate employment.

Employment Contracts

- For whom?
- Term?
- Compensation?

Protection of Proprietary Information

- What protection is afforded to proprietary information?

Stockholders Agreement or Operating Agreement

- Tag-along rights.
- Drag-along rights and other provisions.

Registration Rights

- How early can investor require registration?
- How many demand registration rights and piggy-back rights?
- Other covenants.

VALUATION ISSUES

The negotiations begin with the professional investor providing the entrepreneur with a term sheet. The term sheet is a very brief summary of the major deal terms.

The valuation of a business determines the amount of equity which the owner must give to the professional investor in exchange for his or her investment in the business. As discussed in Chapter 6, the percentage of the equity to which the investor is entitled is determined by the following formula:

$$\frac{\text{Amount of investment}}{\text{Pre-money value of company} + \text{Amount of investment in company}}.$$

The term "pre-money" value of a company refers to its value prior to the investment. For example, if a company has a pre-money value of $1 million and the professional investor is investing $500,000 in the company, the investor is entitled to $33\frac{1}{3}$% of the equity computed as follows:

$$\frac{\$500,000}{\$1 \text{ million} + \$500,000} = 33\frac{1}{3}\%$$

The term "post-money" valuation refers to the value of the business after the investment. In the above example, the post-money valuation is $1.5 million. See Chapter 6.

In most negotiations, the professional investor will advise the owner as to what they consider to be the pre-money value of the business. However, a better strategy for the entrepreneur is to develop their own valuation model and to convince the investor of the correctness of the entrepreneur's valuation.

A financial advisor is the owner's best source of information on pre-money valuation. A competent financial advisor will be able to provide the owner with analogies to other businesses, particularly publicly-traded companies, and extrapolate a pre-money valuation from these analogies. Since the valuation of the business involves more educated guesses than science, the owner's financial advisor's educated guesses are just as good as the professional investor's educated guesses and should be given to the investor early in the negotiation.

SUBTLE METHODS OF DECREASING VALUATION

There are at least five methods used by the professional investor to increase the percentage of equity in the company to which they are entitled through the legal drafting of the venture capital agreement:

* Requiring the company to issue participating preferred instead of non-participating preferred stock or equity.
* Requiring accrued dividends on preferred stock or equity to be converted into additional equity.
* Requiring full ratchet anti-dilution clauses, rather than average price anti-dilution clauses.
* If the investment is made in stages, accruing preferred stock or equity dividends on all of the staged investments before it has all been received.
* Counting stock options as outstanding stock or equity.

PARTICIPATING VERSUS NON-PARTICIPATING PREFERRED STOCK

For purposes of the remainder of this chapter, we will assume that the company is a U.S. corporation rather than a limited liability company, limited partnership, etc. If the U.S. company is organized as a limited liability company, all references to "preferred stock" should be considered references to preferred equity interests and all references to "common stock" should be considered references to equity interests which are not so preferred.

The characteristics of the preferred stock which must be issued to the professional investor can significantly affect the valuation of the business.

For example, assume that the investor creates a term sheet which states that the pre-valuation of the business is $4.75 million and plans the injection in stages of $3.5 million into the company. In return, the professional investor receives shares of "participating preferred stock" of the company. One would presume that the post-money valuation of the business would therefore be $8.25 million ($4.75 million + $3.5 million).

Shares of "participating preferred stock" permit the holder to receive, in the event of the sale or other liquidation of the business, their original investment back, plus accrued but unpaid dividends.

For example, suppose all of the assets of the business were sold for $8.25 million in cash plus the assumption by the buyer of all of its liabilities. Under these circumstances, $8.25 million would be available for distribution among all of the holders of preferred stock and common stock.

With a "participating" preferred stock, the holder of the preferred stock receives the first slice of the $8.25 million by taking back their original investment of $3.5 million.

Assume further that the $3.5 million injection by the professional investor may also be increased by accrued but unpaid dividends at the rate of 4% per annum. For purposes of this computation, we assume that the accrued but unpaid dividends are not added to the $3.5 million.

The payment of $3.5 million to the preferred stock reduces the amount available to further distribution to $4.75 million ($8.25 million less $3.5 million).

The remaining $4.75 million is then divided between the participating preferred stock and the common stock in accordance with the ratio of preferred stock investment ($3.5 million) over the pre-money value of $4.75 million plus the $3.5 million, or 42%.

Thus, the percentage of the remaining $4.75 million paid to the participating preferred stock is computed as follows:

42% of $4.75 million = $1.995 million to preferred stock.
58% of $4.75 million = $2.755 million to common stock.

The effect of this sale of the business at $8.25 million is that the preferred stock receives a total of $5.495 million ($1.995 million + $3.5 million) and common stock receives a total of $2.755 million.

If the common stock receives only $2.755 out of a total of sale proceeds of $8.25 million, what is the meaning of the $4.75 million "pre-money" value set forth in the term sheet? The answer is that it has no meaning because participating preferred stock is to be received by the professional investor.

The correct pre-money value of this business is really only $2.755 million. The entrepreneur who believes the term sheet "pre-money" valuation of $4.75 million is incorrect. The only purpose of the $4.75 million "pre-money" value in the term sheet was to provide a mechanism to divide the sale or liquidation proceeds *after* the original investment of the preferred stock has been repaid.

If the preferred stock had not been "participating," but instead was "non-participating," the $4.75 million pre-money valuation would have been correct. Under those circumstances, the preferred stock would have been entitled to receive its original investment (possibly, plus 4% dividend) before the split with the common stock. Thus, if the assets of the company had been sold for $8.25 million and the buyer had assumed all liabilities, the $8.25 million would have been divided as follows, using the 42–58% division between the preferred stock and common stock:

42% of $8.25 million = $3.5 million (with rounding) to the preferred stock.
58% of $8.25 million = $4.75 million to the common stock.

CONVERTING ACCRUED DIVIDENDS INTO ADDITIONAL EQUITY

Suppose the preferred stock purchased by the professional investor contains a dividend rate of 4% per annum. The 4% per annum dividend is applied to the original investment of $3.5 million and increases the liquidation preference of the preferred stock each year by 4%. Some professional investors, in computing the number of shares of common stock into which the preferred stock is convertible, also require that the accrued dividends be convertible as well as the original investment.

The discussion in the previous section assumes that the accrued but unpaid dividend on the preferred stock did not increase the conversion percentage of the preferred stock. If such unpaid dividends did increase the conversion percentage of the preferred stock, the split would become even more unfavorable for the common stock.

For example, if non-participating preferred stock had an accrued dividend rate of 4% per annum, convertible into additional shares of common stock, and was outstanding for five years before the sale at $8.25 million, the split would be computed as follows: preferred stock receives approximately 47% of the net proceeds (versus 42% if the dividend was not convertible into additional common stock) and common stock receives 53% of proceeds (versus 58% if the dividend was not convertible into additional common stock).

ANTI-DILUTION CLAUSES

There are two general types of anti-dilution clauses typically used by professional investors and sophisticated angel investors in their legal documents:

- Full ratchet anti-dilution clause.
- Weighted average anti-dilution clause.

In the full ratchet anti-dilution clause, if the company issues more stock after the closing of the venture capital financing at a lower valuation than that used by the professional investor at the closing, the investor obtains the benefit of the lower valuation. For example, suppose the company issued 50,000 shares of Series A Convertible Preferred Stock at $20 per share to the investors and the entrepreneur owned 100,000 shares of common stock. Assume further that each of the 50,000 shares of Series A Preferred Stock is convertible into 50,000 shares of common stock, which represents approximately $33\frac{1}{3}$% of the common stock (50,000 divided by 100,000 plus 50,000).

If, after the closing, the company were to issue shares at $10 per share, the conversion rate on the Series A Convertible Preferred Stock would, as a result of the full ratchet clause, increase so that the 50,000 shares of preferred stock would convert into 100,000 shares of common stock, or approximately 50% of the company. This reduces the entrepreneur's percentage of the company by an additional $16\frac{2}{3}$% and increases the professional investor's percentage by the same amount.

The problem with the full ratchet anti-dilution clause is that the increase in the professional investor's percentage occurs even if only one share is issued at $10 per share. The full ratchet clause does not proportionalize the dilution by the number of shares actually issued below the initial valuation of the investor.

The weighted average anti-dilution clause takes into account how many shares were issued at $10 per share. Thus, if only one share were issued at $10 per share, there would be virtually no change in the percentage of the common stock to which the professional investor was entitled upon conversion of its preferred stock.

Even the weighted average clauses can be unfair to the entrepreneur if these clauses have either of the following characteristics:

- The clause does not average sales above the professional investor's valuation (e.g., $20 per share) with sales below that price.
- The clause measures dilution by looking only to the number of actual common shares outstanding before and after the dilutive event, rather than considering the total number of shares of common stock computed on a fully diluted basis (i.e., treating convertible securities as if they were converted and stock options as if they were exercised).

Although most professional investors or sophisticated angel investors will require either a full ratchet or weighted average anti-dilution clause, other investors will not necessarily require such clauses. This is a matter of negotiation with the investor. In many cases, it is possible to sell common stock of the company to investors, so that these anti-dilution provisions never become an issue.

DILUTION THROUGH CERTAIN TYPES OF STAGED FINANCING

Staged financing refers to a financing structure in which the professional investor's funds are not paid in full at the closing. The business may not be able to absorb all of the investment immediately and therefore it makes sense to provide the money in installments.

In early-stage companies, the professional investor may require the achievement of certain milestones as a condition to further investment. This reduces the investor's risk and requires the owner to demonstrate the ability of his or her business to achieve these milestones before receiving further funding.

Staged financing does not reduce the pre-money valuation of the business unless one of the following two provisions is contained in the venture capital agreement:

- The professional investor receives preferred stock representing all of its investment at closing even though all of the professional investor's money is not invested at closing and preferred stock dividends on all of the investments start to accrue at closing.
- In the case of investment based on milestones, the company is worth significantly more upon achievement of the milestones than the valuation initially given by the professional investor.

An example of the first form of dilution is as follows: Assume that a professional investor invests $1 million in exchange for 50,000 shares of Series A Convertible Preferred Stock of a software company, at a cost of $20 per share. The Series A Convertible Preferred Stock requires the software company to accrue a dividend equal to the higher of $3.00 per share or any dividend paid on the common stock of the software company. $500,000 is paid at the closing and $500,000 is required to be paid six months after the closing and this obligation is evidenced by a promissory note executed by the professional investor, which note bears no interest.

Assume further that even though only $500,000 (rather than $1 million) is paid at the closing by the professional investor, all 50,000 shares of Series A Convertible Preferred Stock are issued at the closing. As a result of issuing all 50,000 shares at closing, not just the 25,000 preferred shares which were paid for by the $500,000, the common stockholders are diluted by the accrual of dividends on the unpaid for 25,000 preferred shares. Since these dividends accrue at the rate of $3 per year, the dividend preference on the preferred stock has been increased by $37,500 (25,000 × $1.50 per share for six months), even though no interest is paid on the $500,000 note.

COUNTING STOCK OPTIONS AS OUTSTANDING STOCK

If the professional investor's valuation shows that they are entitled to $33\frac{1}{3}\%$ of the company's equity for their investment in the company, and the company has 6,000 shares of common stock outstanding, the professional investor should clearly receive preferred stock convertible into 3,000 shares of the company's common stock. The 3,000 shares produce a fraction of $33\frac{1}{3}\%$ of the total of 9,000 shares of common stock outstanding after the conversion of the preferred stock (6,000 existing shares of common stock plus an additional 3,000 resulting from the conversion of preferred stock).

If the company also has employee stock options outstanding for 600 shares of common stock in the foregoing example, some professional investors would want their preferred stock convertible into 3,200 shares of common stock, rather than 3,000 shares of common stock. Their theory is that they should not be diluted by employee stock options, if and when they are exercised.

There is some merit to this argument if the employee stock options have exercise prices for common stock below the price paid per share for common stock by the professional investors (assuming the preferred stock were converted to common stock). However, some professional investors require the inclusion of employee stock options in the calculation even if the option exercise price equals or exceeds the price paid per share by the professional investor.

The effect is that the entrepreneur's equity percentage is diluted by the outstanding employee stock options, thereby effectively indirectly reducing the valuation of the entrepreneur's share of the company. Employee stock options are many times issued *in lieu* of salary which would otherwise have been borne by the business as a whole. Therefore, it may be argued that it is unfair to saddle the entrepreneur with the entire cost of the employee stock options.

HIGH REDEMPTION PRICE AND MISCELLANEOUS METHODS

The typical professional investor may require the company to buy back the shares of preferred stock through a redemption right exercisable three to seven years after the date of the investment. The redemption right is intended to afford the professional investor an exit if the company is not sold and does not effectuate a traditional U.S. IPO that provides for a satisfactory return to the professional investor.

Usually, the redemption price is equal to the original investment plus the amount of the accrued but unpaid dividends. However, some professional investors require a redemption price that is three or more times the original investment, often accompanied by a similar liquidation preference.

For example, suppose a professional investor declares that the company has a pre-money valuation of $10 million and the professional investor invests $5 million (thereby creating a $15 million post-money valuation of the company). The professional investor would typically acquire preferred stock convertible into one-third of the company's outstanding common stock (after conversion). If the professional investor requires a redemption right after five years that entitles the professional investor to receive three times the original investment (i.e., 3 × $5 million, or $15 million), this redemption right completely undermines the original $10 million pre-money valuation. Thus, if the business was sold after five years for $15 million, all of the proceeds would belong to the professional investor because of the redemption right or similar liquidation preference.

The owner and any other common stockholders of the company would not benefit from the sale until the valuation exceeded $15 million and then only to the extent of the excess.

If the business was sold for $17 million, only $2 million would be distributed to the common stockholders, thereby rendering meaningless the $10 million pre-money valuation.

There are various other methods used by professional investors that undermine the pre-money valuation contained in the professional investor's term sheet. For example, some professional investors increase the conversion right of their preferred stock if certain goals are not satisfied. Other professional investors obtain warrants that entitle them to purchase additional common stock of the company for a nominal consideration if certain adverse events occur.

There is no limit to the number of methods that can be used by a professional investor to effectively change the valuation of the business. A careful review of the term sheet by a knowledgeable securities lawyer who has experience in this area should detect these subtle methods of undermining the pre-money valuation given to the owner by the professional investor.

CONTROL OF THE COMPANY

Before negotiating with a professional investor, it is important to understand what rights of control over the company or its business will be required by the professional investor. Since control is an extremely important issue, the results of this inquiry are a major factor in selecting a professional investor.

The board of directors of a corporation makes all significant decisions of importance to the corporation, as noted in Chapter 7. The shareholders have certain veto rights on major transactions and elect the board. Therefore, the venture capital agreement must be carefully examined to determine who controls the company's board of directors.

Control of the shareholder vote, as illustrated in Chapter 7, is much less important to the entrepreneur than control of the board vote. Control of the board vote means that the entrepreneur needs a majority of all of the members of the board, *assuming* that each board member has one vote and the majority rules.

The typical professional investor will require representation on the company's board of directors. Many professional investors require a board of directors consisting of five persons: two selected by the common stock (which the owner controls), two selected by the preferred stock (which the professional investor controls), and one director selected who is either independent or selected from among the officers. The tie-breaking director may be elected by the preferred stock and common stock voting together. If there are more shares of common stock than shares of preferred stock, the common stock should control that selection.

However, some venture capital agreements permit the preferred stock a veto right over the selection of the tie-breaking directors. If the tie-breaking director is to be selected from among the officers, the entrepreneur should ask who controls the compensation of those officers. If the majority of the compensation committee of the board of directors must consist of representatives of the professional investor, the tie-breaking director may not be completely neutral.

Even though the professional investor does not require the owner to give up control, they typically will give themselves (1) veto rights over any major corporate action and (2) provide both overt and subtle methods of exercising control. These veto rights typically include the following subjects at a minimum:

- Issuing more stock;
- Buying back stock;
- Dividends;
- Sales, mergers or consolidations, divisions or dissolution; and
- Changes in the company's charter or by-laws.

Professional investors may require veto rights over the following decisions:

- Selection or termination of the CEO or CFO;
- Incurrence of debt; and
- Changes in board structure or in the company.

REDEMPTION RIGHTS

Another control mechanism utilized by professionally managed venture capital is to permit their preferred stock to be redeemable on certain events. Typically, the redemption rights will become effective around the fifth year. However, some professional investors add provisions permitting redemption even earlier if certain milestones or projections in the business plan are not met.

This redemption right gives the professional investor an important control mechanism. If they can force the company to repurchase the preferred stock (plus accumulated but unpaid dividends), they can exercise substantial influence over the company, particularly if the company cannot afford to redeem the preferred stock.

Most state corporate statutes do not permit a forced redemption of stock if the redemption would cause the company to be unable to satisfy its other debts in the ordinary course of business. State law may also contain other limitations on the legal ability of the professional investor to force redemption.

DRAG-ALONG RIGHTS

A "drag-along" clause permits the professional investor to force the sale of the company, including the stock of the entrepreneur. It is used by some, but not all, professional investors, particularly in early-stage businesses.

If the professional investor insists upon a "drag-along" clause, the entrepreneur should attempt to eliminate it or place significant limitations on the use of this powerful clause. The existence of a "drag-along" clause also provides significant leverage and control to the professional investor.

If the "drag-along" clause cannot be eliminated, the owner of the business might negotiate with a professional investor for possible limitations on the "drag-along" clause, such as to following:

- Limiting the ability to exercise the "drag-along" clause for the first several years on the theory that a sale should not be forced until management has had a reasonable opportunity to operate the business.
- Limiting the ability to exercise the "drag-along" clause to situations in which the goals of the business plan have not been satisfied by a wide margin over a significant period of time.
- Conditioning the professional investor's right to exercise the "drag-along" on a right of first refusal given to the entrepreneur, or at least the right to make the first offer to purchase the business.

FORM OF INVESTMENTS

Professionally managed private equity will typically require the company to issue preferred stock, convertible into common stock, in exchange for their investment. (If the company is a limited liability company, the analog would be equity interests which are preferred over the equity interests issued to the owner.) The preferred stock will typically contain provisions permitting the holder to force the company to redeem it at the end of five years, and earlier if certain conditions occur. In effect, the preferred stock investment of the professional investor is really just a disguised long-term debt, convertible into the company's stock if things go well.

There are three major reasons for requiring the company to issue preferred stock:

- If the company is liquidated, the professional investors will receive their money as preferred stockholders (plus accrued but unpaid dividends) prior to any distribution on the common stock. For this purpose, "liquidation" may include a sale or merger.
- For purposes of balance sheet presentation, preferred stock might be classified under the stockholder equity section of the company's balance sheet. If the professional investor received notes, they would be viewed as an additional liability of the company, thereby making the company less attractive to potential suppliers and bankers.
- The use of preferred stock also permits the preferred stock, voting as a separate class, to have veto rights over certain corporation transactions.

If the professional investor uses preferred stock, the following issues would typically be covered in the term sheet, many of which were previously discussed:

- What is the dividend rate and when does it commence?

  Note: The dividend rate, typically ranging from 4% to 15% per annum on the original investment by the professional investor is really a form of disguised interest which adds to the liquidation preference of the preferred stock. If the company is sold or otherwise liquidated, the accrued dividends may be convertible into addi-tional shares of common stock.

- What are the liquidation rights?

  Note: The liquidation rights are typically equal to the original investment by the professional investor plus accrued but unpaid dividends.

- What are the conversion rights (do accrued but unpaid dividends also convert)?

  Note: The number of shares of common stock into which the preferred stock is convertible is determined by the pre-money valuation of the business. See Chapter 6.

- Is preferred stock participating or not?

   Note: Participating preferred stock typically permits the professional investor, in the event of a sale or other liquidation, to receive back the original investment *and* the right to convert to a certain percentage of the company's common stock for purposes of dividing the remaining proceeds. Non-participating preferred stock does not permit the professional investor to receive back the original investment in addition to the right to convert into common stock.

- What voting rights for directors and on other shareholder issues?
- What special protections (e.g., veto rights) are given preferred stock over corporate actions?
- What redemption rights are given to holder of preferred stock and to company?

   Note: A "redemption right" is the right of the preferred stock to demand the repayment from the company of the original investment plus accrued but unpaid dividends. Typically, the preferred stock redemption rights commence five years after the date of the original investment or earlier if certain default events occur.

- Anti-dilution protections: full ratchet, weighted average (how determined?), and other protective clauses.

The terms of the preferred stock should be negotiated, to the extent the entrepreneur has bargaining power, to avoid provisions that overtly or subtly reduce the valuation of the company as previously set forth. For example, efforts should be made to avoid conversion rights with respect to accrued but unpaid dividends. So-called "participating" preferred stock should be avoided because of its equity dilution, and weighted average dilution clauses should be negotiated *in lieu of* so-called full-ratchet clauses.

MANAGEMENT INCENTIVES AND DISINCENTIVES

The owner's negotiation with a professional investor should include the reservation of a certain percentage of shares of common stock for the company's key employees. Typically, professional investors will permit a reservation of 5–10% of the outstanding common stock for that purpose.

However, as previously noted, certain professional investors will consider the reserved stock as if it was part of the outstanding shares of common stock for purposes of computing the pre-money valuation of the company and the percentage of the company's stock to which they are entitled for their investment. Thus, if the professional investor is entitled to one-third of the company's outstanding stock in exchange for their investment, the one-third will also apply to the reserved management stock. Under these circumstances, the reserved stock will be diluting the owner's own equity interest.

Professional investors differ on this issue; the owner may be able to negotiate a provision whereby the reserved stock does not increase the percentage of shares to which the professional investor is entitled.

Professional investors typically will not object to a stock option plan in which the option price is based upon the valuation given to the company by the professional investor. This gives the key employees an incentive to grow the company above the professional investor's valuation. If there is no growth, the option becomes valueless.

Professional investors also provide disincentives to the key employees, including the entrepreneur, if they terminate their employment with the company. These disincentives are usually provided for in a stock restriction agreement which requires the forfeiture of a percentage of the stockholdings of the key employee if he or she leaves his or her employment or is terminated with cause.

EMPLOYMENT CONTRACTS AND AGREEMENTS

The professional investor will typically require the entrepreneur and his or her key employees to enter into employment contracts and agreements to preserve proprietary information and to prevent competition.

Typically, the employment contract is reserved for the top one or two executives, whereas the employee agreement protecting proprietary information is required to be signed by all key employees and possibly all employees.

The entrepreneur should not take great comfort in his or her employment contracts. The primary purpose of the employment contract is to legally bind the entrepreneur to a minimum period of employment and a fixed compensation.

If the entrepreneur does not control the board of directors, there is nothing to prevent the board of directors from terminating the entrepreneur's employment even before the end of the term of the employment contract. This is true whether or not the entrepreneur has created any "cause" for the termination. If the entrepreneur's employment is terminated in breach of the employment agreement, he or she must mitigate damages by seeking another position and offsetting any income earned from this other position against the damages caused by the premature termination of the entrepreneur's employment contract.

If the entrepreneur wishes to assure that he or she cannot be fired by the board of directors, and assuming that entrepreneur is a member of the board, he or she must negotiate a clause in the corporate charter which requires unanimous consent of the board for any employment contract termination. Merely placing a clause in the employment agreement that the entrepreneur cannot be terminated during the term of the contract is legally ineffective since the board of directors normally has a legal right to breach any executive employment contract.

It may also be worthwhile to place a clause in the employment contract which eliminates any duty the entrepreneur might have to mitigate damages for breach of the employment contract by the company. The effect of such a clause would be that, if the entrepreneur were terminated without cause, the company would owe the entrepreneur compensation for the remaining term of the contract and that compensation could not be reduced by the income the entrepreneur earns elsewhere.

STOCKHOLDERS AGREEMENT

The Stockholders Agreement (or Operating Agreement in the case of a limited liability company) typically prevents entrepreneur from selling the stock without giving a right of first refusal to the preferred stock-holders. It may also contain the "tag-along" and "drag-along" clauses previously discussed.

REGISTRATION RIGHTS

Professional investors typically require the company, upon request, to register their stock under the 1933 Act. The costs of preparing and filing such a registration statement can be considerable, generally exceeding $1 million for a first-time registrant.

The professional venture capitalist requires registration rights in order to facilitate a public offering exit strategy. Since only the company can register stock under the 1933 Act or qualify the stock pursuant to Tier 2 or Regulation A, the professional investor registration rights clause contractually requires the company to register upon request a minimum percentage of the preferred stock.

It would be foolish for the professional investor to request registration unless an underwriter or other purchaser of the stock was ready to acquire the stock once the registration becomes effective. However, the existence of the registration rights clause creates leverage which the entrepreneur should attempt to reasonably limit.

For example, most professional investors will negotiate extending the date when the registration rights commence from one year to two or more years after the initial investment. Since only the company can file a registration statement with the Securities and Exchange Commission (SEC) under the 1933 Act, the entrepreneur may also need a registration rights covenant if the entrepreneur could lose control of the board of directors. In such a situation, the entrepreneur could wind up with a significant amount of stock which could not be publicly sold after the IPO (with the possible exception of sales after the lock-up period under SEC Rule 144, which permits at least 1% of the outstanding stock to be sold every three months if certain conditions are satisfied).

OTHER COVENANTS

The typical venture capital agreement contains a variety of covenants, such as:

- A requirement that monthly, quarterly, and annual financial reports be sent to preferred stockholders.
- A requirement to permit preferred stock investors certain observation rights, including the right to attend board of director meetings.

- A requirement not to issue employee stock options without approval of the compensation committee of the board of directors (usually controlled by investor designees).
- A requirement to give preemptive rights for any new stock insurance to holders of preferred stock.
- A requirement to maintain life insurance on the life of the entrepreneur(s), payable solely to the company usually in an amount at least equal to the venture capital investment.
- A requirement as to the number of preferred stockholder designees who must sit on the board of directors and its compensation committee.
- A requirement to pay tax and maintain adequate insurance, preserve corporate existence, comply with laws, maintain adequate books and records, maintain properties and assets, comply with ERISA, etc.
- A requirement to obtain approval by the majority of the preferred stock of capital and operating expense budgets, cash flow projections, profit and loss projections, and company's business plan.
- A requirement to obtain approval from the compensation committee of the board of directors of all compensation and fringe benefits for officers.
- Limitations on transactions with affiliates and major corporation transactions.
- Prohibition on repurchase of shares or charter or by-law amendments or changes in the nature of the business.

Many (but not all) of these covenants disappear when the company has a "qualified public offering."

A "qualified public offering" typically requires an IPO at a valuation which is at least five times the price per share paid by the professional investor and which raises a minimum amount of IPO proceeds, typically $50 million or more. If there is an IPO, but it is not a "qualified public offering," the covenants will continue in effect.

However, most underwriters will usually insist upon changes in the covenant as a condition to the underwriting. If the IPO valuation gives some benefit to the investor (even though not the five times or more multiple), most investors will negotiate covenant changes.

These registration covenants are fairly standard and it is difficult to negotiate major changes. However, minor changes to certain clauses can be made in appropriate circumstances.

For example, many professional investors may waive the requirement for monthly financial statements and budgets and will agree to quarterly or semi-annual financial statements and budgets. Likewise, the amount of life insurance in the entrepreneur's life may be negotiable if the cost is too high.

This concludes our last chapter. Good luck with your financing!

APPENDICES

APPENDIX 1

SEC REGULATION D

§230.500 USE OF REGULATION D.

Users of Regulation D (§§230.500 *et seq.*) should note the following:

(a) Regulation D relates to transactions exempted from the registration requirements of section 5 of the Securities Act of 1933 (the Act) (15 U.S.C.77a *et seq.,* as amended). Such transactions are not exempt from the antifraud, civil liability, or other provisions of the federal securities laws. Issuers are reminded of their obligation to provide such further material information, if any, as may be necessary to make the information required under Regulation D, in light of the circumstances under which it is furnished, not misleading.

(b) Nothing in Regulation D obviates the need to comply with any applicable state law relating to the offer and sale of securities. Regulation D is intended to be a basic element in a uniform system of federal-state limited offering exemptions consistent with the provisions of sections 18 and 19(c) of the Act (15 U.S.C. 77r and 77(s)(c)). In those states that have adopted Regulation D, or any version of Regulation D, special attention should be directed to the applicable state laws and regulations, including those relating to registration of persons who receive remuneration in connection with the offer and sale of securities, to disqualification of issuers and other persons associated with offerings based on state administrative orders or judgments, and to requirements for filings of notices of sales.

(c) Attempted compliance with any rule in Regulation D does not act as an exclusive election; the issuer can also claim the availability of any other applicable exemption. For instance, an issuer's failure to satisfy all the terms and conditions of rule 506(b) (§230.506(b)) shall not raise any presumption that the exemption provided by section 4(a)(2) of the Act (15 U.S.C. 77d(2)) is not available.

(d) Regulation D is available only to the issuer of the securities and not to any affiliate of that issuer or to any other person for resales of the issuer's securities. Regulation D provides an exemption only for the transactions in which the securities are offered or sold by the issuer, not for the securities themselves.

(e) Regulation D may be used for business combinations that involve sales by virtue of rule 145(a) (§230.145(a)) or otherwise.

(f) In view of the objectives of Regulation D and the policies underlying the Act, Regulation D is not available to any issuer for any transaction or chain of transactions that, although in technical compliance with Regulation D, is part of a plan or scheme to evade the registration provisions of the Act. In such cases, registration under the Act is required.

(g) Securities offered and sold outside the United States in accordance with Regulation S (§230.901 through 905) need not be registered under the Act. See Release No. 33-6863. Regulation S may be relied upon for such offers and sales even if coincident offers and sales are made in accordance with Regulation D inside the United States. Thus, for example, persons who are offered and sold securities in accordance with Regulation S would not be counted in the calculation of the number of purchasers under Regulation D. Similarly, proceeds from such sales would not be included in the aggregate offering price. The provisions of this paragraph (g), however, do not apply if the issuer elects to rely solely on Regulation D for offers or sales to persons made outside the United States.

[77 FR 18684, Mar. 28, 2012, as amended at 78 FR 44804, July 24, 2013]

§230.501 DEFINITIONS AND TERMS USED IN REGULATION D.

As used in Regulation D (§230.500 *et seq.* of this chapter), the following terms shall have the meaning indicated:

(a) *Accredited investor. Accredited investor* shall mean any person who comes within any of the following categories, or who the issuer reasonably believes comes within any of the following categories, at the time of the sale of the securities to that person:

(1) Any bank as defined in section 3(a)(2) of the Act, or any savings and loan association or other institution as defined in section 3(a)(5)(A) of the Act whether acting in its individual or fiduciary capacity; any broker or dealer registered pursuant to section 15 of the Securities Exchange Act of 1934; any insurance company as defined in section 2(a)(13) of the Act; any investment company registered under the Investment Company Act of 1940 or a business development company as defined in section 2(a)(48) of that Act; any Small Business Investment Company licensed by the U.S. Small Business Administration under section 301(c) or (d) of the Small Business Investment Act of 1958; any plan established and maintained by a state, its political subdivisions, or any agency or instrumentality of a state or its political subdivisions, for the benefit of its employees, if such plan has total assets in excess of $5,000,000; any employee benefit plan within the meaning of the Employee Retirement Income Security Act of 1974 if the investment decision is made by a plan fiduciary, as defined in section 3(21) of such act, which is either a bank, savings and loan association, insurance company, or registered investment adviser, or if the employee benefit plan has total assets in excess of $5,000,000 or, if a self-directed plan, with investment decisions made solely by persons that are accredited investors;

(2) Any private business development company as defined in section 202(a)(22) of the Investment Advisers Act of 1940;

(3) Any organization described in section 501(c)(3) of the Internal Revenue Code, corporation, Massachusetts or similar business trust, or partnership, not formed for the specific purpose of acquiring the securities offered, with total assets in excess of $5,000,000;

(4) Any director, executive officer, or general partner of the issuer of the securities being offered or sold, or any director, executive officer, or general partner of a general partner of that issuer;

(5) Any natural person whose individual net worth, or joint net worth with that person's spouse, exceeds $1,000,000.

(i) Except as provided in paragraph (a)(5)(ii) of this section, for purposes of calculating net worth under this paragraph (a)(5):

(A) The person's primary residence shall not be included as an asset;

(B) Indebtedness that is secured by the person's primary residence, up to the estimated fair market value of the primary residence at the time of the sale of securities, shall not be included as a liability (except that if the amount of such indebtedness outstanding at the time of sale of securities exceeds the amount outstanding 60 days before such time, other than as a result of the acquisition of the primary residence, the amount of such excess shall be included as a liability); and

(C) Indebtedness that is secured by the person's primary residence in excess of the estimated fair market value of the primary residence at the time of the sale of securities shall be included as a liability;

(ii) Paragraph (a)(5)(i) of this section will not apply to any calculation of a person's net worth made in connection with a purchase of securities in accordance with a right to purchase such securities, provided that:

(A) Such right was held by the person on July 20, 2010;

(B) The person qualified as an accredited investor on the basis of net worth at the time the person acquired such right; and

(C) The person held securities of the same issuer, other than such right, on July 20, 2010.

(6) Any natural person who had an individual income in excess of $200,000 in each of the two most recent years or joint income with that person's spouse in excess of $300,000 in each of those years and has a reasonable expectation of reaching the same income level in the current year;

(7) Any trust, with total assets in excess of $5,000,000, not formed for the specific purpose of acquiring the securities offered, whose purchase is directed by a sophisticated person as described in §230.506(b)(2)(ii); and

(8) Any entity in which all of the equity owners are accredited investors.

(b) *Affiliate.* An *affiliate* of, or person *affiliated* with, a specified person shall mean a person that directly, or indirectly through one or more intermediaries, controls or is controlled by, or is under common control with, the person specified.

(c) *Aggregate offering price.* *Aggregate offering price* shall mean the sum of all cash, services, property, notes, cancellation of debt, or other consideration to be received by an issuer for issuance of its securities. Where securities are being offered for both cash and non-cash consideration, the aggregate offering price shall be based on the price at which the securities are offered for cash. Any portion of the aggregate offering price attributable to cash received in a foreign currency shall be translated into United States currency at the currency exchange rate in effect at a reasonable time prior to or on the date of the sale of the securities. If securities are not offered for cash, the aggregate offering price shall be based on the value of the consideration as established by bona fide sales of that consideration made within a reasonable time, or, in the absence of sales, on the fair value as determined by an accepted standard. Such valuations of non-cash consideration must be reasonable at the time made.

(d) *Business combination.* *Business combination* shall mean any transaction of the type specified in paragraph (a) of Rule 145 under the Act (17 CFR 230.145) and any transaction involving the acquisition by one issuer, in exchange for all or a part of its own or its parent's stock, of stock of another issuer if, immediately after the acquisition, the acquiring issuer has control of the other issuer (whether or not it had control before the acquisition).

(e) *Calculation of number of purchasers.* For purposes of calculating the number of purchasers under §§230.505(b) and 230.506(b) only, the following shall apply:

(1) The following purchasers shall be excluded:

(i) Any relative, spouse or relative of the spouse of a purchaser who has the same primary residence as the purchaser;

(ii) Any trust or estate in which a purchaser and any of the persons related to him as specified in paragraph (e)(1)(i) or (e)(1)(iii) of this section collectively have more than 50% of the beneficial interest (excluding contingent interests);

(iii) Any corporation or other organization of which a purchaser and any of the persons related to him as specified in paragraph (e)(1)(i) or (e)(1)(ii) of this section collectively are beneficial owners of more than 50% of the equity securities (excluding directors' qualifying shares) or equity interests; and

(iv) Any accredited investor.

(2) A corporation, partnership or other entity shall be counted as one purchaser. If, however, that entity is organized for the specific purpose of acquiring the securities offered and is not an accredited investor under paragraph (a)(8) of this section, then each beneficial owner of equity securities or equity interests in the entity shall count as a separate purchaser for all provisions of Regulation D (§§230.501-230.508), except to the extent provided in paragraph (e)(1) of this section.

(3) A non-contributory employee benefit plan within the meaning of Title I of the Employee Retirement Income Security Act of 1974 shall be counted as one purchaser where the trustee makes all investment decisions for the plan.

Note: The issuer must satisfy all the other provisions of Regulation D for all purchasers whether or not they are included in calculating the number of purchasers. Clients of an investment adviser or customers of a broker or dealer shall be considered the "purchasers" under Regulation D regardless of the amount of discretion given to the investment adviser or broker or dealer to act on behalf of the client or customer.

(f) *Executive officer. Executive officer* shall mean the president, any vice president in charge of a principal business unit, division or function (such as sales, administration or finance), any other officer who performs a policy making function, or any other person who performs similar policy making functions for the issuer. Executive officers of subsidiaries may be deemed executive officers of the issuer if they perform such policy making functions for the issuer.

(g) *Final order.* *Final order* shall mean a written directive or declaratory statement issued by a federal or state agency described in §230.506(d)(1)(iii) under applicable statutory authority that provides for notice and an opportunity for hearing, which constitutes a final disposition or action by that federal or state agency.

(h) *Issuer.* The definition of the term *issuer* in section 2(a)(4) of the Act shall apply, except that in the case of a proceeding under the Federal Bankruptcy Code (11 U.S.C. 101 *et seq.*), the trustee or debtor in possession shall be considered the issuer in an offering under a plan or reorganization, if the securities are to be issued under the plan.

(i) *Purchaser representative.* *Purchaser representative* shall mean any person who satisfies all of the following conditions or who the issuer reasonably believes satisfies all of the following conditions:

(1) Is not an affiliate, director, officer or other employee of the issuer, or beneficial owner of 10% or more of any class of the equity securities or 10% or more of the equity interest in the issuer, except where the purchaser is:

(i) A relative of the purchaser representative by blood, marriage or adoption and not more remote than a first cousin;

(ii) A trust or estate in which the purchaser representative and any persons related to him as specified in paragraph (h)(1)(i) or (h)(1)(iii) of this section collectively have more than 50% of the beneficial interest (excluding contingent interest) or of which the purchaser representative serves as trustee, executor, or in any similar capacity; or

(iii) A corporation or other organization of which the purchaser representative and any persons related to him as specified in paragraph (h)(1)(i) or (h)(1)(ii) of this section collectively are the beneficial owners of more than 50% of the equity securities (excluding directors' qualifying shares) or equity interests;

(2) Has such knowledge and experience in financial and business matters that he is capable of evaluating, alone, or together with other purchaser representatives of the purchaser, or together with the purchaser, the merits and risks of the prospective investment;

(3) Is acknowledged by the purchaser in writing, during the course of the transaction, to be his purchaser representative in connection with evaluating the merits and risks of the prospective investment; and

(4) Discloses to the purchaser in writing a reasonable time prior to the sale of securities to that purchaser any material relationship between himself or his affiliates and the issuer or its affiliates that then exists, that is mutually understood to be contemplated, or that has existed at any time during the previous two years, and any compensation received or to be received as a result of such relationship.

Note 1 to §230.501: A person acting as a purchaser representative should consider the applicability of the registration and antifraud provisions relating to brokers and dealers under the Securities Exchange Act of 1934 (Exchange Act) (15 U.S.C. 78a et seq., as amended) and relating to investment advisers under the Investment Advisers Act of 1940.

Note 2 to §230.501: The acknowledgment required by paragraph (h)(3) and the disclosure required by paragraph (h)(4) of this section must be made with specific reference to each prospective investment. Advance blanket acknowledgment, such as for all securities transactions or all private placements, is not sufficient.

Note 3 to §230.501: Disclosure of any material relationships between the purchaser representative or his affiliates and the issuer or its affiliates does not relieve the purchaser representative of his obligation to act in the interest of the purchaser.

[47 FR 11262, Mar. 16, 1982, as amended at 53 FR 7868, Mar. 10, 1988; 54 FR 11372, Mar. 20, 1989; 76 FR 81806, Dec. 29, 2011; 77 FR 18685, Mar. 28, 2012; 78 FR 44770, 44804, July 24, 2013]

§230.502 GENERAL CONDITIONS TO BE MET.

The following conditions shall be applicable to offers and sales made under Regulation D (§230.500 et seq. of this chapter):

(a) Integration. All sales that are part of the same Regulation D offering must meet all of the terms and conditions of Regulation D. Offers and sales that are made more than six months before the start of a Regulation D offering or are made more than six months after completion of a Regulation D offering will not be considered part of that Regulation D offering, so long as during those six-month periods there are no offers or sales of securities by or for the issuer that are of the same or a similar class as those offered or sold under Regulation D, other than those offers or sales of securities under an employee benefit plan as defined in rule 405 under the Act (17 CFR 230.405).

Note: The term offering is not defined in the Act or in Regulation D. If the issuer offers or sells securities for which the safe harbor rule in paragraph (a) of this §230.502 is unavailable, the determination as to whether separate sales of securities are part of the same offering (i.e., are considered integrated) depends on the particular facts and circumstances. Generally, transactions otherwise meeting the requirements of an exemption will not be integrated with simultaneous offerings being made outside the United States in compliance with Regulation S. See Release No. 33-6863.

The following factors should be considered in determining whether offers and sales should be integrated for purposes of the exemptions under Regulation D:

(a) Whether the sales are part of a single plan of financing;

(b) Whether the sales involve issuance of the same class of securities;

(c) Whether the sales have been made at or about the same time;

(d) Whether the same type of consideration is being received; and

(e) Whether the sales are made for the same general purpose.

See Release 33-4552 (November 6, 1962) [27 FR 11316].

(b) Information requirements—(1) When information must be furnished. If the issuer sells securities under §230.505 or §230.506(b) to any purchaser that is not an accredited investor, the issuer shall furnish the information specified in paragraph (b)(2) of this section to such purchaser a reasonable time prior to sale. The issuer is not required to furnish the specified information to purchasers when it sells securities under §230.504, or to any accredited investor.

Note: When an issuer provides information to investors pursuant to paragraph (b)(1), it should consider providing such information to accredited investors as well, in view of the anti-fraud provisions of the federal securities laws.

(2) Type of information to be furnished. (i) If the issuer is not subject to the reporting requirements of section 13 or 15(d) of the Exchange Act, at a reasonable time prior to the sale of securities the issuer shall furnish to the purchaser, to the extent material to an understanding of the issuer, its business and the securities being offered:

(A) Non-financial statement information. If the issuer is eligible to use Regulation A (§230.251-263), the same kind of information as would be required in Part II of Form 1-A (§239.90 of this chapter). If the issuer is not eligible to use Regulation A, the same kind of information as required in Part I of a registration statement filed under the Securities Act on the form that the issuer would be entitled to use.

(B) Financial statement information—(1) Offerings up to $2,000,000. The information required in Article 8 of Regulation S-X (§210.8 of this chapter), except that only the issuer's balance sheet, which shall be dated within 120 days of the start of the offering, must be audited.

(2) Offerings up to $7,500,000. The financial statement information required in Form S-1 (§239.10 of this chapter) for smaller reporting companies. If an issuer, other than a limited partnership, cannot obtain audited financial statements without unreasonable effort or expense, then only the issuer's balance sheet, which shall be dated within 120 days of the start of

the offering, must be audited. If the issuer is a limited partnership and cannot obtain the required financial statements without unreasonable effort or expense, it may furnish financial statements that have been prepared on the basis of Federal income tax requirements and examined and reported on in accordance with generally accepted auditing standards by an independent public or certified accountant.

(3) Offerings over $7,500,000. The financial statement as would be required in a registration statement filed under the Act on the form that the issuer would be entitled to use. If an issuer, other than a limited partnership, cannot obtain audited financial statements without unreasonable effort or expense, then only the issuer's balance sheet, which shall be dated within 120 days of the start of the offering, must be audited. If the issuer is a limited partnership and cannot obtain the required financial statements without unreasonable effort or expense, it may furnish financial statements that have been prepared on the basis of Federal income tax requirements and examined and reported on in accordance with generally accepted auditing standards by an independent public or certified accountant.

(C) If the issuer is a foreign private issuer eligible to use Form 20-F (§249.220f of this chapter), the issuer shall disclose the same kind of information required to be included in a registration statement filed under the Act on the form that the issuer would be entitled to use. The financial statements need be certified only to the extent required by paragraph (b)(2)(i) (B) (1), (2) or (3) of this section, as appropriate.

(ii) If the issuer is subject to the reporting requirements of section 13 or 15(d) of the Exchange Act, at a reasonable time prior to the sale of securities the issuer shall furnish to the purchaser the information specified in paragraph (b)(2)(ii)(A) or (B) of this section, and in either event the information specified in paragraph (b)(2)(ii)(C) of this section:

(A) The issuer's annual report to shareholders for the most recent fiscal year, if such annual report meets the requirements of Rules 14a-3 or 14c-3 under the Exchange Act (§240.14a-3 or 37§240.14c-3 of this chapter), the definitive proxy statement filed in connection with that annual report, and if requested by the purchaser in writing, a copy of the issuer's most recent Form 10-K (§249.310 of this chapter) under the Exchange Act.

(B) The information contained in an annual report on Form 10-K (§249.310 of this chapter) under the Exchange Act or in a registration statement on Form S-1 (§239.11 of this chapter) or S-11 (§239.18 of this chapter) under the Act or on Form 10 (§249.210 of this chapter) under the Exchange Act, whichever filing is the most recent required to be filed.

(C) The information contained in any reports or documents required to be filed by the issuer under sections 13(a), 14(a), 14(c), and 15(d) of the Exchange Act since the distribution or filing of the report or registration statement specified in paragraphs (b)(2)(ii) (A) or (B), and a brief description of the securities being offered, the use of the proceeds from the offering, and any material changes in the issuer's affairs that are not disclosed in the documents furnished.

(D) If the issuer is a foreign private issuer, the issuer may provide in lieu of the information specified in paragraph (b)(2)(ii) (A) or (B) of this section, the information contained in its most recent filing on Form 20-F or Form F-1 (§239.31 of the chapter).

(iii) Exhibits required to be filed with the Commission as part of a registration statement or report, other than an annual report to shareholders or parts of that report incorporated by reference in a Form 10-K report, need not be furnished to each purchaser that is not an accredited investor if the contents of material exhibits are identified and such exhibits are made available to a purchaser, upon his or her written request, a reasonable time before his or her purchase.

(iv) At a reasonable time prior to the sale of securities to any purchaser that is not an accredited investor in a transaction under §230.505 or §230.506(b), the issuer shall furnish to the purchaser a brief description in writing of any material written information concerning the offering that has been provided by the issuer to any accredited investor but not previously delivered to such unaccredited purchaser. The issuer shall furnish any portion or all of this information to the purchaser, upon his written request a reasonable time prior to his purchase.

(v) The issuer shall also make available to each purchaser at a reasonable time prior to his purchase of securities in a transaction under §230.505 or §230.506(b) the opportunity to ask questions and receive answers concerning the terms and conditions of the offering and to obtain any additional information which the issuer possesses or can acquire without unreasonable effort or expense that is necessary to verify the accuracy of information furnished under paragraph (b)(2) (i) or (ii) of this section.

(vi) For business combinations or exchange offers, in addition to information required by Form S-4 (17 CFR 239.25), the issuer shall provide to each purchaser at the time the plan is submitted to security holders, or, with an exchange, during the course of the transaction and prior to sale, written information about any terms or arrangements of the proposed transactions that are materially different from those for all other security holders. For purposes of this subsection, an issuer which is not subject to the reporting requirements of section 13 or 15(d) of the Exchange Act may satisfy the requirements of Part I.B. or C. of Form S-4 by compliance with paragraph (b)(2)(i) of this §230.502.

(vii) At a reasonable time prior to the sale of securities to any purchaser that is not an accredited investor in a transaction under §230.505 or §230.506(b), the issuer shall advise the purchaser of the limitations on resale in the manner contained in paragraph (d)(2) of this section. Such disclosure may be contained in other materials required to be provided by this paragraph.

(c) Limitation on manner of offering. Except as provided in §230.504(b)(1) or §230.506(c), neither the issuer nor any person acting on its behalf shall offer or sell the securities by any form of general solicitation or general advertising, including, but not limited to, the following:

(1) Any advertisement, article, notice or other communication published in any newspaper, magazine, or similar media or broadcast over television or radio; and

(2) Any seminar or meeting whose attendees have been invited by any general solicitation or general advertising; Provided, however, that publication by an issuer of a notice in accordance with §230.135c or filing with the

Commission by an issuer of a notice of sales on Form D (17 CFR 239.500) in which the issuer has made a good faith and reasonable attempt to comply with the requirements of such form, shall not be deemed to constitute general solicitation or general advertising for purposes of this section; Provided further, that, if the requirements of §230.135e are satisfied, providing any journalist with access to press conferences held outside of the United States, to meetings with issuer or selling security holder representatives conducted outside of the United States, or to written press-related materials released outside the United States, at or in which a present or proposed offering of securities is discussed, will not be deemed to constitute general solicitation or general advertising for purposes of this section.

(d) Limitations on resale. Except as provided in §230.504(b)(1), securities acquired in a transaction under Regulation D shall have the status of securities acquired in a transaction under section 4(a)(2) of the Act and cannot be resold without registration under the Act or an exemption therefrom. The issuer shall exercise reasonable care to assure that the purchasers of the securities are not underwriters within the meaning of section 2(a)(11) of the Act, which reasonable care may be demonstrated by the following:

(1) Reasonable inquiry to determine if the purchaser is acquiring the securities for himself or for other persons;

(2) Written disclosure to each purchaser prior to sale that the securities have not been registered under the Act and, therefore, cannot be resold unless they are registered under the Act or unless an exemption from registration is available; and

(3) Placement of a legend on the certificate or other document that evidences the securities stating that the securities have not been registered under the Act and setting forth or referring to the restrictions on transferability and sale of the securities.

While taking these actions will establish the requisite reasonable care, it is not the exclusive method to demonstrate such care. Other actions by the issuer may satisfy this provision. In addition, §230.502(b)(2)(vii) requires the delivery of written disclosure of the limitations on resale to investors in certain instances.

[47 FR 11262, Mar. 16, 1982, as amended at 47 FR 54771, Dec. 6, 1982; 53 FR 7869, Mar. 11, 1988; 54 FR 11372, Mar. 20, 1989; 55 FR 18322, May 2, 1990; 56 FR 30054, 30055, July 1, 1991; 57 FR 47409, Oct. 16, 1992; 58 FR 26514, May 4, 1993; 59 FR 21650, Apr. 26, 1994; 62 FR 53954, Oct. 17, 1997; 73 FR 969, Jan. 4, 2008; 73 FR 10615, Feb. 27, 2008; 77 FR 18685, Mar. 28, 2012; 78 FR 44804, July 24, 2013]

§230.503 FILING OF NOTICE OF SALES.

(a) *When notice of sales on Form D is required and permitted to be filed.* (1) An issuer offering or selling securities in reliance on §230.504, §230.505, or §230.506 must file with the Commission a notice of sales containing the information required by Form D (17 CFR 239.500) for each new offering of securities no later than 15 calendar days after the first sale of securities in the offering, unless the end of that period falls on a Saturday, Sunday or holiday, in which case the due date would be the first business day following.

(2) An issuer may file an amendment to a previously filed notice of sales on Form D at any time.

(3) An issuer must file an amendment to a previously filed notice of sales on Form D for an offering:

(i) To correct a material mistake of fact or error in the previously filed notice of sales on Form D, as soon as practicable after discovery of the mistake or error;

(ii) To reflect a change in the information provided in the previously filed notice of sales on Form D, as soon as practicable after the change, except that no amendment is required to reflect a change that occurs after the offering terminates or a change that occurs solely in the following information:

(A) The address or relationship to the issuer of a related person identified in response to Item 3 of the notice of sales on Form D;

(B) An issuer's revenues or aggregate net asset value;

(C) The minimum investment amount, if the change is an increase, or if the change, together with all other changes in that amount since the previously filed notice of sales on Form D, does not result in a decrease of more than 10%;

(D) Any address or state(s) of solicitation shown in response to Item 12 of the notice of sales on Form D;

(E) The total offering amount, if the change is a decrease, or if the change, together with all other changes in that amount since the previously filed notice of sales on Form D, does not result in an increase of more than 10%;

(F) The amount of securities sold in the offering or the amount remaining to be sold;

(G) The number of non-accredited investors who have invested in the offering, as long as the change does not increase the number to more than 35;

(H) The total number of investors who have invested in the offering; or

(I) The amount of sales commissions, finders' fees or use of proceeds for payments to executive officers, directors or promoters, if the change is a decrease, or if the change, together with all other changes in that amount since the previously filed notice of sales on Form D, does not result in an increase of more than 10%; and

(iii) Annually, on or before the first anniversary of the filing of the notice of sales on Form D or the filing of the most recent amendment to the notice of sales on Form D, if the offering is continuing at that time.

(4) An issuer that files an amendment to a previously filed notice of sales on Form D must provide current information in response to all requirements of the notice of sales on Form D regardless of why the amendment is filed.

(b) *How notice of sales on Form D must be filed and signed.* (1) A notice of sales on Form D must be filed with the Commission in electronic format by means of the Commission's Electronic Data Gathering,

Analysis, and Retrieval System (EDGAR) in accordance with EDGAR rules set forth in Regulation S-T (17 CFR Part 232).

(2) Every notice of sales on Form D must be signed by a person duly authorized by the issuer.

[73 FR 10615, Feb. 27, 2008]

§230.504 EXEMPTION FOR LIMITED OFFERINGS AND SALES OF SECURITIES NOT EXCEEDING $1,000,000.

(a) *Exemption.* Offers and sales of securities that satisfy the conditions in paragraph (b) of this §230.504 by an issuer that is not:

(1) Subject to the reporting requirements of section 13 or 15(d) of the Exchange Act,;

(2) An investment company; or

(3) A development stage company that either has no specific business plan or purpose or has indicated that its business plan is to engage in a merger or acquisition with an unidentified company or companies, or other entity or person, shall be exempt from the provision of section 5 of the Act under section 3(b) of the Act.

(b) *Conditions to be met*—(1) *General conditions.* To qualify for exemption under this §230.504, offers and sales must satisfy the terms and conditions of §§230.501 and 230.502 (a), (c) and (d), except that the provisions of §230.502 (c) and (d) will not apply to offers and sales of securities under this §230.504 that are made:

(i) Exclusively in one or more states that provide for the registration of the securities, and require the public filing and delivery to investors of a substantive disclosure document before sale, and are made in accordance with those state provisions;

(ii) In one or more states that have no provision for the registration of the securities or the public filing or delivery of a disclosure document before sale, if the securities have been registered in at least one state that provides for such registration, public filing and delivery before sale, offers and sales are made in that state in accordance with such provisions, and the disclosure document is delivered before sale to all purchasers (including those in the states that have no such procedure); or

(iii) Exclusively according to state law exemptions from registration that permit general solicitation and general advertising so long as sales are made only to "accredited investors" as defined in §230.501(a).

(2) The aggregate offering price for an offering of securities under this §230.504, as defined in §230.501(c), shall not exceed $1,000,000, less the aggregate offering price for all securities sold within the 12 months before the start of and during the offering of securities under this §230.504, in reliance on any exemption under section 3(b), or in violation of section 5(a) of the Securities Act.

Note 1: The calculation of the aggregate offering price is illustrated as follows:

If an issuer sold $900,000 on June 1, 1987 under this §230.504 and an additional $4,100,000 on December 1, 1987 under §230.505, the issuer could not sell any of its securities under this §230.504 until December 1, 1988. Until then the issuer must count the December 1, 1987 sale towards the $1,000,000 limit within the preceding 12 months.

Note 2: If a transaction under §230.504 fails to meet the limitation on the aggregate offering price, it does not affect the availability of this §230.504 for the other transactions considered in applying such limitation. For example, if an issuer sold $1,000,000 worth of its securities on January 1, 1988 under this §230.504 and an additional $500,000 worth on July 1, 1988, this §230.504 would not be available for the later sale, but would still be applicable to the January 1, 1988 sale.

[57 FR 36473, Aug. 13, 1992, as amended at 61 FR 30402, June 14, 1996; 64 FR 11094, Mar. 8, 1999]

§230.505 EXEMPTION FOR LIMITED OFFERS AND SALES OF SECURITIES NOT EXCEEDING $5,000,000.

(a) *Exemption.* Offers and sales of securities that satisfy the conditions in paragraph (b) of this section by an issuer that is not an investment company shall be exempt from the provisions of section 5 of the Act under section 3(b) of the Act.

(b) *Conditions to be met*—(1) *General conditions.* To qualify for exemption under this section, offers and sales must satisfy the terms and conditions of §§230.501 and 230.502.

(2) *Specific conditions*—(i) *Limitation on aggregate offering price.* The aggregate offering price for an offering of securities under this §230.505, as defined in §203.501(c), shall not exceed $5,000,000, less the aggregate offering price for all securities sold within the 12 months before the start of and during the offering of securities under this section in reliance on any exemption under section 3(b) of the Act or in violation of section 5(a) of the Act.

Note: The calculation of the aggregate offering price is illustrated as follows:

Example 1: If an issuer sold $2,000,000 of its securities on June 1, 1982 under this §230.505 and an additional $1,000,000 on September 1, 1982, the issuer would be permitted to sell only $2,000,000 more under this §230.505 until June 1, 1983. Until that date the issuer must count both prior sales towards the $5,000,000 limit. However, if the issuer made its third sale on June 1, 1983, the issuer could then sell $4,000,000 of its securities because the June 1, 1982 sale would not be within the preceding 12 months.

Example 2: If an issuer sold $500,000 of its securities on June 1, 1982 under §230.504 and an additional $4,500,000 on December 1, 1982 under this section, then the issuer could not sell any of its securities under this section until June 1, 1983. At that time it could sell an additional $500,000 of its securities.

(ii) *Limitation on number of purchasers.* There are no more than or the issuer reasonably believes that there are no more than 35 purchasers of securities from the issuer in any offering under this section.

(iii) *Disqualifications.* No exemption under this section shall be available for the securities of any issuer described in §230.262 of Regulation A, except that for purposes of this section only:

(A) The term "filing of the offering statement required by §230.252" as used in §230.262(a), (b) and (c) shall mean the first sale of securities under this section;

(B) The term "underwriter" as used in §230.262 (b) and (c) shall mean a person that has been or will be paid directly or indirectly remuneration for solicitation of purchasers in connection with sales of securities under this section; and

(C) Paragraph (b)(2)(iii) of this section shall not apply to any issuer if the Commission determines, upon a showing of good cause, that it is not necessary under the circumstances that the exemption be denied. Any such determination shall be without prejudice to any other action by the Commission in any other proceeding or matter with respect to the issuer or any other person.

[47 FR 11262, Mar. 16, 1982, as amended at 54 FR 11373, Mar. 20, 1989; 57 FR 36473, Aug. 13, 1992]

§230.506 EXEMPTION FOR LIMITED OFFERS AND SALES WITHOUT REGARD TO DOLLAR AMOUNT OF OFFERING.

(a) *Exemption.* Offers and sales of securities by an issuer that satisfy the conditions in paragraph (b) or (c) of this section shall be deemed to be transactions not involving any public offering within the meaning of section 4(a)(2) of the Act.

(b) *Conditions to be met in offerings subject to limitation on manner of offering—*(1) *General conditions.* To qualify for an exemption under this section, offers and sales must satisfy all the terms and conditions of §§230.501 and 230.502.

(2) *Specific conditions*—(i) *Limitation on number of purchasers.* There are no more than or the issuer reasonably believes that there are no more than 35 purchasers of securities from the issuer in any offering under this section.

Note to paragraph (b)(2)(i): See §230.501(e) for the calculation of the number of purchasers and §230.502(a) for what may or may not constitute an offering under paragraph (b) of this section.

(ii) *Nature of purchasers.* Each purchaser who is not an accredited investor either alone or with his purchaser representative(s) has such knowledge and experience in financial and business matters that he is capable of evaluating the merits and risks of the prospective investment, or the issuer reasonably believes immediately prior to making any sale that such purchaser comes within this description.

(c) *Conditions to be met in offerings not subject to limitation on manner of offering*—(1) *General conditions.* To qualify for exemption under this section, sales must satisfy all the terms and conditions of §§230.501 and 230.502(a) and (d).

(2) *Specific conditions*—(i) *Nature of purchasers.* All purchasers of securities sold in any offering under paragraph (c) of this section are accredited investors.

(ii) *Verification of accredited investor status.* The issuer shall take reasonable steps to verify that purchasers of securities sold in any offering under paragraph (c) of this section are accredited investors. The issuer shall be deemed to take reasonable steps to verify if the issuer uses, at its option, one of the following non-exclusive and non-mandatory methods of verifying that a natural person who purchases securities in such offering is an accredited investor; provided, however, that the issuer does not have knowledge that such person is not an accredited investor:

(A) In regard to whether the purchaser is an accredited investor on the basis of income, reviewing any Internal Revenue Service form that reports the purchaser's income for the two most recent years (including, but not limited to, Form W-2, Form 1099, Schedule K-1 to Form 1065, and Form 1040) and obtaining a written representation from the purchaser that he or she has a reasonable expectation of reaching the income level necessary to qualify as an accredited investor during the current year;

(B) In regard to whether the purchaser is an accredited investor on the basis of net worth, reviewing one or more of the following types of documentation dated within the prior three months and obtaining a written representation from the purchaser that all liabilities necessary to make a determination of net worth have been disclosed:

(1) With respect to assets: Bank statements, brokerage statements and other statements of securities holdings, certificates of deposit, tax assessments, and appraisal reports issued by independent third parties; and

(2) With respect to liabilities: A consumer report from at least one of the nationwide consumer reporting agencies; or

(C) Obtaining a written confirmation from one of the following persons or entities that such person or entity has taken reasonable steps to verify that the purchaser is an accredited investor within the prior three months and has determined that such purchaser is an accredited investor:

(1) A registered broker-dealer;

(2) An investment adviser registered with the Securities and Exchange Commission;

(3) A licensed attorney who is in good standing under the laws of the jurisdictions in which he or she is admitted to practice law; or

(4) A certified public accountant who is duly registered and in good standing under the laws of the place of his or her residence or principal office.

(D) In regard to any person who purchased securities in an issuer's Rule 506(b) offering as an accredited investor prior to September 23, 2013 and continues to hold such securities, for the same issuer's Rule 506(c) offering, obtaining a certification by such person at the time of sale that he or she qualifies as an accredited investor.

Instructions to paragraph (c)(2)(ii)(A) through (D) of this section:

1. The issuer is not required to use any of these methods in verifying the accredited investor status of natural persons who are purchasers. These methods are examples of the types of non-exclusive and non-mandatory methods that satisfy the verification requirement in §230.506(c)(2)(ii).

2. In the case of a person who qualifies as an accredited investor based on joint income with that person's spouse, the issuer would be deemed to satisfy the verification requirement in §230.506(c)(2)(ii)(A) by reviewing copies of Internal Revenue Service forms that report income for the two most recent years in regard to, and obtaining written representations from, both the person and the spouse.

3. In the case of a person who qualifies as an accredited investor based on joint net worth with that person's spouse, the issuer would be deemed to satisfy the verification requirement in §230.506(c)(2)(ii)(B) by reviewing such documentation in regard to, and obtaining written representations from, both the person and the spouse.

(d) *"Bad Actor" disqualification.* (1) No exemption under this section shall be available for a sale of securities if the issuer; any predecessor of the issuer; any affiliated issuer; any director, executive officer, other officer participating in the offering, general partner or managing member of the issuer; any beneficial owner of 20% or more of the issuer's outstanding voting equity securities, calculated on the basis of voting power; any promoter connected with the issuer in any capacity at the time of such sale; any investment manager of an issuer that is a pooled investment fund; any person that has been or will be paid (directly or indirectly) remuneration for solicitation of purchasers in connection with such sale of securities; any general partner or managing member of any such investment manager or solicitor; or any director, executive officer or other officer participating in the offering of any such investment manager or solicitor or general partner or managing member of such investment manager or solicitor:

(i) Has been convicted, within 10 years before such sale (or five years, in the case of issuers, their predecessors and affiliated issuers), of any felony or misdemeanor:

(A) In connection with the purchase or sale of any security;

(B) Involving the making of any false filing with the Commission; or

(C) Arising out of the conduct of the business of an underwriter, broker, dealer, municipal securities dealer, investment adviser or paid solicitor of purchasers of securities;

(ii) Is subject to any order, judgment or decree of any court of competent jurisdiction, entered within five years before such sale that, at the time of such sale, restrains or enjoins such person from engaging or continuing to engage in any conduct or practice:

(A) In connection with the purchase or sale of any security;

(B) Involving the making of any false filing with the Commission; or

(C) Arising out of the conduct of the business of an underwriter, broker, dealer, municipal securities dealer, investment adviser or paid solicitor of purchasers of securities;

(iii) Is subject to a final order of a state securities commission (or an agency or officer of a state performing like functions); a state authority that supervises or examines banks, savings associations, or credit unions; a state insurance commission (or an agency or officer of a state performing like functions); an appropriate federal banking agency; the U.S. Commodity Futures Trading Commission; or the National Credit Union Administration that:

(A) At the time of such sale, bars the person from:

(1) Association with an entity regulated by such commission, authority, agency, or officer;

(2) Engaging in the business of securities, insurance or banking; or

(3) Engaging in savings association or credit union activities; or

(B) Constitutes a final order based on a violation of any law or regulation that prohibits fraudulent, manipulative, or deceptive conduct entered within 10 years before such sale;

(iv) Is subject to an order of the Commission entered pursuant to section 15(b) or 15B(c) of the Securities Exchange Act of 1934 (15 U.S.C. 78*o*(b) or 78*o*-4(c)) or section 203(e) or (f) of the Investment Advisers Act of 1940 (15 U.S.C. 80b-3(e) or (f)) that, at the time of such sale:

(A) Suspends or revokes such person's registration as a broker, dealer, municipal securities dealer or investment adviser;

(B) Places limitations on the activities, functions or operations of such person; or

(C) Bars such person from being associated with any entity or from participating in the offering of any penny stock;

(v) Is subject to any order of the Commission entered within five years before such sale that, at the time of such sale, orders the person to cease and desist from committing or causing a violation or future violation of:

(A) Any scienter-based anti-fraud provision of the federal securities laws, including without limitation section 17(a)(1) of the Securities Act of 1933 (15 U.S.C. 77q(a)(1)), section 10(b) of the Securities Exchange Act of 1934 (15 U.S.C. 78j(b)) and 17 CFR 240.10b-5, section 15(c)(1) of the Securities Exchange Act of 1934 (15 U.S.C. 78*o*(c)(1)) and section 206(1) of the Investment Advisers Act of 1940 (15 U.S.C. 80b-6(1)), or any other rule or regulation thereunder; or

(B) Section 5 of the Securities Act of 1933 (15 U.S.C. 77e).

(vi) Is suspended or expelled from membership in, or suspended or barred from association with a member of, a registered national securities exchange or a registered national or affiliated securities association for any act or omission to act constituting conduct inconsistent with just and equitable principles of trade;

(vii) Has filed (as a registrant or issuer), or was or was named as an underwriter in, any registration statement or Regulation A offering statement filed with the Commission that, within five years before such sale, was the subject of a refusal order, stop order, or order suspending the Regulation A exemption, or is, at the time of such sale, the subject of an investigation or proceeding to determine whether a stop order or suspension order should be issued; or

(viii) Is subject to a United States Postal Service false representation order entered within five years before such sale, or is, at the time of such sale, subject to a temporary restraining order or preliminary injunction with respect to conduct alleged by the United States Postal Service to constitute a scheme or device for obtaining money or property through the mail by means of false representations.

(2) Paragraph (d)(1) of this section shall not apply:

(i) With respect to any conviction, order, judgment, decree, suspension, expulsion or bar that occurred or was issued before September 23, 2013;

(ii) Upon a showing of good cause and without prejudice to any other action by the Commission, if the Commission determines that it is not necessary under the circumstances that an exemption be denied;

(iii) If, before the relevant sale, the court or regulatory authority that entered the relevant order, judgment or decree advises in writing (whether contained in the relevant judgment, order or decree or separately to the Commission or its staff) that disqualification under paragraph (d)(1) of this section should not arise as a consequence of such order, judgment or decree; or

(iv) If the issuer establishes that it did not know and, in the exercise of reasonable care, could not have known that a disqualification existed under paragraph (d)(1) of this section.

Instruction to paragraph (d)(2)(iv). An issuer will not be able to establish that it has exercised reasonable care unless it has made, in light of the circumstances, factual inquiry into whether any disqualifications exist. The nature and scope of the factual inquiry will vary based on the facts and circumstances concerning, among other things, the issuer and the other offering participants.

(3) For purposes of paragraph (d)(1) of this section, events relating to any affiliated issuer that occurred before the affiliation arose will be not considered disqualifying if the affiliated entity is not:

(i) In control of the issuer; or

(ii) Under common control with the issuer by a third party that was in control of the affiliated entity at the time of such events.

(e) *Disclosure of prior "bad actor" events.* The issuer shall furnish to each purchaser, a reasonable time prior to sale, a description in writing of any matters that would have triggered disqualification under paragraph (d)(1) of this section but occurred before September 23, 2013. The failure to furnish such information timely shall not prevent an issuer from relying on this section if the issuer establishes that it did not know and, in the exercise of reasonable care, could not have known of the existence of the undisclosed matter or matters.

Instruction to paragraph (e). An issuer will not be able to establish that it has exercised reasonable care unless it has made, in light of the circumstances, factual inquiry into whether any disqualifications exist. The nature and scope of the factual inquiry will vary based on the facts and circumstances concerning, among other things, the issuer and the other offering participants.

[47 FR 11262, Mar. 6, 1982, as amended at 54 FR 11373, Mar. 20, 1989; 78 FR 44770, 44804, July 24, 2013]

§230.507 DISQUALIFYING PROVISION RELATING TO EXEMPTIONS UNDER §§230.504, 230.505 AND 230.506.

(a) No exemption under §230.505, §230.505 or §230.506 shall be available for an issuer if such issuer, any of its predecessors or affiliates have been subject to any order, judgment, or decree of any court of competent jurisdiction temporarily, preliminary or permanently enjoining such person for failure to comply with §230.503.

(b) Paragraph (a) of this section shall not apply if the Commission determines, upon a showing of good cause, that it is not necessary under the circumstances that the exemption be denied.

[54 FR 11374, Mar. 20, 1989]

§230.508 INSIGNIFICANT DEVIATIONS FROM A TERM, CONDITION OR REQUIREMENT OF REGULATION D.

(a) A failure to comply with a term, condition or requirement of §230.504, §230.505 or §230.506 will not result in the loss of the exemption from the requirements of section 5 of the Act for any offer or sale to a particular individual or entity, if the person relying on the exemption shows:

(1) The failure to comply did not pertain to a term, condition or requirement directly intended to protect that particular individual or entity; and

(2) The failure to comply was insignificant with respect to the offering as a whole, provided that any failure to comply with paragraph (c) of §230.502, paragraph (b)(2) of §230.504, paragraphs (b)(2)(i) and (ii) of §230.505 and paragraph (b)(2)(i) of §230.506 shall be deemed to be significant to the offering as a whole; and

(3) A good faith and reasonable attempt was made to comply with all applicable terms, conditions and requirements of §230.504, §230.505 or §230.506.

(b) A transaction made in reliance on §230.504, §230.505 or §230.506 shall comply with all applicable terms, conditions and requirements of Regulation D. Where an exemption is established only through reliance upon paragraph (a) of this section, the failure to comply shall nonetheless be actionable by the Commission under section 20 of the Act.

[54 FR 11374, Mar. 20, 1989, as amended at 57 FR 36473, Aug. 13, 1992]

APPENDIX 2

FORM D TO BE FILED UNDER SEC REGULATION D

(This form does not reflect changes proposed by the SEC
in Rel. No. 33-9416, which has not been adopted
as of December 1, 2015.)

FORM D

Notice of Exempt Offering of Securities

U.S. Securities and Exchange Commission
Washington, DC 20549

(See instructions beginning on page 5)

Intentional misstatements or omissions of fact constitute federal criminal violations. See 18 U.S.C. 1001.

OMB APPROVAL
OMB Number: 3235-0076
Expires: September 30, 2016
Estimated average burden hours per response: 4.00

Item 1. Issuer's Identity

Name of Issuer

Previous Name(s) ☐ None

Entity Type (Select one)
- ☐ Corporation
- ☐ Limited Partnership
- ☐ Limited Liability Company
- ☐ General Partnership
- ☐ Business Trust
- ☐ Other (Specify)

Jurisdiction of Incorporation/Organization

Year of Incorporation/Organization
(Select one)
- ○ Over Five Years Ago   ○ Within Last Five Years (specify year)   ○ Yet to Be Formed

(If more than one issuer is filing this notice, check this box ☐ and identify additional issuer(s) by attaching Items 1 and 2 Continuation Page(s).)

Item 2. Principal Place of Business and Contact Information

Street Address 1

Street Address 2

City

State/Province/Country

ZIP/Postal Code

Phone No.

Item 3. Related Persons

Last Name

First Name

Middle Name

Street Address 1

Street Address 2

City

State/Province/Country

ZIP/Postal Code

Relationship(s):   ☐ Executive Officer   ☐ Director   ☐ Promoter

Clarification of Response (if necessary)

(Identify additional related persons by checking this box ☐ and attaching Item 3 Continuation Page(s).)

Item 4. Industry Group   (Select one)

- ○ **Agriculture**

  Banking and Financial Services
  - ○ Commercial Banking
  - ○ Insurance
  - ○ Investing
  - ○ Investment Banking
  - ○ Pooled Investment Fund

  If selecting this industry group, also select one fund type below and answer the question below:
  - ○ Hedge Fund
  - ○ Private Equity Fund
  - ○ Venture Capital Fund
  - ○ Other Investment Fund

  Is the issuer registered as an investment company under the Investment Company Act of 1940? ○ Yes   ○ No
  - ○ Other Banking & Financial Services

- ○ **Business Services**

  Energy
  - ○ Electric Utilities
  - ○ Energy Conservation
  - ○ Coal Mining
  - ○ Environmental Services
  - ○ Oil & Gas
  - ○ Other Energy

  Health Care
  - ○ Biotechnology
  - ○ Health Insurance
  - ○ Hospitals & Physicians
  - ○ Pharmaceuticals
  - ○ Other Health Care

- ○ **Manufacturing**

  Real Estate
  - ○ Commercial

- ○ Construction
- ○ REITS & Finance
- ○ Residential
- ○ Other Real Estate

○ **Retailing**
○ **Restaurants**
Technology
- ○ Computers
- ○ Telecommunications
- ○ Other Technology

Travel
- ○ Airlines & Airports
- ○ Lodging & Conventions
- ○ Tourism & Travel Services
- ○ Other Travel

○ **Other**

SEC1972 (9/13)

Form D   1

FORM D

U.S. Securities and Exchange Commission
Washington, DC 20549

Item 5. Issuer Size   (Select one)

Revenue Range (for issuer not specifying "hedge" or "other investment" fund in Item 4 above)		Aggregate Net Asset Value Range (for issuer specifying "hedge" or "other investment" fund in Item 4 above)
○ No Revenues		○ No Aggregate Net Asset Value
○ $1 - $1,000,000	**OR**	○ $1 - $5,000,000
○ $1,000,001 - $5,000,000		○ $5,000,001 - $25,000,000
○ $5,000,001 - $25,000,000		○ $25,000,001 - $50,000,000
○ $25,000,001 - $100,000,000		○ $50,000,001 - $100,000,000
○ Over $100,000,000		○ Over $100,000,000
○ Decline to Disclose		○ Decline to Disclose
○ Not Applicable		○ Not Applicable

Item 6. Federal Exemptions and Exclusions Claimed   (Select all that apply)

Investment Company Act Section 3(c)

☐ Rule 504(b)(1) (not (i), (ii) or (iii))	☐ Section 3(c)(1)	☐ Section 3(c)(9)
☐ Rule 504(b)(1)(i)	☐ Section 3(c)(2)	☐ Section 3(c)(10)
☐ Rule 504(b)(1)(ii)	☐ Section 3(c)(3)	☐ Section 3(c)(11)
☐ Rule 504(b)(1)(iii)	☐ Section 3(c)(4)	☐ Section 3(c)(12)
☐ Rule 505	☐ Section 3(c)(5)	☐ Section 3(c)(13)
☐ Rule 506(b)	☐ Section 3(c)(6)	☐ Section 3(c)(14)
☐ Rule 506(c)	☐ Section 3(c)(7)	
☐ Securities Act Section 4(a)(5)		

Item 7. Type of Filing

○ New Notice   **OR**   ○ Amendment

Date of First Sale in this Offering: [   ]   **OR**   ☐ First Sale Yet to Occur

Item 8. Duration of Offering

Does the issuer intend this offering to last more than one year?   ☐ Yes   ☐ No

Item 9. Type(s) of Securities Offered   (Select all that apply)

☐ Equity	☐ Pooled Investment Fund Interests
☐ Debt	☐ Tenant-in-Common Securities
☐ Option, Warrant or Other Right to Acquire Another Security	☐ Mineral Property Securities
	☐ Other (describe)
☐ Security to be Acquired Upon Exercise of Option, Warrant or Other Right to Acquire Security	

Item 10. Business Combination Transaction

Is this offering being made in connection with a business combination transaction, such as a merger, acquisition or exchange offer?   ☐ Yes   ☐ No

Clarification of Response (if necessary)

FORM D

U.S. Securities and Exchange Commission
Washington, DC 20549

Item 11. Minimum Investment

Minimum investment accepted from any outside investor $ [_____]

Item 12. Sales Compensation

Recipient

[_____]

Recipient CRD Number

[_____] ☐ No CRD Number

(Associated) Broker or Dealer   ☐ None

[_____]

(Associated) Broker or Dealer CRD Number

[_____] ☐ No CRD Number

Street Address 1

[_____]

Street Address 2

[_____]

City

[_____]

State/Province/Country

[_____]

ZIP/Postal Code

[_____]

States of Solicitation   ☐ All States

☐ AL	☐ AK	☐ AZ	☐ AR	☐ CA	☐ CO	☐ CT	☐ DE	☐ DC	☐ FL	☐ GA	☐ HI	☐ ID
☐ IL	☐ IN	☐ IA	☐ KS	☐ KY	☐ LA	☐ ME	☐ MD	☐ MA	☐ MI	☐ MN	☐ MS	☐ MO
☐ MT	☐ NE	☐ NV	☐ NH	☐ NJ	☐ NM	☐ NY	☐ NC	☐ ND	☐ OH	☐ OK	☐ OR	☐ PA
☐ RI	☐ SC	☐ SD	☐ TN	☐ TX	☐ UT	☐ VT	☐ VA	☐ WA	☐ WV	☐ WI	☐ WY	☐ PR

(Identify additional person(s) being paid compensation by checking this box ☐ and attaching Item 12 Continuation Page(s).)

Item 13. Offering and Sales Amounts

(a) Total Offering Amount $ [_____]   **OR** ☐ Indefinite

(b) Total Amount Sold $ [_____]

(c) Total Remaining to be Sold $ [_____]   **OR** ☐ Indefinite
(Subtract (a) from (b))

Clarification of Response (if necessary)

[_____]

Item 14. Investors

Check this box ☐ if securities in the offering have been or may be sold to persons who do not qualify as accredited investors, and enter the number of such non-accredited investors who already have invested in the offering: [_____]

Enter the total number of investors who already have invested in the offering: [_____]

Item 15. Sales Commissions and Finders' Fees Expenses

Provide separately the amounts of sales commissions and finders' fees expenses, if any. If an amount is not known, provide an estimate and check the box next to the amount.

Sales Commissions $ [_____] ☐ Estimate

Clarification of Response (if necessary)

Finders' Fees $ [_____] ☐ Estimate

[_____]

Form D 3

FORM D

U.S. Securities and Exchange Commission

Washington, DC 20549

Item 16. Use of Proceeds

Provide the amount of the gross proceeds of the offering that has been or is proposed to be used for payments to any of the persons required to be named as executive officers, directors or promoters in response to Item 3 above. If the amount is unknown, provide an estimate and check the box next to the amount.

$ [   ]   ☐ Estimate

Clarification of Response (if necessary)

Signature and Submission

Please verify the information you have entered and review the Terms of Submission below before signing and submitting this notice.

Terms of Submission. In Submitting this notice, each identified issuer is:

Notifying the SEC and/or each State in which this notice is filed of the offering of securities described and undertaking to furnish them, upon written request, in accordance with applicable law, the information furnished to offerees.[*]

Irrevocably appointing each of the Secretary of the SEC and the Securities Administrator or other legally designated officer of the State in which the issuer maintains its principal place of business and any State in which this notice is filed, as its agents for service of process, and agreeing that these persons may accept service on its behalf, of any notice, process or pleading, and further agreeing that such service may be made by registered or certified mail, in any Federal or state action, administrative proceeding, or arbitration brought against the issuer in any place subject to the jurisdiction of the United States, if the action, proceeding or arbitration (a) arises out of any activity in connection with the offering of securities that is the subject of this notice, and (b) is founded, directly or indirectly, upon the provisions of: (i) the Securities Act of 1933, the Securities Exchange Act of 1934, the Trust Indenture Act of 1939, the Investment Company Act of 1940, or the Investment Advisers Act of 1940, or any rule or regulation under any of these statutes; or (ii) the laws of the State in which the issuer maintains its principal place of business or any State in which this notice is filed.

Certifying that, if the issuer is claiming a Regulation D exemption for the offering, the issuer is not disqualified from relying on Regulation D for one of the reasons stated in Rule 505(b)(2)(iii) or Rule 506(d).

[*] This undertaking does not affect any limits Section 102(a) of the National Securities Markets Improvement Act of 1996 ("NSMIA") [Pub. L. No. 104-290, 110 Stat. 3416 (Oct. 11, 1996)] imposes on the ability of States to require information. As a result, if the securities that are the subject of this Form D are "covered securities" for purposes of NSMIA, whether in all instances or due to the nature of the offering that is the subject of this Form D, States cannot routinely require offering materials under this undertaking or otherwise and can require offering materials only to the extent NSMIA permits them to do so under NSMIA's preservation of their anti-fraud authority.

Each identified issuer has read this notice, knows the contents to be true, and has duly caused this notice to be signed on its behalf by the undersigned duly authorized person. (Check this box ☐ and attach Signature Continuation Pages for signatures of issuers identified in Item 1 above but not represented by signer below.)

Issuer(s)

Name of Signer

Signature

Title

Date

Number of continuation pages attached: [   ]

Persons who respond to the collection of information contained in this form are not required to respond unless the form displays a currently valid OMB number.

FORM D

U.S. Securities and Exchange Commission
Washington, DC 20549

Instructions for Submitting a Form D Notice

General Instructions

Who must file: Each issuer of securities that sells its securities in reliance on an exemption provided in Regulation D or Section 4(a)(5) of the Securities Act of 1933 must file this notice containing the information requested with the U.S. Securities and Exchange Commission (SEC) and with the state(s) requiring it. If more than one issuer has sold its securitie in the same transaction, all issuers should be identified in one filing with the SEC, but some states may require a separate filing for each issuer or security sold.

When to file:

o An issuer must file a new notice with the SEC for each new offering of securities no later than 15 calendar days after the "date of first sale" of securities in the offering as explained in the Instruction to Item 7. For this purpose, the date of first sale is the date on which the first investor is irrevocably contractually committed to invest, which, depending on the terms and conditions of the contract, could be the date on which the issuer receives the investor's subscription agreement or check. An issuer may file the notice at any time before that if it has determined to make the offering. An issuer must file a new notice with each state that requires it at the time set by the state. For state filing information, go to www.NASAA.org. A mandatory capital commitment call does not constitute a new offering, but is made under the original offering, so no new Form D filing is required.

o An issuer may file an amendment to a previously filed notice at any time.

o An issuer must file an amendment to a previously filed notice for an offering:

- to correct a material mistake of fact or error in the previously filed notice, as soon as practicable after discovery of the mistake or error;

- to reflect a change in the information provided in the previously filed notice, except as provided below, as soon as practicable after the change; and

- annually, on or before the first anniversary of the most recent previously filed notice, if the offering is continuing at that time.

When amendment is not required: An issuer is not required to file an amendment to a previously filed notice to reflect a change that occurs after the offering terminates or a change that occurs solely in the following information:

- the address or relationship to the issuer of a related person identified in response to Item 3;

- an issuer's revenues or aggregate net asset value;

- the minimum investment amount, if the change is an increase, or if the change, together with all other changes in that amount since the previously filed notice, does not result in a decrease of more than 10%;

- any address or state(s) of solicitation shown in response to Item 12;

- the total offering amount, if the change is a decrease, or if the change, together with all other changes in that amount since the previously filed notice, does not result in an increase of more than 10%;

- the amount of securities sold in the offering or the amount remaining to be sold;

- the number of non-accredited investors who have invested in the offering, as long as the change does not increase the number to more than 35;

- the total number of investors who have invested in the offering; and

- the amount of sales commissions, finders' fees or use of proceeds for payments to executive officers, directors or promoters, if the change is a decrease, or if the change, together with all other changes in that amount since the previously filed notice, does not result in an increase of more than 10%.

Saturdays, Sundays and holidays: If the date on which a notice or an amendment to a previously filed notice is required to be filed falls on a Saturday, Sunday or holiday, the due date is the first business day following.

Amendment content: An issuer that files an amendment to a previously filed notice must provide current information in response to all items of this Form D, regardless of why the amendment is filed.

How to file: Issuers must file this notice with the SEC in electronic format. For state filing information, go to www.NASAA.org.

Filing fee: There is no federal fiing fee. For information on state filing fees, go to www. NASAA.org.

Definitions of terms: Terms used but not defined in this form that are defined in Rule 405 and Rule 501 under the Securities Act of 1933, 17 CFR 230.405 and 230.501, have the meanings given to them in those rules.

FORM D

Item-by-Item Instructions

Item 1. Issuer's Identity. Identify each legal entity issuing any securities being reported as being offered by entering its full name; any previous name used within the past five years; and its jurisdiction of incorporation or organization, type of legal entity, and year of incorporation or organization within the past five years or status as formed over five years ago or not yet formed. If more than one entity is issuing the securities, identify a primary issuer in the first fields shown on the first page of the form, checking the box provided, and identify additional issuers by attaching Items 1 and 2 continuation page(s).

Item 2. Principal Place of Business and Contact Information. Enter a full street address of the issuer's principal place of business. Post office box numbers and "In care of" addresses are not acceptable. Enter a contact telephone number for the issuer. If you identified more than one issuer in response to Item 1, enter the requested information for the primary issuer you identified in response to that item and, at your option, for any or all of the other issuers you identified on your Item 1 and 2 continuation page(s).

Item 3. Related Persons. Enter the full name and address of each person having the specified relationships with any issuer and identify each relationship:

 • Each executive officer and director of the issuer and person performing similar functions (title alone is not determinative) for the issuer, such as the general and managing partners of partnerships and managing members of limited liability companies; and

 • Each person who has functioned directly or indirectly as a promoter of the issuer within the past five years of the later of the first sale of securities or the date upon which the Form D filing was required to be made.

If necessary to prevent the information supplied from being misleading, also provide a clarification in the space provided.

Identify additional persons having the specified relationships by checking the box provided and attaching Item 3 continuation page(s).

Item 4. Industry Group. Select the issuer's industry group. If the issuer or issuers can be categorized in more than one industry group, select the industry group that most accurately reflects the use of the bulk of the proceeds of the offering. For purposes of this filing, use the ordinary dictionary and commonly understood meanings of the terms identifying the industry group.

Item 5. Issuer Size.

 • **Revenue Range** (for issuers that do not specify "Hedge Fund" or "Other Investment Fund" in response to Item 4): Enter the revenue range of the issuer or of all the issuers together for the most recently completed fiscal year available, or, if not in existence for a fiscal year, revenue range to date. Domestic SEC reporting companies should state revenues in accordance with Regulation S-X under the Securities Exchange Act of 1934. Domestic non-reporting companies should state revenues in accordance with U.S. Generally Accepted Accounting Principles (GAAP). Foreign issuers should calculate revenues in U.S. dollars and state them in accordance with U.S. GAAP, home country GAAP or International Financial Reporting Standards. If the issuer(s) declines to disclose its revenue range, enter "Decline to Disclose." If the issuer's(s') business is intended to produce revenue but did not, enter "No Revenues." If the business is not intended to produce revenue (for example, the business seeks asset appreciation only), enter "Not Applicable."

 • **Aggregate Net Asset Value** (for issuers that specify "Hedge Fund" or "Other Investment Fund" in response to Item 4): Enter the aggregate net asset value range of the issuer or of all the issuers together as of the most recent practicable date. If the issuer(s) declines to disclose its aggregate net asset value range, enter "Decline to Disclose."

Item 6. Federal Exemption(s) and Exclusion(s) Claimed. Select the provision(s) being claimed to exempt the offering and resulting sales from the federal registration requirements under the Securities Act of 1933 and, if applicable, to exclude the issuer from the definition of "investment company" under the Investment Company Act of 1940. Select "Rule 504(b)(1) (not (i), (ii) or (iii))" only if the issuer is relying on the exemption in the introductory sentence of Rule 504 for offers and sales that satisfy all the terms and conditions of Rules 501 and 502(a), (c) and (d).

Item 7. Type of Filing. Indicate whether the issuer is filing a new notice or an amendment to a notice that was filed previously. If this is a new notice, enter the date of the first sale of securities in the offering or indicate that the first sale has "Yet to Occur." For this purpose, the date of first sale is the date on which the first investor is irrevocably contractually committed to invest, which, depending on the terms and conditions of the contract, could be the date on which the issuer receives the investor's subscription agreement or check.

Item 8. Duration of Offering. Indicate whether the issuer intends the offering to last for more than one year.

FORM D

Item-by-Item Instructions (Continued)

Item 9. Type(s) of Securities Offered. Select the appropriate type or types of securities offered as to which this notice is filed. If the securities are debt convertible into other securities, however, select "Debt" and any other appropriate types of securities except for "Equity." For purposes of this filing, use the ordinary dictionary and commonly understood meanings of these categories. For instance, equity securities would be securities that represent proportional ownership in an issuer, such as ordinary common and preferred stock of corporations and partnership and limited liability company interests; debt securities would be securities representing money loaned to an issuer that must be repaid to the investor at a later date; pooled investment fund interests would be securities that represent ownership interests in a pooled or collective investment vehicle; tenant-in-common securities would be securities that include an undivided fractional interest in real property other than a mineral property; and mineral property securities would be securities that include an undivided interest in an oil, gas or other mineral property.

Item 10. Business Combination Transaction. Indicate whether or not the offering is being made in connection with a business combination, such as an exchange (tender) offer or a merger, acquisition, or other transaction of the type described in paragraph (a)(1), (2) or (3) of Rule 145 under the Securities Act of 1933. Do not include an exchange (tender) offer for a class of the issuer's own securities. If necessary to prevent the information supplied from being misleading, also provide a clarification in the space provided.

Item 11. Minimum Investment. Enter the minimum dollar amount of investment that will be accepted from any outside investor. If the offering provides a minimum investment amount for outside investors that can be waived, provide the lowest amount below which a waiver will not be granted. If there is no minimum investment amount, enter "0." Investors will be considered outside investors if they are not employees, officers, directors, general partners, trustees (where the issuer is a business trust), consultants, advisors or vendors of the issuer, its parents, its majority owned subsidiaries, or majority owned subsidiaries of the issuer's parent.

Item 12. Sales Compensation. Enter the requested information for each person that has been or will be paid directly or indirectly any commission or other similar compensation in cash or other consideration in connection with sales of securities in the offering, including finders. Enter the CRD number for every person identified and any broker and dealer listed that has a CRD number. CRD numbers can be found at http://brokercheck.finra.org. A person that does not have a CRD number need not obtain one in order to be listed, and must be listed when required regardless of whether the person has a CRD number. In addition, check the State(s) in which the named person has solicited or intends to solicit investors. If more than five persons to be listed are associated persons of the same broker or dealer, enter only the name of the broker or dealer, its CRD number and street address, and the State(s) in which the named person has solicited or intends to solicit investors.

Item 13. Offering and Sales Amounts. Enter the dollar amount of securities being offered under a claim of federal exemption identified in Item 6 above. Also enter the dollar amount of securities sold in the offering as of the filing date. Select the "Indefinite" box if the amount being offered is undetermined or cannot be calculated at the present time, such as if the offering includes securities to be acquired upon the exercise or exchange of other securities or property and the exercise price or exchange value is not currently known or knowable. If an amount is definite but difficult to calculate without unreasonable effort or expense, provide a good faith estimate. The total offering and sold amounts should include all cash and other consideration to be received for the securities, including cash to be paid in the future under mandatory capital commitments. In offerings for consideration other than cash, the amounts entered should be based on the issuer's good faith valuation of the consideration. If necessary to prevent the information supplied from being misleading, also provide a clarification in the space provided.

Item 14. Investors. Indicate whether securities in the offering have been or may be sold to persons who do not qualify as accredited investors as defined in Rule 501(a), 17 CFR 230.501(a), and provide the number of such investors who have already invested in the offering. In addition, regardless of whether securities in the offering have been or may be sold to persons who do not qualify as accredited investors, specify the total number of investors who already have invested.

Item 15. Sales Commission and Finders' Fees Expenses. The information on sales commissions and finders' fees expenses may be given as subject to future contingencies.

Item 16. Use of Proceeds. No additional instructions.

Signature and Submission. An individual who is a duly authorized representative of each issuer identified must sign, date and submit this notice for the issuer. The capacity in which the individual is signing should be set forth in the "Title" field underneath the individual's name.

The name of the issuer(s) on whose behalf the notice is being submitted should be set forth in the "Issuer" field beside the individual's name; if the individual is signing on behalf of all issuers submitting the notice, the word "All" may be set forth in the "Issuer" field. Attach signature continuation page(s) to have different individuals sign on behalf of different issuer(s). Enter the number of continuation pages attached and included in the filing. If no continuation pages are attached, enter "0".

FORM D

U.S. Securities and Exchange Commission
Washington, DC 20549
Items 1 and 2 Continuation Page

Item 1 and 2. Issuer's Identity and Contact Information (Continued)

Name of Issuer

Previous Name(s) ☐ None

Entity Type (Select one)
- ○ Corporation
- ○ Limited Partnership
- ○ Limited Liability Company
- ○ General Partnership
- ○ Business Trust
- ○ Other (Specify)

Jurisdiction of Incorporation/Organization

Year of Incorporation/Organization
(Select one)
○ Over Five Years Ago   ○ Within Last Five Years
(specify year)   ○ Yet to Be Formed

At your option, supply separate contact information for this issuer:

Street Address 1

Street Address 2

City

State/Province/Country   ZIP/Postal Code   Phone No.

Name of Issuer

Previous Name(s) ☐ None

Entity Type (Select one)
- ○ Corporation
- ○ Limited Partnership
- ○ Limited Liability Company
- ○ General Partnership
- ○ Business Trust
- ○ Other (Specify)

Jurisdiction of Incorporation/Organization

Year of Incorporation/Organization
(Select one)
○ Over Five Years Ago   ○ Within Last Five Years
(specify year)   ○ Yet to Be Formed

At your option, supply separate contact information for this issuer:

Street Address 1

Street Address 2

City

State/Province/Country   ZIP/Postal Code   Phone No.

Name of Issuer

Previous Name(s) ☐ None

Entity Type (Select one)
- ○ Corporation
- ○ Limited Partnership
- ○ Limited Liability Company
- ○ General Partnership
- ○ Business Trust
- ○ Other (Specify)

Jurisdiction of Incorporation/Organization

Year of Incorporation/Organization
(Select one)
○ Over Five Years Ago   ○ Within Last Five Years
(specify year)   ○ Yet to Be Formed

At your option, supply separate contact information for this issuer:

Street Address 1

Street Address 2

City

State/Province/Country   ZIP/Postal Code   Phone No.

(Copy and use additional copies of this page as necessary.)
Form D 8

FORM D   U.S. Securities and Exchange Commission

Washington, DC 20549

Item 3 Continuation Page

Item 3. Related Persons (Continued)

Last Name	First Name	Middle Name

Street Address 1	Street Address 2

City	State/Province/Country	ZIP/Postal Code

Relationship(s): ☐ Executive Officer ☐ Director ☐ Promoter

Clarification of Response (if necessary) [   ]

- -

Last Name	First Name	Middle Name

Street Address 1	Street Address 2

City	State/Province/Country	ZIP/Postal Code

Relationship(s): ☐ Executive Officer ☐ Director ☐ Promoter

Clarification of Response (if necessary) [   ]

- -

Last Name	First Name	Middle Name

Street Address 1	Street Address 2

City	State/Province/Country	ZIP/Postal Code

Relationship(s): ☐ Executive Officer ☐ Director ☐ Promoter

Clarification of Response (if necessary) [   ]

- -

Last Name	First Name	Middle Name

Street Address 1	Street Address 2

City	State/Province/Country	ZIP/Postal Code

Relationship(s): ☐ Executive Officer ☐ Director ☐ Promoter

Clarification of Response (if necessary) [   ]

(Copy and use additional copies of this page as necessary.)

Form D 9

FORM D

U.S. Securities and Exchange Commission
Washington, DC 20549

Item 12 Continuation Page

Item 12. Sales Compensation (Continued)

Recipient

Recipient CRD Number

☐ No CRD Number

(Associated) Broker or Dealer ☐ None

(Associated) Broker or Dealer CRD Number

☐ No CRD Number

Street Address 1

Street Address 2

City

State/Province/Country

ZIP/Postal Code

States of Solicitation ☐ All States

☐ AL	☐ AK	☐ AZ	☐ AR	☐ CA	☐ CO	☐ CT	☐ DE	☐ DC	☐ FL	☐ GA	☐ HI	☐ ID
☐ IL	☐ IN	☐ IA	☐ KS	☐ KY	☐ LA	☐ ME	☐ MD	☐ MA	☐ MI	☐ MN	☐ MS	☐ MO
☐ MT	☐ NE	☐ NV	☐ NH	☐ NJ	☐ NM	☐ NY	☐ NC	☐ ND	☐ OH	☐ OK	☐ OR	☐ PA
☐ RI	☐ SC	☐ SD	☐ TN	☐ TX	☐ UT	☐ VT	☐ VA	☐ WA	☐ WV	☐ WI	☐ WY	☐ PR

- - - - - - - - - - - - - - -

Recipient

Recipient CRD Number

☐ No CRD Number

(Associated) Broker or Dealer ☐ None

(Associated) Broker or Dealer CRD Number

☐ No CRD Number

Street Address 1

Street Address 2

City

State/Province/Country

ZIP/Postal Code

States of Solicitation ☐ All States

☐ AL	☐ AK	☐ AZ	☐ AR	☐ CA	☐ CO	☐ CT	☐ DE	☐ DC	☐ FL	☐ GA	☐ HI	☐ ID
☐ IL	☐ IN	☐ IA	☐ KS	☐ KY	☐ LA	☐ ME	☐ MD	☐ MA	☐ MI	☐ MN	☐ MS	☐ MO
☐ MT	☐ NE	☐ NV	☐ NH	☐ NJ	☐ NM	☐ NY	☐ NC	☐ ND	☐ OH	☐ OK	☐ OR	☐ PA
☐ RI	☐ SC	☐ SD	☐ TN	☐ TX	☐ UT	☐ VT	☐ VA	☐ WA	☐ WV	☐ WI	☐ WY	☐ PR

- - - - - - - - - - - - - - -

(Copy and use additional copies of this page as necessary.)

FORM D

U.S. Securities and Exchange Commission
Washington, DC 20549

Signature Continuation Page

Signature and Submission

The undersigned is the duly authorized representative of the issuer(s), identied in the field beside the individual's name below.

Issuer

Name of Signer

Signature

Title

Date

Issuer

Name of Signer

Signature

Title

Date

Issuer

Name of Signer

Signature

Title

Date

Issuer

Name of Signer

Signature

Title

Date

(Copy and use additional copies of this page as necessary.)

Form D 11

APPENDIX 3

FORM C
UNDER THE SECURITIES ACT
OF 1933

(Mark one.)
☐ **Form C: Offering Statement**
☐ **Form C-U: Progress Update:** _____
☐ **Form C/A: Amendment to Offering Statement:** _____
    ☐ **Check box if Amendment is material and investors must reconfirm within five business days.**
☐ **Form C-AR: Annual Report**
☐ **Form C-AR/A: Amendment to Annual Report**
☐ **Form C-TR: Termination of Reporting**

Name of issuer: _____
Legal status of issuer:
    Form: _____
    Jurisdiction of Incorporation/Organization: _____
    Date of organization): _____
Physical address of issuer: _____
Website of issuer: _____
Name of intermediary through which the offering will be conducted: ___

CIK number of intermediary: _____

SEC file number of intermediary: _____

CRD number, if applicable, of intermediary:_____

Amount of compensation to be paid to the intermediary, whether as a dollar amount or a percentage of the offering amount, or a good faith estimate if the exact amount is not available at the time of the filing, for conducting the offering, including the amount of referral and any other fees associated with the offering:

_____

Any other direct or indirect interest in the issuer held by the intermediary, or any arrangement for the intermediary to acquire such an interest:

_____

Type of security offered: _____

Target number of securities to be offered: _____

Price (or method for determining price):_____

Target offering amount: _____

Oversubscriptions accepted: ☐ Yes ☐ No

If yes, disclose how oversubscriptions will be allocated: ☐ Pro-rata basis
☐ First-come, first-served basis
☐ Other — provide a description:_____
Maximum offering amount (if different from target offering amount): ___

_____

Deadline to reach the target offering amount:_____

NOTE: If the sum of the investment commitments does not equal or exceed the target offering amount at the offering deadline, no securities will be sold in the offering, investment commitments will be canceled and committed funds will be returned.

Current number of employees: _____

Total Assets:	Most recent fiscal year-end: _____	Prior fiscal year-end: _____
Cash & Cash Equivalents:	Most recent fiscal year-end: _____	Prior fiscal year-end: _____
Accounts Receivable:	Most recent fiscal year-end: _____	Prior fiscal year-end: _____
Short-term Debt:	Most recent fiscal year-end: _____	Prior fiscal year-end: _____
Long-term Debt:	Most recent fiscal year-end: _____	Prior fiscal year-end: _____
Revenues/Sales:	Most recent fiscal year-end: _____	Prior fiscal year-end: _____
Cost of Goods Sold:	Most recent fiscal year-end: _____	Prior fiscal year-end: _____
Taxes Paid:	Most recent fiscal year-end: _____	Prior fiscal year-end: _____
Net Income:	Most recent fiscal year-end: _____	Prior fiscal year-end: _____

Using the list below, select the jurisdictions in which the issuer intends to offer the securities:

[List will include all U.S. jurisdictions, with an option to add and remove them individually, add all and remove all.]

GENERAL INSTRUCTIONS

I. Eligibility Requirements for Use of Form C

This Form shall be used for the offering statement, and any related amendments and progress reports, required to be filed by any issuer offering or selling securities in reliance on the exemption in Securities Act Section 4(a)(6) and in accordance with Section 4A and Regulation Crowdfunding (§ 227.100 *et. seq.*). This Form also shall be used for an annual report required pursuant to Rule 202 of Regulation Crowdfunding (§ 227.202) and for the termination of reporting required pursuant to Rule 203(b)(2) of Regulation Crowdfunding (§ 227.203(b)(2)). Careful attention should be directed to the terms, conditions and requirements of the exemption.

II. Preparation and Filing of Form C

Information on the cover page will be generated based on the information provided in XML format. Other than the cover page, this Form is not to be used as a blank form to be filled in, but only as a guide in the preparation of Form C. General information regarding the preparation, format and how to file this Form is contained in Regulation S-T (§ 232 *et. seq.*).

III. Information to be Included in the Form

Item 1. Offering Statement Disclosure Requirements

An issuer filing this Form for an offering in reliance on Section 4(a)(6) of the Securities Act and pursuant to Regulation Crowdfunding (§ 227.100 *et. seq.*) must file the Form prior to the commencement of the offering and include the information required by Rule 201 of Regulation Crowdfunding (§ 227.201).

An issuer must include in the XML-based portion of this Form: the information required by paragraphs (a), (e), (g), (h), (l), (n), and (o) of Rule 201 of Regulation Crowdfunding (§ 227.201(a), (e), (g), (h), (l), (n), and (o)); selected financial data for the prior two fiscal years (including total assets, cash and cash equivalents, accounts receivable, short-term debt, long-term debt, revenues/sales, cost of goods sold, taxes paid and net income); the jurisdictions in which the issuer intends to offer the securities; and any information required by Rule 203(a)(3) of Regulation Crowdfunding (§ 227.203(a)(3)).

Other than the information required to be provided in XML format, an issuer may provide the required information in the optional Question and Answer format included herein or in any other format included on the intermediary's platform, by filing such information as an exhibit to this Form, including copies of screen shots of the relevant information, as appropriate and necessary.

If disclosure in response to any paragraph of Rule 201 of Regulation Crowdfunding (§ 227.201) or Rule 203(a)(3) is responsive to one or more other paragraphs of Rule 201 of Regulation Crowdfunding (§ 227.201) or to Rule 203(a)(3) of Regulation Crowdfunding (§ 227.203(a)(3)), issuers are not required to make duplicate disclosures.

Item 2. Legends

(a) An issuer filing this Form for an offering in reliance on Section 4(a)(6) of the Securities Act and pursuant to Regulation Crowdfunding (§ 227.100 *et. seq.*) must include the following legends:

A crowdfunding investment involves risk. You should not invest any funds in this offering unless you can afford to lose your entire investment.

In making an investment decision, investors must rely on their own examination of the issuer and the terms of the offering, including the merits and risks involved. These securities have not been recommended or approved by any federal or state securities commission or regulatory authority. Furthermore, these authorities have not passed upon the accuracy or adequacy of this document.

The U.S. Securities and Exchange Commission does not pass upon the merits of any securities offered or the terms of the offering, nor does it pass upon the accuracy or completeness of any offering document or literature.

These securities are offered under an exemption from registration; however, the U.S. Securities and Exchange Commission has not made an independent determination that these securities are exempt from registration.

(b) An issuer filing this Form for an offering in reliance on Section 4(a)(6) of the Securities Act and pursuant to Regulation Crowdfunding (§ 227.100 *et. seq.*) must disclose in the offering statement that it will file a report with the Commission annually and post the report on its website, no later than 120 days after the end of each fiscal year covered by the report. The issuer must also disclose how an issuer may terminate its reporting obligations in the future in accordance with Rule 202(b) of Regulation Crowdfunding (§ 227.202(b)).

Item 3. Annual Report Disclosure Requirements

An issuer filing this Form for an annual report, as required by Regulation Crowdfunding (§ 227.100 *et. seq.*), must file the Form no later than 120 days after the issuer's fiscal year end covered by the report and include the information required by Rule 201(a), (b), (c), (d), (e), (f), (m), (p), (q), (r), (s), (t), (x) and (y) of Regulation Crowdfunding (§§ 227.201(a), (b), (c), (d), (e), (f), (m), (p), (q), (r), (s), (t), (x) and (y)). For purposes of paragraph (t), the issuer shall provide financial statements certified by the principal executive officer of the issuer to be true and complete in all material respects. If, however, the issuer has available financial statements prepared in accordance with U.S. generally accepted accounting principles (U.S. GAAP) that have been reviewed or audited by an independent certified public accountant, those financial statements must be provided and the principal executive officer certification will not be required.

An issuer must include in the XML-based portion of this Form: the information required by paragraphs (a), and (e) of Rule 201 of Regulation Crowdfunding (§ 227.201(a) and (e)); and selected financial data for the prior two fiscal years (including total assets, cash and cash equivalents, accounts receivable, short-term debt, long-term debt, revenues/sales, cost of goods sold, taxes paid and net income).

SIGNATURE

Pursuant to the requirements of Sections 4(a)(6) and 4A of the Securities Act of 1933 and Regulation Crowdfunding (§ 227.100 *et. seq.*), the issuer certifies that it has reasonable grounds to believe that it meets all of the requirements for filing on Form C and has duly caused this Form to be signed on its behalf by the duly authorized undersigned.

_____

(Issuer)

By

_____

(Signature and Title)

Pursuant to the requirements of Sections 4(a)(6) and 4A of the Securities Act of 1933 and Regulation Crowdfunding (§ 227.100 *et. seq.*), this Form C has been signed by the following persons in the capacities and on the dates indicated.

_____

(Signature)

_____

(Title)

_____

(Date)

Instructions.

1. The form shall be signed by the issuer, its principal executive officer or officers, its principal financial officer, its controller or principal accounting officer and at least a majority of the board of directors or persons performing similar functions.
2. The name of each person signing the form shall be typed or printed beneath the signature.

Intentional misstatements or omissions of facts constitute federal criminal violations. *See* 18 U.S.C. 1001.

OPTIONAL QUESTION & ANSWER FORMAT

FOR AN OFFERING STATEMENT

Respond to each question in each paragraph of this part. Set forth each question and any notes, but not any instructions thereto, in their entirety. If disclosure in response to any question is responsive to one or more other questions, it is not necessary to repeat the disclosure. If a question or series of questions is inapplicable or the response is available elsewhere in the Form, either state that it is inapplicable, include a cross-reference to the responsive disclosure, or omit the question or series of questions.

Be very careful and precise in answering all questions. Give full and complete answers so that they are not misleading under the circumstances involved. Do not discuss any future performance or other anticipated event unless you have a reasonable basis to believe that it will actually occur within the foreseeable future. If any answer requiring significant information is materially inaccurate, incomplete or misleading, the Company, its management and principal shareholders may be liable to investors based on that information.

THE COMPANY

1. Name of issuer: _____

ELIGIBILITY

2. ☐ Check this box to certify that all of the following statements are true for the issuer:

- Organized under, and subject to, the laws of a State or territory of the United States or the District of Columbia.
- Not subject to the requirement to file reports pursuant to Section 13 or Section 15(d) of the Securities Exchange Act of 1934.
- Not an investment company registered or required to be registered under the Investment Company Act of 1940.
- Not ineligible to rely on this exemption under Section 4(a)(6) of the Securities Act as a result of a disqualification specified in Rule 503(a) of Regulation Crowdfunding. (For more information about these disqualifications, see Question 30 of this Question and Answer format).
- Has filed with the Commission and provided to investors, to the extent required, the ongoing annual reports required by Regulation Crowdfunding during the two years immediately preceding the filing of this offering statement (or for such shorter period that the issuer was required to file such reports).
- Not a development stage company that (a) has no specific business plan or (b) has indicated that its business plan is to engage in a merger or acquisition with an unidentified company or companies.

INSTRUCTION TO QUESTION 2: If any of these statements is not true, then you are NOT eligible to rely on this exemption under Section 4(a)(6) of the Securities Act.

3. Has the issuer or any of its predecessors previously failed to comply with the ongoing reporting requirements of Rule 202 of Regulation Crowdfunding? ☐ Yes ☐ No
   Explain: _____

DIRECTORS OF THE COMPANY

4. Provide the following information about each director (and any persons occupying a similar status or performing a similar function) of the issuer:

Name:_____ Dates of Board Service:_____
    Principal Occupation:_____
    Employer:_____ Dates of Service: _____
    Employer's principal business: _____

List all positions and offices with the issuer held and the period of time in which the director served in the position or office:

Position: _____ Dates of Service: _____
Position: _____ Dates of Service: _____
Position: _____ Dates of Service: _____

Business Experience: List the employers, titles and dates of positions held during past three years with an indication of job responsibilities:

Employer:_____
Employer's principal business:_____
Title:_____ Dates of Service:_____
Responsibilities:_____

Employer:_____
Employer's principal business:_____
Title:_____ Dates of Service:_____
Responsibilities:_____

Employer:_____
Employer's principal business:_____
Title:_____ Dates of Service:_____
Responsibilities:_____

OFFICERS OF THE COMPANY

5. Provide the following information about each officer (and any persons occupying a similar status or performing a similar function) of the issuer:

Name:_____

Title:_____   Dates of Service:_____

Responsibilities:_____

List any prior positions and offices with the issuer and the period of time in which the officer served in the position or office:

Position: _____   Dates of Service: _____

Responsibilities:_____

Position: _____   Dates of Service: _____

Responsibilities:_____

Position: _____   Dates of Service: _____

Responsibilities:_____

Business Experience: List any other employers, titles and dates of positions held during past three years with an indication of job responsibilities:

Employer:_____

Employer's principal business:_____

Title:_____   Dates of Service:_____

Responsibilities:_____

Employer:_____

Employer's principal business:_____

Title:_____   Dates of Service:_____

Responsibilities:_____

Employer:_____

Employer's principal business:_____

Title:_____ Dates of Service:_____

Responsibilities:_____

INSTRUCTION TO QUESTION 5: For purposes of this Question 5, the term officer means a president, vice president, secretary, treasurer or principal financial officer, comptroller or principal accounting officer, and any person routinely performing similar functions.

PRINCIPAL SECURITY HOLDERS

6. Provide the name and ownership level of each person, as of the most recent practicable date, who is the beneficial owner of 20% or more of the issuer's outstanding voting equity securities, calculated on the basis of voting power.

Name of Holder	No. and Class of Securities Now Held	% of Voting Power Prior to Offering
_____	_____	_____ %
_____	_____	_____ %
_____	_____	_____ %
_____	_____	_____ %

INSTRUCTION TO QUESTION 6: The above information must be provided as of a date that is no more than 120 days prior to the date of filing of this offering statement.

To calculate total voting power, include all securities for which the person directly or indirectly has or shares the voting power, which includes the power to vote or to direct the voting of such securities. If the person has the right to acquire voting power of such securities within 60 days, including through the exercise of any option, warrant or right, the conversion of a security, or other arrangement, or if securities are held by a member of the family, through corporations or partnerships, or otherwise in a manner that would allow a person to direct or control the voting of the securities (or share in such direction or control — as, for example, a co-trustee) they should be included as being "beneficially owned." You should include an explanation of these circumstances in a footnote to the "Number of and Class of Securities Now Held." To calculate outstanding voting equity securities, assume all outstanding options are exercised and all outstanding convertible securities converted.

BUSINESS AND ANTICIPATED BUSINESS PLAN

7. Describe in detail the business of the issuer and the anticipated business plan of the issuer.

RISK FACTORS

A crowdfunding investment involves risk. You should not invest any funds in this offering unless you can afford to lose your entire investment.

In making an investment decision, investors must rely on their own examination of the issuer and the terms of the offering, including the merits and risks involved. These securities have not been recommended or approved by any federal or state securities commission or regulatory authority. Furthermore, these authorities have not passed upon the accuracy or adequacy of this document.

The U.S. Securities and Exchange Commission does not pass upon the merits of any securities offered or the terms of the offering, nor does it pass upon the accuracy or completeness of any offering document or literature.

These securities are offered under an exemption from registration; however, the U.S. Securities and Exchange Commission has not made an independent determination that these securities are exempt from registration.

8. Discuss the material factors that make an investment in the issuer speculative or risky:

(1) _____

(2) _____

(3) _____

(4) _____

(5) _____

(6) _____

(7) _____

(8) _____

(9) _____

(10) _____

INSTRUCTION TO QUESTION 8: Avoid generalized statements and include only those factors that are unique to the issuer. Discussion should be tailored to the issuer's business and the offering and should not repeat the factors addressed in the legends set forth above. No specific number of risk factors is required to be identified. Add additional lines and number as appropriate.

THE OFFERING

9. What is the purpose of this offering?

10. How does the issuer intend to use the proceeds of this offering?

	If Target Offering Amount Sold	If Maximum Amount Sold
Total Proceeds	$	$
Less: Offering Expenses		
(A)		
(B)		
(C)		
Net Proceeds	$	$

(*Continued*)

	If Target Offering Amount Sold	If Maximum Amount Sold
Use of Net Proceeds		
(A)		
(B)		
(C)		
Total Use of Net Proceeds	$	$

INSTRUCTION TO QUESTION 10: An issuer must provide a reasonably detailed description of any intended use of proceeds, such that investors are provided with an adequate amount of information to understand how the offering proceeds will be used. If an issuer has identified a range of possible uses, the issuer should identify and describe each probable use and the factors the issuer may consider in allocating proceeds among the potential uses. If the issuer will accept proceeds in excess of the target offering amount, the issuer must describe the purpose, method for allocating oversubscriptions, and intended use of the excess proceeds with similar specificity.

11. How will the issuer complete the transaction and deliver securities to the investors?

12. How can an investor cancel an investment commitment?

   NOTE: Investors may cancel an investment commitment until 48 hours prior to the deadline identified in these offering materials.
   The intermediary will notify investors when the target offering amount has been met.
   If the issuer reaches the target offering amount prior to the deadline identified in the offering materials, it may close the offering early if it provides notice about the new offering deadline at least five business days prior to such new offering deadline (absent a material change that would require an extension of the offering and reconfirmation of the investment commitment).

If an investor does not cancel an investment commitment before the 48-hour period prior to the offering deadline, the funds will be released to the issuer upon closing of the offering and the investor will receive securities in exchange for his or her investment.

If an investor does not reconfirm his or her investment commitment after a material change is made to the offering, the investor's investment commitment will be cancelled and the committed funds will be returned.

OWNERSHIP AND CAPITAL STRUCTURE

The Offering

13. Describe the terms of the securities being offered.

14. Do the securities offered have voting rights?   ☐ Yes ☐ No

15. Are there any limitations on any voting or other rights identified above? ☐ Yes ☐ No

    Explain: _____

16. How may the terms of the securities being offered be modified?

Restrictions on Transfer of the Securities Being Offered

The securities being offered may not be transferred by any purchaser of such securities during the one-year period beginning when the securities were issued, unless such securities are transferred:

(1) to the issuer;

(2) to an accredited investor;

(3) as part of an offering registered with the U.S. Securities and Exchange Commission; or

(4) to a member of the family of the purchaser or the equivalent, to a trust controlled by the purchaser, to a trust created for the benefit of a member of the family of the purchaser or the equivalent, or in connection with the death or divorce of the purchaser or other similar circumstance.

NOTE: The term "accredited investor" means any person who comes within any of the categories set forth in Rule 501(a) of Regulation D, or who the seller reasonably believes comes within any of such categories, at the time of the sale of the securities to that person.

The term "member of the family of the purchaser or the equivalent" includes a child, stepchild, grandchild, parent, stepparent, grandparent, spouse or spousal equivalent, sibling, mother-in-law, father-in-law, son-in-law, daughter-in-law, brother-in-law, or sister-in-law of the purchaser, and includes adoptive relationships. The term "spousal equivalent" means a cohabitant occupying a relationship generally equivalent to that of a spouse.

Description of Issuer's Securities

17. What other securities or classes of securities of the issuer are outstanding? Describe the material terms of any other outstanding securities or classes of securities of the issuer.

Class of Security	Securities (or Amount) Authorized	Securities (or Amount) Outstanding	Voting Rights	Other Rights
Preferred Stock (list each class in order of preference):				
_____			☐ Yes ☐ No	☐ Yes ☐ No Specify: ____
_____			☐ Yes ☐ No	☐ Yes ☐ No Specify: ____
Common Stock:			☐ Yes ☐ No	☐ Yes ☐ No Specify: ____
Debt Securities:			☐ Yes ☐ No	☐ Yes ☐ No Specify: ____

Other:

_____   ☐ Yes ☐ No ☐ Yes   ☐ No
                                          Specify: ____

_____   ☐ Yes ☐ No ☐ Yes   ☐ No
                                          Specify: ____

| | **Securities Reserved for Issuance upon Exercise or** |
Class of Security	**Conversion**
Warrants:	
Options:	
Other Rights:	

_____

_____

18. How may the rights of the securities being offered be materially limited, diluted or qualified by the rights of any other class of security identified above?

19. Are there any differences not reflected above between the securities being offered and each other class of security of the issuer? ☐ Yes ☐ No
Explain: _____

20. How could the exercise of rights held by the principal shareholders identified in Question 6 above affect the purchasers of the securities being offered?

21. How are the securities being offered being valued? Include examples of methods for how such securities may be valued by the issuer in the future, including during subsequent corporate actions.

22. What are the risks to purchasers of the securities relating to minority ownership in the issuer?

23. What are the risks to purchasers associated with corporate actions including:

- additional issuances of securities,
- issuer repurchases of securities,
- a sale of the issuer or of assets of the issuer or
- transactions with related parties?

24. Describe the material terms of any indebtedness of the issuer:

Creditor(s)	Amount Outstanding	Interest Rate	Maturity Date	Other Material Terms
	$_____	_____ %		
	$_____	_____ %		
	$_____	_____ %		

25. What other exempt offerings has the issuer conducted within the past three years?

Date of Offering	Exemption Relied Upon	Securities Offered	Amount Sold	Use of Proceeds
			$_____	
			$_____	
			$_____	

26. Was or is the issuer or any entities controlled by or under common control with the issuer a party to any transaction since the beginning of the issuer's last fiscal year, or any currently proposed transaction, where the amount involved exceeds 5% of the aggregate amount of capital raised by the issuer in reliance on Section 4(a)(6) of the Securities Act during the preceding 12-month period, including the amount the issuer seeks to raise in the current offering, in which any of the following persons had or is to have a direct or indirect material interest:

(1) any director or officer of the issuer;

(2) any person who is, as of the most recent practicable date, the beneficial owner of 20% or more of the issuer's outstanding voting equity securities, calculated on the basis of voting power;

(3) if the issuer was incorporated or organized within the past three years, any promoter of the issuer; or

(4) any immediate family member of any of the foregoing persons.

If yes, for each such transaction, disclose the following:

Specified Person	Relationship to Issuer	Nature of Interest in Transaction	Amount of Interest
			$ _____
			$ _____
			$ _____

INSTRUCTIONS TO QUESTION 26:

The term transaction includes, but is not limited to, any financial transaction, arrangement or relationship (including any indebtedness or guarantee of indebtedness) or any series of similar transactions, arrangements or relationships.

Beneficial ownership for purposes of paragraph (2) shall be determined as of a date that is no more than 120 days prior to the date of filing of this offering statement and using the same calculation described in Question 6 of this Question and Answer format.

The term "member of the family" includes any child, stepchild, grandchild, parent, stepparent, grandparent, spouse or spousal equivalent, sibling, mother-in-law, father-in-law, son-in-law, daughter-in-law, brother-in-law, or sister-in-law of the person, and includes adoptive relationships. The term "spousal equivalent" means a cohabitant occupying a relationship generally equivalent to that of a spouse.

Compute the amount of a related party's interest in any transaction without regard to the amount of the profit or loss involved in the transaction. Where it is not practicable to state the approximate amount of the interest, disclose the approximate amount involved in the transaction.

FINANCIAL CONDITION OF THE ISSUER

27. Does the issuer have an operating history? ☐ Yes ☐ No

28. Describe the financial condition of the issuer, including, to the extent material, liquidity, capital resources and historical results of operations.

INSTRUCTIONS TO QUESTION 28:

The discussion must cover each year for which financial statements are provided. Include a discussion of any known material changes or trends in the financial condition and results of operations of the issuer during any time period subsequent to the period for which financial statements are provided.

For issuers with no prior operating history, the discussion should focus on financial milestones and operational, liquidity and other challenges.

For issuers with an operating history, the discussion should focus on whether historical results and cash flows are representative of what investors should expect in the future.

Take into account the proceeds of the offering and any other known or pending sources of capital. Discuss how the proceeds from the offering will affect liquidity, whether receiving these funds and any other additional funds is necessary to the viability of the business, and how quickly the issuer anticipates using its available cash. Describe the other available sources of capital to the business, such as lines of credit or required contributions by shareholders.

References to the issuer in this Question 28 and these instructions refer to the issuer and its predecessors, if any.

FINANCIAL INFORMATION

29. Include the financial information specified below covering the two most recently completed fiscal years or the period(s) since inception, if shorter:

Aggregate Offering Amount (defined below):	Financial Information Required:	Financial Statement Requirements:
(a) $100,000 or less:	• The following information or their equivalent line items as reported on the federal income tax return filed by the issuer for the most recently completed year (if any): ○ Total income ○ Taxable income; and ○ Total tax; certified by the principal executive officer of the issuer to reflect accurately the information reported on the issuer's federal income tax returns; and • Financial statements of the issuer and its predecessors, if any.	Financial statements must be **certified** by the principal executive officer of the issuer as set forth below. If financial statements are available that have either been reviewed or audited by a public accountant that is independent of the issuer, the issuer must provide those financial statements instead along with a signed audit or review report and need not include the information reported on the federal income tax returns or the certification of the principal executive officer.
(b) More than $100,000, but not more than $500,000:	• Financial statements of the issuer and its predecessors, if any.	Financial statements must be **reviewed** by a public accountant that is independent of the issuer and must include a signed review report. If financial statements of the issuer are available that have been audited by a public accountant that is independent of the issuer, the issuer must provide those financial statements instead along with a signed audit report and need not include the reviewed financial statements.

(Continued)

(Continued)

Aggregate Offering Amount (defined below):	Financial Information Required:	Financial Statement Requirements:
(c) More than $500,000:	• Financial statements of the issuer and its predecessors, if any.	If the issuer **has** previously sold securities in reliance on Regulation Crowdfunding:
		Financial statements must be **audited** by a public accountant that is independent of the issuer and must include a signed audit report.
		If the issuer **has not** previously sold securities in reliance on Regulation Crowdfunding and it is offering more than $500,000 but not more than $1,000,000:
		Financial statements must be **reviewed** by a public accountant that is independent of the issuer and must include a signed review report.
		If financial statements of the issuer are available that have been audited by a public accountant that is independent of the issuer, the issuer must provide those financial statements instead along with a signed audit report and need not include the reviewed financial statements.

INSTRUCTIONS TO QUESTION 29: To determine the financial statements required, the Aggregate Offering Amount for purposes of this Question 29 means the aggregate amounts offered and sold by the issuer, all entities controlled by or under common control with the issuer, and all predecessors of the issuer in reliance on Section 4(a)(6) of the Securities Act within the preceding 12-month period plus the current maximum offering amount provided on the cover of this Form.

To determine whether the issuer has previously sold securities in reliance on Regulation Crowdfunding for purposes of paragraph (c) of this Question 29, "issuer" means the issuer, all entities controlled by or under common control with the issuer, and all predecessors of the issuer.

Financial statements must be prepared in accordance with U.S. generally accepted accounting principles and must include balance sheets, statements of comprehensive income, statements of cash flows, statements of changes in stockholders' equity and notes to the financial statements. If the financial statements are not audited, they shall be labeled as "unaudited."

Issuers offering securities and required to provide the information set forth in row (a) before filing a tax return for the most recently completed fiscal year may provide information from the tax return filed for the prior year (if any), provided that the issuer provides information from the tax return for the most recently completed fiscal year when it is filed, if filed during the offering period. An issuer that requested an extension of the time to file would not be required to provide information from the tax return until the date when the return is filed, if filed during the offering period.

A principal executive officer certifying financial statements as described above must provide the following certification**:

I, [identify the certifying individual], certify that:

(1) the financial statements of [identify the issuer] included in this Form are true and complete in all material respects; and

(2) the tax return information of [identify the issuer] included in this Form reflects accurately the information reported on the tax return for

---

** Intentional misstatements or omissions of facts constitute federal criminal violations. *See* 18 U.S.C. 1001.

[identify the issuer] filed for the fiscal year ended [date of most recent tax return].

[Signature]
[Title]

To qualify as a public accountant that is independent of the issuer for purposes of this Question 29, the accountant must satisfy the independence standards of either:

(i) Rule 2-01 of Regulation S-X or
(ii) the AICPA.

The public accountant that audits or reviews the financial statements provided by an issuer must be (1) duly registered and in good standing as a certified public accountant under the laws of the place of his or her residence or principal office or (2) in good standing and entitled to practice as a public accountant under the laws of his or her place of residence or principal office.

An issuer will not be in compliance with the requirement to provide reviewed financial statement if the issuer received a review report that includes modifications. An issuer will not be in compliance with the requirement to provide audited financial statements if the issuer received a qualified opinion, an adverse opinion, or a disclaimer of opinion.

The issuer must notify the public accountant of the issuer's intended use of the public accountant's audit or review report in the offering.

For an offering conducted in the first 120 days of a fiscal year, the financial statements provided may be for the two fiscal years prior to the issuer's most recently completed fiscal year; however, financial statements for the two most recently completed fiscal years must be provided if they are otherwise available. If more than 120 days have passed since the end of the issuer's most recently completed fiscal year, the financial statements provided must be for the issuer's two most recently completed fiscal years. If the 120th day falls on a Saturday, Sunday, or holiday, the next business day shall be considered the 120th day for purposes of determining the age of the financial statements.

An issuer may elect to delay complying with any new or revised financial accounting standard until the date that a company that is not an issuer (as defined under section 2(a) of the Sarbanes-Oxley Act of 2002 is required to comply with such new or revised accounting standard, if such standard also applies to companies that are not issuers. Issuers electing such extension of time accommodation must disclose it at the time the issuer files its offering statement and apply the election to all standards. Issuers electing not to use this accommodation must forgo this accommodation for all financial accounting standards and may not elect to rely on this accommodation in any future filings.

30. With respect to the issuer, any predecessor of the issuer, any affiliated issuer, any director, officer, general partner or managing member of the issuer, any beneficial owner of 20% or more of the issuer's outstanding voting equity securities, calculated in the same form as described in Question 6 of this Question and Answer format, any promoter connected with the issuer in any capacity at the time of such sale, any person that has been or will be paid (directly or indirectly) remuneration for solicitation of purchasers in connection with such sale of securities, or any general partner, director, officer or managing member of any such solicitor, prior to May 16, 2016:

(1) Has any such person been convicted, within 10 years (or five years, in the case of issuers, their predecessors and affiliated issuers) before the filing of this offering statement, of any felony or misdemeanor:

   (i) in connection with the purchase or sale of any security? ☐ Yes ☐ No
   (ii) involving the making of any false filing with the Commission? ☐ Yes ☐ No
   (iii) arising out of the conduct of the business of an underwriter, broker, dealer, municipal securities dealer, investment adviser, funding portal or paid solicitor of purchasers of securities? ☐ Yes ☐ No
   If Yes to any of the above, explain: _____

(2) Is any such person subject to any order, judgment or decree of any court of competent jurisdiction, entered within five years before the filing of the information required by Section 4A(b) of the Securities Act that, at the time of filing of this offering statement, restrains or enjoins such person from engaging or continuing to engage in any conduct or practice:

    (i) in connection with the purchase or sale of any security? □ Yes □ No;

    (ii) involving the making of any false filing with the Commission? □ Yes □ No

    (iii) arising out of the conduct of the business of an underwriter, broker, dealer, municipal securities dealer, investment adviser, funding portal or paid solicitor of purchasers of securities? □ Yes □ No

    If Yes to any of the above, explain: _____

(3) Is any such person subject to a final order of a state securities commission (or an agency or officer of a state performing like functions); a state authority that supervises or examines banks, savings associations or credit unions; a state insurance commission (or an agency or officer of a state performing like functions); an appropriate federal banking agency; the U.S. Commodity Futures Trading Commission; or the National Credit Union Administration that:

    (i) at the time of the filing of this offering statement bars the person from:

        (A) association with an entity regulated by such commission, authority, agency or officer? □ Yes □ No

        (B) engaging in the business of securities, insurance or banking? □ Yes □ No

        (C) engaging in savings association or credit union activities? □ Yes □ No

(ii) constitutes a final order based on a violation of any law or regulation that prohibits fraudulent, manipulative or deceptive conduct and for which the order was entered within the 10-year period ending on the date of the filing of this offering statement? ☐ Yes ☐ No

If Yes to any of the above, explain: _____

(4) Is any such person subject to an order of the Commission entered pursuant to Section 15(b) or 15B(c) of the Exchange Act or Section 203(e) or (f) of the Investment Advisers Act of 1940 that, at the time of the filing of this offering statement:

    (i) suspends or revokes such person's registration as a broker, dealer, municipal securities dealer, investment adviser or funding portal? ☐ Yes ☐ No

   (ii) places limitations on the activities, functions or operations of such person? ☐ Yes ☐ No

  (iii) bars such person from being associated with any entity or from participating in the offering of any penny stock? ☐ Yes ☐ No

If Yes to any of the above, explain:_____

(5) Is any such person subject to any order of the Commission entered within five years before the filing of this offering statement that, at the time of the filing of this offering statement, orders the person to cease and desist from committing or causing a violation or future violation of:

    (i) any scienter-based anti-fraud provision of the federal securities laws, including without limitation Section 17(a)(1) of the Securities Act, Section 10(b) of the Exchange Act, Section 15(c) (1) of the Exchange Act and Section 206(1) of the Investment Advisers Act of 1940 or any other rule or regulation thereunder? ☐ Yes ☐ No

   (ii) Section 5 of the Securities Act? ☐ Yes ☐ No

If Yes to either of the above, explain: _____

(6) Is any such person suspended or expelled from membership in, or suspended or barred from association with a member of, a

registered national securities exchange or a registered national or affiliated securities association for any act or omission to act constituting conduct inconsistent with just and equitable principles of trade? ☐ Yes ☐ No

If Yes, explain: _____

(7) Has any such person filed (as a registrant or issuer), or was any such person or was any such person named as an underwriter in, any registration statement or Regulation A offering statement filed with the Commission that, within five years before the filing of this offering statement, was the subject of a refusal order, stop order, or order suspending the Regulation A exemption, or is any such person, at the time of such filing, the subject of an investigation or proceeding to determine whether a stop order or suspension order should be issued? ☐ Yes ☐ No

If Yes, explain: _____

(8) Is any such person subject to a United States Postal Service false representation order entered within five years before the filing of the information required by Section 4A(b) of the Securities Act, or is any such person, at the time of filing of this offering statement, subject to a temporary restraining order or preliminary injunction with respect to conduct alleged by the United States Postal Service to constitute a scheme or device for obtaining money or property through the mail by means of false representations? ☐ Yes ☐ No

If Yes, explain: _____

If you would have answered "Yes" to any of these questions had the conviction, order, judgment, decree, suspension, expulsion or bar occurred or been issued after May 16, 2016 then you are NOT eligible to rely on this exemption under Section 4(a)(6) of the Securities Act.

INSTRUCTIONS TO QUESTION 30: Final order means a written directive or declaratory statement issued by a federal or state agency, described in Rule 503(a)(3) of Regulation Crowdfunding, under applicable statutory authority that provides for notice and an opportunity for hearing, which constitutes a final disposition or action by that federal or state agency.

No matters are required to be disclosed with respect to events relating to any affiliated issuer that occurred before the affiliation arose if the affiliated entity is not (i) in control of the issuer or (ii) under common control with the issuer by a third party that was in control of the affiliated entity at the time of such events.

OTHER MATERIAL INFORMATION

31. In addition to the information expressly required to be included in this Form, include:

   (1) any other material information presented to investors; and
   (2) such further material information, if any, as may be necessary to make the required statements, in the light of the circumstances under which they are made, not misleading.

INSTRUCTIONS TO QUESTION 31: If information is presented to investors in a format, media or other means not able to be reflected in text or portable document format, the issuer should include

   (a) a description of the material content of such information;
   (b) a description of the format in which such disclosure is presented; and
   (c) in the case of disclosure in video, audio or other dynamic media or format, a transcript or description of such disclosure.

ONGOING REPORTING

The issuer will file a report electronically with the Securities & Exchange Commission annually and post the report on its website, no later than:

_____

(120 days after the end of each fiscal year covered by the report).

Once posted, the annual report may be found on the issuer's website at:

_____

The issuer must continue to comply with the ongoing reporting requirements until:

(1) the issuer is required to file reports under Section 13(a) or Section 15(d) of the Exchange Act;

(2) the issuer has filed at least one annual report pursuant to Regulation Crowdfunding and has fewer than 300 holders of record and has total assets that do not exceed $10,000,000;

(3) the issuer has filed at least three annual reports pursuant to Regulation Crowdfunding;

(4) the issuer or another party repurchases all of the securities issued in reliance on Section 4(a)(6) of the Securities Act, including any payment in full of debt securities or any complete redemption of redeemable securities; or

(5) the issuer liquidates or dissolves its business in accordance with state law.

APPENDIX 4

FORM 1-A REGULATION A OFFERING STATEMENT UNDER THE SECURITIES ACT OF 1933

GENERAL INSTRUCTIONS

I. Eligibility Requirements for Use of Form 1-A

This Form is to be used for securities offerings made pursuant to Regulation A (17 CFR 230.251 *et seq.*). Careful attention should be directed to the terms, conditions and requirements of Regulation A, especially Rule 251, because the exemption is not available to all issuers or for every type of securities transaction. Further, the aggregate offering price and aggregate sales of securities in any 12-month period is strictly limited to $20 million for Tier 1 offerings and $50 million for Tier 2 offerings, including no more than $6 million offered by all selling securityholders that are affiliates of the issuer for Tier 1 offerings and $15 million by all selling securityholders that are affiliates of the issuer for Tier 2 offerings. Please refer to Rule 251 of Regulation A for more details.

II. Preparation, Submission and Filing of the Offering Statement

An offering statement must be prepared by all persons seeking exemption under the provisions of Regulation A. Parts I, II and III must be addressed by all issuers. Part II, which relates to the content of the required offering circular, provides alternative formats, of which the issuer must choose one. General information regarding the preparation, format, content, and submission or filing of the offering statement is contained in Rule 252. Information regarding non-public submission of the offering statement is contained in Rule 252(d). Requirements relating to the offering circular are contained in Rules 253 and 254. The offering statement must be submitted or filed with the Securities and Exchange Commission in electronic format by means of the Commission's Electronic Data Gathering, Analysis and Retrieval System (EDGAR) in accordance with the EDGAR rules set forth in Regulation S-T (17 CFR Part 232) for such submission or filing.

III. Incorporation by Reference and Cross-Referencing

An issuer may incorporate by reference to other documents previously submitted or filed on EDGAR. Cross-referencing within the offering statement is also encouraged to avoid repetition of information. For example, you may respond to an item of this Form by providing a cross-reference to the location of the information in the financial statements, instead of repeating such information. Incorporation by reference and cross-referencing are subject to the following additional conditions:

(a) The use of incorporation by reference and cross-referencing in Part II of this Form is limited to the following items:

   (1) Items 2–14 of Part II if following the Offering Circular format;
   (2) Items 3–11 (other than Item 11(e)) of Form S-1 if following the Part I of Form S-1 format; or
   (3) Items 3–26, 28, and 30 of Form S-11 if following the Part I of Form S-11 format.

(b) Descriptions of where the information incorporated by reference or cross-referenced can be found must be specific and must clearly identify the relevant document and portion thereof where such information can be found. For exhibits incorporated by reference, this description must be noted in the exhibits index for each relevant exhibit. All descriptions of where information incorporated by reference can be found must be accompanied by a hyperlink to the incorporated document on EDGAR, which hyperlink need not remain active after the filing of the offering statement. Inactive hyperlinks must be updated in any amendment to the offering statement otherwise required.

(c) Reference may not be made to any document if the portion of such document containing the pertinent information includes an incorporation by reference to another document. Incorporation by reference to documents not available on EDGAR is not permitted. Incorporating information into the financial statements from elsewhere is not permitted. Information shall not be incorporated by reference or cross-referenced in any case where such incorporation would render the statement or report incomplete, unclear, or confusing.

(d) If any substantive modification has occurred in the text of any document incorporated by reference since such document was filed, the issuer must file with the reference a statement containing the text and date of such modification.

IV. Supplemental Information

The information specified below must be furnished to the Commission as supplemental information, if applicable. Supplemental information shall not be required to be filed with or deemed part of the offering statement, unless otherwise required. The information shall be returned to the issuer upon request made in writing at the time of submission, provided that the return of such information is consistent with the protection of investors and the provisions of the Freedom of Information Act [5 U.S.C. 552] and the information was not filed in electronic format.

(a) A statement as to whether or not the amount of compensation to be allowed or paid to the underwriter has been cleared with the Financial Industry Regulatory Authority (FINRA).

(b) Any engineering, management, market, or similar report referenced in the offering circular or provided for external use by the issuer or by a principal underwriter in connection with the proposed offering. There must also be furnished at the same time a statement as to the actual or proposed use and distribution of such report or memorandum. Such statement must identify each class of persons who have received or will receive the report or memorandum, and state the number of copies distributed to each such class along with a statement as to the actual or proposed use and distribution of such report or memorandum.

(c) Such other information as requested by the staff in support of statements, representations and other assertions contained in the offering statement or any correspondence to the staff.

Correspondence appropriately responding to any staff comments made on the offering statement must also be furnished electronically. When applicable, such correspondence must clearly indicate where changes responsive to the staff's comments may be found in the offering statement.

PART I — NOTIFICATION

The following information must be provided in the XML-based portion of Form 1-A available through the EDGAR portal and must be completed or updated before uploading each offering statement or amendment thereto. The format of Part I shown below may differ from the electronic version available on EDGAR. The electronic version of Part I will allow issuers to attach Part II and Part III for filing by means of EDGAR. All items must be addressed, unless otherwise indicated.

******

☐   No changes to the information required by Part I have occurred since the last filing of this offering statement.

Item 1.   Issuer Information

Exact name of issuer as specified in the issuer's charter: _____
Jurisdiction of incorporation/organization: _____
Year of incorporation: _____

CIK: _____

Primary Standard Industrial Classification Code: _____

I.R.S. Employer Identification Number: _____

Total number of full-time employees: _____

Total number of part-time employees: _____

Contact Information

Address of Principal Executive Offices: _____

Telephone: ( ) _____

Provide the following information for the person the Securities and Exchange Commission's staff should call in connection with any pre-qualification review of the offering statement:

Name: _____

Address: _____

Telephone: ( ) _____

Provide up to two e-mail addresses to which the Securities and Exchange Commission's staff may send any comment letters relating to the offering statement. After qualification of the offering statement, such e-mail addresses are not required to remain active: _____

Financial Statements

Industry Group (select one): ☐   Banking   ☐   Insurance   ☐   Other

Use the financial statements for the most recent fiscal period contained in this offering statement to provide the following information about the issuer. The following table does not include all of the line items from the financial statements. Long-Term Debt would include notes payable, bonds, mortgages, and similar obligations. To determine "Total Revenues" for all companies selecting "Other" for their industry group, refer to Article 5-03(b)(1) of Regulation S-X. For companies selecting "Insurance," refer to Article 7-04 of Regulation S-X for calculation of "Total Revenues" and paragraphs 5 and 7(a) for "Costs and Expenses Applicable to Revenues."

[If "Other" is selected, display the following options in the Financial Statements table:]

Balance Sheet Information   _____
Cash and Cash Equivalents: _____
Investment Securities: _____
Accounts and Notes Receivable: _____
Property, Plant and Equipment (PP&E): _____
Total Assets: _____
Accounts Payable and Accrued Liabilities: _____
Long-Term Debt: _____
Total Liabilities: _____
Total Stockholders' Equity: _____
Total Liabilities and Equity: _____

Income Statement Information   _____
Total Revenues: _____
Costs and Expenses Applicable to Revenues: _____
Depreciation and Amortization: _____
Net Income: _____
Earnings Per Share – Basic: _____
Earnings Per Share – Diluted: _____

[If "Banking" is selected, display the following options in the Financial Statements table]

Balance Sheet Information   _____
Cash and Cash Equivalents: _____
Investment Securities: _____
Loans: _____
Property and Equipment: _____
Total Assets: _____
Accounts Payable and Accrued Liabilities: _____
Deposits: _____
Long-Term Debt: _____
Total Liabilities: _____
Total Stockholders' Equity: _____
Total Liabilities and Equity: _____

Income Statement Information _____
Total Interest Income: _____
Total Interest Expense: _____
Depreciation and Amortization: _____
Net Income: _____
Earnings Per Share – Basic: _____
Earnings Per Share – Diluted: _____

[If "Insurance" is selected, display the following options in the Financial Statements table]

Balance Sheet Information _____
Cash and Cash Equivalents: _____
Total Investments: _____
Accounts and Notes Receivable: _____
Property and Equipment: _____
Total Assets: _____
Accounts Payable and Accrued Liabilities: _____
Policy Liabilities and Accruals: _____
Long-Term Debt: _____
Total Liabilities: _____
Total Stockholders' Equity: _____
Total Liabilities and Equity: _____

Income Statement Information _____
Total Revenues: _____
Costs and Expenses Applicable to Revenues: _____
Depreciation and Amortization: _____
Net Income: _____
Earnings Per Share – Basic: _____
Earnings Per Share – Diluted: _____

[End of section that varies based on the selection of Industry Group]

Name of Auditor (if any): _____

Outstanding Securities

	Name of Class (if any)	Units Outstanding	CUSIP (if any)	Name of Trading Center or Quotation Medium (if any)
Common Equity				
Preferred Equity				
Debt Securities				

Item 2.   Issuer Eligibility

☐   Check this box to certify that all of the following statements are true for the issuer(s):

- Organized under the laws of the United States or Canada, or any State, Province, Territory or possession thereof, or the District of Columbia.
- Principal place of business is in the United States or Canada.
- Not subject to section 13 or 15(d) of the Securities Exchange Act of 1934.
- Not a development stage company that either (a) has no specific business plan or purpose, or (b) has indicated that its business plan is to merge with an unidentified company or companies.
- Not an investment company registered or required to be registered under the Investment Company Act of 1940.
- Not issuing fractional undivided interests in oil or gas rights, or a similar interest in other mineral rights.
- Not issuing asset-backed securities as defined in Item 1101(c) of Regulation AB.
- Not, and has not been, subject to any order of the Commission entered pursuant to Section 12(j) of the Exchange Act (15 U.S.C. 78*l*(j)) within five years before the filing of this offering statement.
- Has filed with the Commission all the reports it was required to file, if any, pursuant to Rule 257 during the two years immediately before the filing of the offering statement (or for such shorter period that the issuer was required to file such reports).

Item 3. Application of Rule 262

☐ Check this box to certify that, as of the time of this filing, each person described in Rule 262 of Regulation A is either not disqualified under that rule or is disqualified but has received a waiver of such disqualification.

☐ Check this box if "bad actor" disclosure under Rule 262(d) is provided in Part II of the offering statement.

Item 4. Summary Information Regarding the Offering and Other Current or Proposed Offerings

Check the appropriate box to indicate whether you are conducting a Tier 1 or Tier 2 offering:

☐ Tier 1   ☐ Tier 2

Check the appropriate box to indicate whether the annual financial statements have been audited:

☐ Unaudited   ☐ Audited

Types of Securities Offered in this Offering Statement (select all that apply):

☐ Equity (common or preferred stock)
☐ Debt
☐ Option, warrant or other right to acquire another security
☐ Security to be acquired upon exercise of option, warrant or other right to acquire security
☐ Tenant-in-common securities
☐ Other (describe) _____

Does the issuer intend to offer the securities on a delayed or continuous basis pursuant to Rule 251(d)(3)?

Yes ☐   No ☐

Does the issuer intend this offering to last more than one year?

Yes ☐   No ☐

Does the issuer intend to price this offering after qualification pursuant to Rule 253(b)?

Yes ☐   No ☐

Will the issuer be conducting a best efforts offering?

Yes ☐   No ☐

Has the issuer used solicitation of interest communications in connection with the proposed offering?

Yes ☐   No ☐

Does the proposed offering involve the resale of securities by affiliates of the issuer?

Yes ☐   No ☐

Number of securities offered: _____

Number of securities of that class already outstanding: _____

The information called for by this item below may be omitted if undetermined at the time of filing or submission, except that if a price range has been included in the offering statement, the midpoint of that range must be used to respond. Please refer to Rule 251(a) for the definition of "aggregate offering price" or "aggregate sales" as used in this item. Please leave the field blank if undetermined at this time and include a zero if a particular item is not applicable to the offering.

Price per security: $_____

The portion of the aggregate offering price attributable to securities being offered on behalf of the issuer:

$_____

The portion of the aggregate offering price attributable to securities being offered on behalf of selling securityholders:

$_____

The portion of aggregate offering attributable to all the securities of the issuer sold pursuant to a qualified offering statement within the 12 months before the qualification of this offering statement: $_____

The estimated portion of aggregate sales attributable to securities that may be sold pursuant to any other qualified offering statement concurrently with securities being sold under this offering statement: $_____

Total: $_____ (the sum of the aggregate offering price and aggregate sales in the four preceding paragraphs).

Anticipated fees in connection with this offering and names of service providers:

	Name of Service Provider	Fees
Underwriters:	_____	$_____
Sales Commissions:	_____	$_____
Finders' Fees:	_____	$_____
Auditor:	_____	$_____
Legal:	_____	$_____
Promoters:	_____	$_____
Blue Sky Compliance:	_____	$_____

CRD Number of any broker or dealer listed: _____

Estimated net proceeds to the issuer: $_____

Clarification of responses (if necessary): _____

Item 5.   Jurisdictions in Which Securities are to be Offered

Using the list below, select the jurisdictions in which the issuer intends to offer the securities:

[List will include all U.S. and Canadian jurisdictions, with an option to add and remove them individually, add all and remove all]

Using the list below, select the jurisdictions in which the securities are to be offered by underwriters, dealers or sales persons or check the appropriate box:

☐   None

☐   Same as the jurisdictions in which the issuer intends to offer the securities.

[List will include all U.S. and Canadian jurisdictions, with an option to add and remove them individually, add all and remove all.]

Item 6.   Unregistered Securities Issued or Sold Within One Year

☐   None

As to any unregistered securities issued by the issuer or any of its predecessors or affiliated issuers within one year before the filing of this Form 1-A, state:

(a)   Name of such issuer.

(b)   (1) Title of securities issued
      (2) Total amount of such securities issued
      (3) Amount of such securities sold by or for the account of any person who at the time was a director, officer, promoter or principal securityholder of the issuer of such securities, or was an underwriter of any securities of such issuer

(c)   (1) Aggregate consideration for which the securities were issued and basis for computing the amount thereof.

_____

_____

_____

      (2) Aggregate consideration for which the securities listed in (b)(3) of this item (if any) were issued and the basis for computing the amount thereof (if different from the basis described in (c)(1)).

(d)   Indicate the section of the Securities Act or Commission rule or regulation relied upon for exemption from the registration requirements of such Act and state briefly the facts relied upon for such exemption:

_____

_____

PART II — INFORMATION REQUIRED IN OFFERING CIRCULAR

(a) Financial statement requirements regardless of the applicable disclosure format are specified in Part F/S of this Form 1-A. The narrative disclosure contents of offering circulars are specified as follows:

(1) The information required by:

(i) the Offering Circular format described below; or

(ii) The information required by Part I of Form S-1 (17 CFR 239.11) or Part I of Form S-11 (17 CFR 239.18), except for the financial statements, selected financial data, and supplementary financial information called for by those forms. An issuer choosing to follow the Form S-1 or Form S-11 format may follow the requirements for smaller reporting companies if it meets the definition of that term in Rule 405 (17 CFR 230.405). An issuer may only use the Form S-11 format if the offering is eligible to be registered on that form;

The cover page of the offering circular must identify which disclosure format is being followed.

(2) The offering circular must describe any matters that would have triggered disqualification under Rule 262(a)(3) or (a)(5) but for the provisions set forth in Rule 262(b)(1);

(3) The legend required by Rule 253(f) of Regulation A must be included on the offering circular cover page (for issuers following the S-1 or S-11 disclosure models this legend must be included instead of the legend required by Item 501(b)(7) of Regulation S-K);

(4) For preliminary offering circulars, the legend required by Rule 254(a) must be included on the offering circular cover page (for issuers

following the S-1 or S-11 disclosure models, this legend must be included instead of the legend required by Item 501(b)(10) of Regulation S-K); and

(5) For Tier 2 offerings where the securities will not be listed on a registered national securities exchange upon qualification, the offering circular cover page must include the following legend highlighted by prominent type or in another manner:

Generally, no sale may be made to you in this offering if the aggregate purchase price you pay is more than 10% of the greater of your annual income or net worth. Different rules apply to accredited investors and non-natural persons. Before making any representation that your investment does not exceed applicable thresholds, we encourage you to review Rule 251(d)(2)(i)(C) of Regulation A. For general information on investing, we encourage you to refer to www.investor.gov.

(b) The Commission encourages the use of management's projections of future economic performance that have a reasonable basis and are presented in an appropriate format. See Rule 175, 17 CFR 230.175.

(c) Offering circulars need not follow the order of the items or the order of other requirements of the disclosure form except to the extent otherwise specifically provided. Such information may not, however, be set forth in such a fashion as to obscure any of the required information or any information necessary to keep the required information from being incomplete or misleading. Information requested to be presented in a specified tabular format must be given in substantially the tabular format specified. For incorporation by reference, please refer to General Instruction III of this Form.

OFFERING CIRCULAR

Item 1.   Cover Page of Offering Circular

The cover page of the offering circular must be limited to one page and must include the information specified in this item.

(a) Name of the issuer.

Instruction to Item 1(a):

If your name is the same as, or confusingly similar to, that of a company that is well known, include information to eliminate any possible confusion with the other company. If your name indicates a line of business in which you are not engaged or you are engaged only to a limited extent, include information to eliminate any misleading inference as to your business. In some circumstances, disclosure may not be sufficient and you may be required to change your name. You will not be required to change your name if you are an established company, the character of your business has changed, and the investing public is generally aware of the change and the character of your current business.

(b) Full mailing address of the issuer's principal executive offices and the issuer's telephone number (including the area code) and, if applicable, website address.

(c) Date of the offering circular.

(d) Title and amount of securities offered. Separately state the amount of securities offered by selling securityholders, if any. Include a cross-reference to the section where the disclosure required by Item 14 of Part II of this Form 1-A has been provided;

(e) The information called for by the applicable table below as to all the securities being offered, in substantially the tabular format indicated. If necessary, you may estimate any underwriting discounts and commissions and the proceeds to the issuer or other persons.

	Price to public	Underwriting discount and commissions	Proceeds to issuer	Proceeds to other persons
Per share/unit:	_____	_____	_____	_____
Total:	_____	_____	_____	_____

If the securities are to be offered on a best efforts basis, the cover page must set forth the termination date, if any, of the offering, any minimum required sale and any arrangements to place the funds received in an escrow, trust, or similar arrangement. The following table must be used instead of the preceding table.

	Price to public	Underwriting discount and commissions	Proceeds to issuer	Proceeds to other persons
Per share/unit:				
Total Minimum:				
Total Maximum:				

Instructions to Item 1(e):

1. *The term "commissions" includes all cash, securities, contracts, or anything else of value, paid, to be set aside, disposed of, or understandings with or for the benefit of any other persons in which any underwriter is interested, made in connection with the sale of such security.*

2. *Only commissions paid by the issuer in cash are to be indicated in the table. Commissions paid by other persons or any form of non-cash compensation must be briefly identified in a footnote to the table with a cross-reference to a more complete description elsewhere in the offering circular.*

3. *Before the commencement of sales pursuant to Regulation A, the issuer must inform the Commission whether or not the amount of compensation to be allowed or paid to the underwriters, as described in the offering statement, has been cleared with FINRA.*

4. *If the securities are not to be offered for cash, state the basis upon which the offering is to be made.*

5. *Any finder's fees or similar payments must be disclosed on the cover page with a reference to a more complete discussion in the offering circular. Such disclosure must identify the finder, the nature of the services rendered and the nature of any relationship between the finder and the issuer, its officers, directors, promoters, principal stockholders and underwriters (including any affiliates of such persons).*

6. *The amount of the expenses of the offering borne by the issuer, including underwriting expenses to be borne by the issuer, must be disclosed in a footnote to the table.*

(f) The name of the underwriter or underwriters.

(g) Any legend or information required by the law of any state in which the securities are to be offered.

(h) A cross-reference to the risk factors section, including the page number where it appears in the offering circular. Highlight this cross-reference by prominent type or in another manner.

(i) Approximate date of commencement of proposed sale to the public.

(j) If the issuer intends to rely on Rule 253(b) and a preliminary offering circular is circulated, provide (1) a bona fide estimate of the range of the maximum offering price and the maximum number of securities offered or (2) a bona fide estimate of the principal amount of the debt securities offered. The range must not exceed $2 for offerings where the upper end of the range is $10 or less and 20% if the upper end of the price range is over $10.

Instruction to Item 1(j):

The upper limit of the price range must be used in determining the aggregate offering price for purposes of Rule 251(a).

Item 2.   Table of Contents

On the page immediately following the cover page of the offering circular, provide a reasonably detailed table of contents. It must show the page numbers of the various sections or subdivisions of the offering circular. Include a specific listing of the risk factors section required by Item 3 of Part II of this Form 1-A.

Item 3.   Summary and Risk Factors

(a) An issuer may provide a summary of the information in the offering circular where the length or complexity of the offering circular makes a summary useful. The summary should be brief and must not contain all of the detailed information in the offering circular.

(b) Immediately following the Table of Contents required by Item 2 or the Summary, there must be set forth under an appropriate caption, a carefully organized series of short, concise paragraphs, summarizing the most significant factors that make the offering speculative or substantially risky. Issuers should avoid generalized statements and include only factors that are specific to the issuer.

Item 4.   Dilution

Where there is a material disparity between the public offering price and the effective cash cost to officers, directors, promoters and affiliated persons for shares acquired by them in a transaction during the past year, or that they have a right to acquire, there must be included a comparison of the public contribution under the proposed public offering and the average effective cash contribution of such persons.

Item 5.   Plan of Distribution and Selling Securityholders

(a) If the securities are to be offered through underwriters, give the names of the principal underwriters, and state the respective amounts underwritten. Identify each such underwriter having a material relationship to the issuer and state the nature of the relationship. State briefly the nature of the underwriters' obligation to take the securities.

Instructions to Item 5(a):

1. *All that is required as to the nature of the underwriters' obligation is whether the underwriters are or will be committed to take and to pay for all of the securities if any are taken, or whether it is merely an agency or the type of best efforts arrangement under which the underwriters are required to take and to pay for only such securities as they may sell to the public. Conditions precedent to the underwriters' taking the securities, including market outs, need not be described except in the case of an agency or best efforts arrangement.*

2. *It is not necessary to disclose each member of a selling group. Disclosure may be limited to those underwriters who are in privity of contract with the issuer with respect to the offering.*

(b) State briefly the discounts and commissions to be allowed or paid to dealers, including all cash, securities, contracts or other consideration to be received by any dealer in connection with the sale of the securities.

(c) Outline briefly the plan of distribution of any securities being issued that are to be offered through the selling efforts of brokers or dealers or otherwise than through underwriters.

(d) If any of the securities are to be offered for the account of security-holders, identify each selling securityholder, state the amount owned by the securityholder prior to the offering, the amount offered for his or her account and the amount to be owned after the offering. Provide such disclosure in a tabular format. At the bottom of the table, provide the total number of securities being offered for the account of all securityholders and describe what percent of the pre-offering out-standing securities of such class the offering represents.

Instruction to Item 5(d):

The term "securityholder" in this paragraph refers to beneficial holders, not nominee holders or other such holders of record. If the selling securityholder is an entity, disclosure of the persons who have sole or shared voting or investment power must be included.

(e) Describe any arrangements for the return of funds to subscribers if all of the securities to be offered are not sold. If there are no such arrangements, so state.

(f) If there will be a material delay in the payment of the proceeds of the offering by the underwriter to the issuer, the salient provisions in this regard and the effects on the issuer must be stated.

(g) Describe any arrangement to (1) limit or restrict the sale of other secu-rities of the same class as those to be offered for the period of distribu-tion, (2) stabilize the market for any of the securities to be offered, or

(3) withhold commissions, or otherwise to hold each underwriter or dealer responsible for the distribution of its participation.

(h) Identify any underwriter that intends to confirm sales to any accounts over which it exercises discretionary authority and include an estimate of the amount of securities so intended to be confirmed.

Instruction to Item 5:

> *Attention is directed to the provisions of Rules 10b-9 [17 CFR 240.10b-9] and 15c2-4 [17 CFR 240.15c2-4] under the Securities Exchange Act of 1934. These rules outline, among other things, antifraud provisions concerning the return of funds to subscribers and the transmission of proceeds of an offering to a seller.*

Item 6.   Use of Proceeds to Issuer

State the principal purposes for which the net proceeds to the issuer from the securities to be offered are intended to be used and the approximate amount intended to be used for each such purpose. If the issuer will not receive any of proceeds from the offering, so state.

Instructions to Item 6:

1. *If any substantial portion of the proceeds has not been allocated for particular purposes, a statement to that effect must be made together with a statement of the amount of proceeds not so allocated.*
2. *State whether or not the proceeds will be used to compensate or otherwise make payments to officers or directors of the issuer or any of its subsidiaries.*
3. *For best efforts offerings, describe any anticipated material changes in the use of proceeds if all of the securities being qualified on the offering statement are not sold.*
4. *If an issuer must provide the disclosure described in Item 9(c) the use of proceeds and plan of operations should be consistent.*
5. *If any material amounts of other funds are to be used in conjunction with the proceeds, state the amounts and sources of such other funds and whether such funds are firm or contingent.*

6. *If any material part of the proceeds is to be used to discharge indebtedness, describe the material terms of such indebtedness. If the indebtedness to be discharged was incurred within one year, describe the use of the proceeds arising from such indebtedness.*

7. *If any material amount of the proceeds is to be used to acquire assets, otherwise than in the ordinary course of business, briefly describe and state the cost of the assets. If the assets are to be acquired from affiliates of the issuer or their associates, give the names of the persons from whom they are to be acquired and set forth the basis used in determining the purchase price to the issuer.*

8. *The issuer may reserve the right to change the use of proceeds, so long as the reservation is prominently disclosed in the section where the use of proceeds is discussed. It is not necessary to describe the possible alternative uses of proceeds unless the issuer believes that a change in circumstances leading to an alternative use of proceeds is likely to occur.*

Item 7.   Description of Business

(a) Narrative description of business.

(1) Describe the business done and intended to be done by the issuer and its subsidiaries and the general development of the business during the past three years or such shorter period as the issuer may have been in business. Such description must include, but not be limited to, a discussion of the following factors if such factors are material to an understanding of the issuer's business:

   (i) The principal products and services of the issuer and the principal market for and method of distribution of such products and services.

   (ii) The status of a product or service if the issuer has made public information about a new product or service that would require the investment of a material amount of the assets of the issuer or is otherwise material.

   (iii) If material, the estimated amount spent during each of the last two fiscal years on company-sponsored research and development activities determined in accordance with generally accepted accounting principles. In addition, state, if material, the estimated dollar amount spent during each of such years on material customer-sponsored research activities relating to the development of new products, services or techniques or the improvement of existing products, services or techniques.

(iv) The total number of persons employed by the issuer, indicating the number employed full time.

(v) Any bankruptcy, receivership or similar proceeding.

(vi) Any legal proceedings material to the business or financial condition of the issuer.

(vii) Any material reclassification, merger, consolidation, or purchase or sale of a significant amount of assets not in the ordinary course of business.

(2) The issuer must also describe those distinctive or special characteristics of the issuer's operation or industry that are reasonably likely to have a material impact upon the issuer's future financial performance. Examples of factors that might be discussed include dependence on one or a few major customers or suppliers (including suppliers of raw materials or financing), effect of existing or probable governmental regulation (including environmental regulation), material terms of and/or expiration of material labor contracts or patents, trademarks, licenses, franchises, concessions or royalty agreements, unusual competitive conditions in the industry, cyclicality of the industry and anticipated raw material or energy shortages to the extent management may not be able to secure a continuing source of supply.

(b) Segment Data. If the issuer is required by generally accepted accounting principles to include segment information in its financial statements, an appropriate cross-reference must be included in the description of business.

(c) Industry Guides. The disclosure guidelines in all Securities Act Industry Guides must be followed. To the extent that the industry guides are codified into Regulation S-K, the Regulation S-K industry disclosure items must be followed.

(d) For offerings of limited partnership or limited liability company interests, an issuer must comply with the Commission's interpretive views on substantive disclosure requirements set forth in Securities Act Release No. 6900 (June 17, 1991).

Item 8. Description of Property

State briefly the location and general character of any principal plants or other material physical properties of the issuer and its subsidiaries. If any such property is not held in fee or is held subject to any major encumbrance, so state and briefly describe how held. Include information regarding the suitability, adequacy, productive capacity and extent of utilization of the properties and facilities used in the issuer's business.

Instruction to Item 8:

Detailed descriptions of the physical characteristics of individual properties or legal descriptions by metes and bounds are not required and should not be given.

Item 9. Management's Discussion and Analysis of Financial Condition and Results of Operations

Discuss the issuer's financial condition, changes in financial condition and results of operations for each year and interim period for which financial statements are required, including the causes of material changes from year to year or period to period in financial statement line items, to the extent necessary for an understanding of the issuer's business as a whole. Information provided also must relate to the segment information of the issuer. Provide the information specified below as well as such other information that is necessary for an investor's understanding of the issuer's financial condition, changes in financial condition and results of operations.

(a) Operating results. Provide information regarding significant factors, including unusual or infrequent events or transactions or new developments, materially affecting the issuer's income from operations, and, in each case, indicating the extent to which income was so affected. Describe any other significant component of revenue or expenses necessary to understand the issuer's results of operations. To the extent that the financial statements disclose material changes in net sales or revenues, provide a narrative discussion of the extent to which such changes are attributable to changes in prices or to changes in the volume or amount of products or services being sold or to the introduction of new products or services.

Instruction to Item 9(a):

1. *The discussion and analysis shall focus specifically on material events and uncertainties known to management that would cause reported financial information not to be necessarily indicative of future operating results or of future financial condition. This would include descriptions and amounts of (A) matters that would have an impact on future operations that have not had an impact in the past, and (B) matters that have had an impact on reported operations that are not expected to have an impact upon future operations.*

2. *Where the consolidated financial statements reveal material changes from year to year in one or more line items, the causes for the changes shall be described to the extent necessary to an understanding of the issuer's businesses as a whole. If the causes for a change in one line item also relate to other line items, no repetition is required and a line-by-line analysis of the financial statements as a whole is not required or generally appropriate. Issuers need not recite the amounts of changes from year to year which are readily computable from the financial statements. The discussion must not merely repeat numerical data contained in the consolidated financial statements.*

3. *When interim period financial statements are included, discuss any material changes in financial condition from the end of the preceding fiscal year to the date of the most recent interim balance sheet provided. Discuss any material changes in the issuer's results of operations with respect to the most recent fiscal year-to-date period for which an income statement is provided and the corresponding year-to-date period of the preceding fiscal year.*

(b) Liquidity and capital resources. Provide information regarding the following:

(1) the issuer's liquidity (both short- and long-term), including a description and evaluation of the internal and external sources of liquidity and a brief discussion of any material unused sources of liquidity. If a material deficiency in liquidity is identified, indicate the course of action that the issuer has taken or proposes to take to remedy the deficiency.

(2) the issuer's material commitments for capital expenditures as of the end of the latest fiscal year and any subsequent interim period and an indication of the general purpose of such commitments and the anticipated sources of funds needed to fulfill such commitments.

(c) Plan of Operations. Issuers (including predecessors) that have not received revenue from operations during each of the three fiscal years immediately before the filing of the offering statement (or since inception, whichever is shorter) must describe, if formulated, their plan of operation for the 12 months following the commencement of the proposed offering. If such information is not available, the reasons for its unavailability must be stated. Disclosure relating to any plan must include, among other things, a statement indicating whether, in the issuer's opinion, the proceeds from the offering will satisfy its cash requirements or whether it anticipates it will be necessary to raise additional funds in the next six months to implement the plan of operations.

(d) Trend information. The issuer must identify the most significant recent trends in production, sales and inventory, the state of the order book and costs and selling prices since the latest financial year. The issuer also must discuss, for at least the current financial year, any known trends, uncertainties, demands, commitments or events that are reasonably likely to have a material effect on the issuer's net sales or revenues, income from continuing operations, profitability, liquidity or capital resources, or that would cause reported financial information not necessarily to be indicative of future operating results or financial condition.

Item 10.   Directors, Executive Officers and Significant Employees

(a) For each of the directors, persons nominated or chosen to become directors, executive officers, persons chosen to become executive officers, and significant employees, provide the information specified below in substantially the following tabular format:

Name	Position	Age	Term of Office[1]	Approximate hours per week for part-time employees[2]
Executive Officers:				
Directors:				
Significant Employees:				

[1] Provide the month and year of the start date and, if applicable, the end date. To the extent you are unable to provide specific dates, provide such other description in the table or in an appropriate footnote clarifying the term of office. If the person is a nominee or chosen to become a director or executive officer, it must be indicated in this column or by footnote.

[2] For executive officers and significant employees that are working part-time, indicate approximately the average number of hours per week or month such person works or is anticipated to work. This column may be left blank for directors. The entire column may be omitted if all those listed in the table work full time for the issuer.

In a footnote to the table, briefly describe any arrangement or understanding between the persons described above and any other persons (naming such persons) pursuant to which the person was or is to be selected to his or her office or position.

Instructions to Item 10(a):

1. *No nominee or person chosen to become a director or person chosen to be an executive officer who has not consented to act as such may be named in response to this item.*

2. The term *"executive officer"* means the president, secretary, treasurer, any vice president in charge of a principal business function (such as sales, administration, or finance) and any other person who performs similar policy making functions for the issuer.

3. The term *"significant employee"* means persons such as production managers, sales managers, or research scientists, who are not executive officers, but who make or are expected to make significant contributions to the business of the issuer.

(b) Family relationships. State the nature of any family relationship between any director, executive officer, person nominated or chosen by the issuer to become a director or executive officer or any significant employee.

Instruction to Item 10(b):

The term "family relationship" means any relationship by blood, marriage, or adoption, not more remote than first cousin.

(c) Business experience. Give a brief account of the business experience during the past five years of each director, executive officer, person nominated or chosen to become a director or executive officer, and each significant employee, including his or her principal occupations and employment during that period and the name and principal business of any corporation or other organization in which such occupations and employment were carried on. When an executive officer or significant employee has been employed by the issuer for less than five years, a brief explanation must be included as to the nature of the responsibilities undertaken by the individual in prior positions to provide adequate disclosure of this prior business experience. What is required is information relating to the level of the employee's professional competence, which may include, depending upon the circumstances, such specific information as the size of the operation supervised.

(d) Involvement in certain legal proceedings. Describe any of the following events which occurred during the past five years and which are material to an evaluation of the ability or integrity of any director, person nominated to become a director or executive officer of the issuer:

(1) A petition under the federal bankruptcy laws or any state insolvency law was filed by or against, or a receiver, fiscal agent or similar officer was appointed by a court for the business or property of such person, or any partnership in which he was general partner at or within two years before the time of such filing, or any corporation or business association of which he was an executive officer at or within two years before the time of such filing; or

(2) Such person was convicted in a criminal proceeding (excluding traffic violations and other minor offenses).

Item 11.　Compensation of Directors and Executive Officers

(a) Provide, in substantially the tabular format indicated, the annual compensation of each of the three highest paid persons who were executive officers or directors during the issuer's last completed fiscal year.

Name	Capacities in which compensation was received (e.g., Chief Executive Officer, director, etc.)	Cash compensation ($)	Other compensation ($)	Total compensation ($)

(b) Provide the aggregate annual compensation of the issuer's directors as a group for the issuer's last completed fiscal year. Specify the total number of directors in the group.

(c) For Tier 1 offerings, the annual compensation of the three highest paid persons who were executive officers or directors and the aggregate annual compensation of the issuer's directors may be provided as a group, rather than as specified in paragraphs (a) and (b) of this item. In such case, issuers must specify the total number of persons in the group.

(d) Briefly describe all proposed compensation to be made in the future pursuant to any ongoing plan or arrangement to the individuals specified in paragraphs (a) and (b) of this item. The description must include a summary of how each plan operates, any performance formula or measure in effect (or the criteria used to determine payment amounts), the time periods over which the measurements of benefits will be determined, payment schedules, and any recent material amendments to the plan. Information need not be included with respect to any group life, health, hospitalization, or medical reimbursement plans that do not discriminate in scope, terms or operation in favor of executive officers or directors of the issuer and that are available generally to all salaried employees.

Instructions to Item 11:

1. *In case of compensation paid or to be paid otherwise than in cash, if it is impracticable to determine the cash value thereof state in a note to the table the nature and amount thereof*

2. *This item is to be answered on an accrual basis if practicable; if not so answered, state the basis used.*

Item 12. Security Ownership of Management and Certain Securityholders

(a) Include the information specified in paragraph (b) of this item as of the most recent practicable date (stating the date used), in substantially the tabular format indicated, with respect to voting securities beneficially owned by:

(1) all executive officers and directors as a group, individually naming each director or executive officer who beneficially owns more than 10% of any class of the issuer's voting securities;

(2) any other securityholder who beneficially owns more than 10% of any class of the issuer's voting securities as such beneficial ownership would be calculated if the issuer were subject to Rule 13d-3(d)(1) of the Securities Exchange Act of 1934.

(b) Beneficial Ownership Table:

Title of class	Name and address of beneficial owner[1]	Amount and nature of beneficial ownership	Amount and nature of beneficial ownership acquirable[2]	Percent of class[3]

[1] The address given in this column may be a business, mailing, or residential address. The address may be included in an appropriate footnote to the table rather than in this column.

[2] This column must include the amount of equity securities each beneficial owner has the right to acquire using the manner specified in Rule 13d-3(d)(1) of the Securities Exchange Act of 1934. An appropriate footnote must be included if the column heading does not sufficiently describe the circumstances upon which such securities could be acquired.

[3] This column must use the amounts contained in the two preceding columns to calculate the percent of class owned by such beneficial owner.

Item 13.   Interest of Management and Others in Certain Transactions

(a) Describe briefly any transactions or any currently proposed transactions during the issuer's last two completed fiscal years and the current fiscal year, to which the issuer or any of its subsidiaries was or is to be a participant and the amount involved exceeds $50,000 for Tier 1 or the lesser of $120,000 and 1% of the average of the issuer's total assets at year end for the last two completed fiscal years for Tier 2, and in which any of the following persons had or is to have a direct or indirect material interest, naming the person and stating his or her relationship to the issuer, the nature of the person's interest in the transaction and, where practicable, the amount of such interest:

(1) Any director or executive officer of the issuer;

(2) Any nominee for election as a director;

(3) Any securityholder named in answer to Item 12(a)(2);

(4) If the issuer was incorporated or organized within the past three years, any promoter of the issuer; or

(5) Any immediate family member of the above persons. An "immediate family member" of a person means such person's child, stepchild, parent, stepparent, spouse, sibling, mother-in-law, father-in-law, son-in-law,

daughter-in-law, brother-in-law, sister-in-law, or any person (other than a tenant or employee) sharing such person's household.

Instructions to Item 13(a):

1. *For purposes of calculating the amount of the transaction described above, all periodic installments in the case of any lease or other agreement providing for periodic payments must be aggregated to the extent they occurred within the time period described in this item.*

2. *No information need be given in answer to this item as to any transaction where:*

   (a) *The rates of charges involved in the transaction are determined by competitive bids, or the transaction involves the rendering of services as a common or contract carrier at rates or charges fixed in conformity with law or governmental authority;*

   (b) *The transaction involves services as a bank depositary of funds, transfer agent, registrar, trustee under a trust indenture, or similar services;*

   (c) *The interest of the specified person arises solely from the ownership of securities of the issuer and the specified person receives no extra or special benefit not shared on a pro-rata basis by all of the holders of securities of the class.*

3. *This item calls for disclosure of indirect as well as direct material interests in transactions. A person who has a position or relationship with a firm, corporation, or other entity which engages in a transaction with the issuer or its subsidiaries may have an indirect interest in such transaction by reason of the position or relationship. However, a person is deemed not to have a material indirect interest in a transaction within the meaning of this item where:*

   (a) *the interest arises only* (i) *from the person's position as a director of another corporation or organization (other than a partnership) that is a party to the transaction, or* (ii) *from the direct or indirect ownership by the person and all other persons specified in paragraphs* (1) *through* (5) *of this item, in the aggregate, of less than a*

> 10% equity interest in another person (other than a partnership) that is a party to the transaction, or (iii) from both such position and ownership;
>
> (b) the interest arises only from the person's position as a limited partner in a partnership in which the person and all other persons specified in paragraphs (1) through (5) of this item had an interest of less than 10%; or
>
> (c) the interest of the person arises solely from the holding of an equity interest (unless the equity interest confers management rights similar to a general partner interest) or a creditor interest in another person that is a party to the transaction with the issuer or any of its subsidiaries and the transaction is not material to the other person.

4. Include the name of each person whose interest in any transaction is described and the nature of the relationships by reason of which such interest is required to be described. The amount of the interest of any specified person must be computed without regard to the amount of the profit or loss involved in the transaction. Where it is not practicable to state the approximate amount of the interest, the approximate amount involved in the transaction must be disclosed.

5. Information must be included as to any material underwriting discounts and commissions upon the sale of securities by the issuer where any of the specified persons was or is to be a principal underwriter or is a controlling person, or member, of a firm which was or is to be a principal underwriter. Information need not be given concerning ordinary management fees paid by underwriters to a managing underwriter pursuant to an agreement among underwriters, the parties to which do not include the issuer or its subsidiaries.

6. As to any transaction involving the purchase or sale of assets by or to any issuer or any subsidiary, otherwise than in the ordinary course of business, state the cost of the assets to the purchaser and, if acquired by the seller within two years before the transaction, the cost to the seller.

7. Information must be included in answer to this item with respect to transactions not excluded above which involve compensation from the

issuer or its subsidiaries, directly or indirectly, to any of the specified persons for services in any capacity unless the interest of such persons arises solely from the ownership individually and in the aggregate of less than 10% of any class of equity securities of another corporation furnishing the services to the issuer or its subsidiaries.

(b) If any expert named in the offering statement as having prepared or certified any part of the offering statement was employed for such purpose on a contingent basis or, at the time of such preparation or certification or at any time thereafter, had a material interest in the issuer or any of its parents or subsidiaries or was connected with the issuer or any of its subsidiaries as a promoter, underwriter, voting trustee, director, officer or employee, describe the nature of such contingent basis, interest or connection.

Item 14. Securities Being Offered

(a) If capital stock is being offered, state the title of the class and furnish the following information regarding all classes of capital stock outstanding:

(1) Outline briefly: (i) dividend rights; (ii) voting rights; (iii) liquidation rights; (iv) preemptive rights; (v) conversion rights; (vi) redemption provisions; (vii) sinking fund provisions; (viii) liability to further calls or to assessment by the issuer; (ix) any classification of the Board of Directors, and the impact of classification where cumulative voting is permitted or required; (x) restrictions on alienability of the securities being offered; (xi) any provision discriminating against any existing or prospective holder of such securities as a result of such security-holder owning a substantial amount of securities; and (xii) any rights of holders that may be modified otherwise than by a vote of a majority or more of the shares outstanding, voting as a class.

(2) Briefly describe potential liabilities imposed on securityholders under state statutes or foreign law, for example, to employees of the issuer, unless such disclosure would be immaterial because the financial resources of the issuer or other factors are such as to make it unlikely that the liability will ever be imposed.

(3) If preferred stock is to be offered or is outstanding, describe briefly any restriction on the repurchase or redemption of shares by the issuer while there is any arrearage in the payment of dividends or sinking fund installments. If there is no such restriction, so state.

(b) If debt securities are being offered, outline briefly the following:

(1) Provisions with respect to interest, conversion, maturity, redemption, amortization, sinking fund or retirement.
(2) Provisions with respect to the kind and priority of any lien securing the issue, together with a brief identification of the principal properties subject to such lien.
(3) Material affirmative and negative covenants.

Instruction to Item 14(b):

In the case of secured debt there mast be stated: (i) *the approximate amount of unbounded property available for use against the issuance of bonds, as of the most recent practicable date, and* (ii) *whether the securities being issued are to be issued against such property, against the deposit of cash, or otherwise.*

(c) If securities described are to be offered pursuant to warrants, rights, or convertible securities, state briefly:

(1) the amount of securities issuable upon the exercise or conversion of such warrants, convertible securities or rights;
(2) the period during which and the price at which the warrants, convertible securities or rights are exercisable;
(3) the amounts of warrants, convertible securities or rights outstanding; and
(4) any other material terms of such securities.

(d) In the case of any other kind of securities, include a brief description with comparable information to that required in (a), (b) and (c) of Item 14.

PART F/S

(a) General Rules

(1) The appropriate financial statements set forth below of the issuer, or the issuer and its predecessors or any businesses to which the issuer is a successor must be filed as part of the offering statement and included in the offering circular that is distributed to investors.

(2) Unless the issuer is a Canadian company, financial statements must be prepared in accordance with generally accepted accounting principles in the United States (US GAAP). If the issuer is a Canadian company, such financial statements must be prepared in accordance with either US GAAP or International Financial Reporting Standards (IFRS) as issued by the International Accounting Standards Board (IASB). If the financial statements comply with IFRS, such compliance must be explicitly and unreservedly stated in the notes to the financial statements and if the financial statements are audited, the auditor's report must include an opinion on whether the financial statements comply with IFRS as issued by the IASB.

(3) The issuer may elect to delay complying with any new or revised financial accounting standard until the date that a company that is not an issuer (as defined under section 2(a) of the Sarbanes-Oxley Act of 2002 (15 U.S.C. 7201(a)) is required to comply with such new or revised accounting standard, if such standard also applies to companies that are not issuers. Issuers electing such extension of time accommodation must disclose it at the time the issuer files its offering statement and apply the election to all standards. Issuers electing not to use this accommodation must forgo this accommodation for all financial accounting standards and may not elect to rely on this accommodation in any future filings.

(b) Financial Statements for Tier 1 Offerings

(1) The financial statements prepared pursuant to this paragraph (b), including (b)(7), need not be prepared in accordance with Regulation S-X.

(2) The financial statements prepared pursuant to paragraph (b), including (b)(7), need not be audited. If the financial statements are not audited, they shall be labeled as "unaudited." However, if an audit of these financial statements is obtained for other purposes and that audit was performed in accordance with either U.S. generally accepted auditing standards or the Standards of the Public Company Accounting Oversight Board by an auditor that is independent pursuant to either the independence standards of the American Institute of Certified Public Accountants (AICPA) or Rule 2-01 of Regulation S-X, those audited financial statements must be filed, and an audit opinion complying with Rule 2-02 of Regulation S-X must be filed along with such financial statements. The auditor may, but need not, be registered with the Public Company Accounting Oversight Board.

(3) *Consolidated Balance Sheets.* Age of balance sheets at filing and at qualification:

(A)   If the filing is made, or the offering statement is qualified, more than three months but no more than nine months after the most recently completed fiscal year end, include a balance sheet as of the two most recently completed fiscal year ends.

(B)   If the filing is made, or the offering statement is qualified, more than nine months after the most recently completed fiscal year end, include a balance sheet as of the two most recently completed fiscal year ends and an interim balance sheet as of a date no earlier than six months after the most recently completed fiscal year end.

(C)   If the filing is made, or the offering statement is qualified, within three months after the most recently completed fiscal year end, include a balance sheet as of the two fiscal year ends preceding the most recently completed fiscal year end and an interim balance sheet as of a date no earlier than six months after the date of the most recent fiscal year end balance sheet that is required.

(D)   If the filing is made, or the offering statement is qualified, during the period from inception until three months after reaching the annual balance sheet date for the first time, include a balance sheet as of a date within nine months of filing or qualification.

(4) *Statements of comprehensive income, cash flows, and changes in stockholders' equity.* File consolidated statements of income, cash flows, and changes in stockholders' equity for each of the two fiscal years preceding the date of the most recent balance sheet being filed or such shorter period as the issuer has been in existence. If a consolidated interim balance sheet is required by (b)(3) above, consolidated interim statements of income and cash flows shall be provided and must cover at least the first six months of the issuer's fiscal year and the corresponding period of the preceding fiscal year.

(5) *Interim financial statements.* Interim financial statements may be condensed as described in Rule 8-03(a) of Regulation S-X. The interim income statements must be accompanied by a statement that in the opinion of management all adjustments necessary in order to make the interim financial statements not misleading have been included.

(6) *Oil and Gas Producing Activities.* Issuers engaged in oil and gas producing activities must follow the financial accounting and reporting standards specified in Rule 4-10 of Regulation S-X.

(7) *Financial Statements of Other Entities.* The circumstances described below may require you to file financial statements of other entities in the offering statement. The financial statements of other entities must be presented for the same periods as if the other entity was the issuer as described above in paragraphs (b)(3) and (b)(4) unless a shorter period is specified by the rules below. The financial statement of other entities shall follow the same audit requirement as paragraph (b)(2) of this Part F/S.

(i) *Financial Statements of Guarantors and Issuers of Guaranteed Securities.* Financial statements of a subsidiary that issues securities guaranteed by the parent or guarantees securities issued by the parent must be presented as required by Rule 3-10 of Regulation S-X.

(ii) *Financial Statements of Affiliates Whose Securities Collateralize an Issuance.* Financial statements for an issuer's affiliates whose securities constitute a substantial portion of the collateral for any class of securities being offered must be presented as required by Rule 3-16 of Regulation S-X.

(iii) *Financial Statements of Businesses Acquired or to be Acquired.* File the financial statements required by Rule 8-04 of Regulation S-X.

(iv) *Pro Forma Financial Information.* If financial statements are presented under paragraph (b)(7)(iii) above, file pro forma information showing the effects of the acquisition as described in Rule 8-05 of Regulation S-X.

(v) *Real Estate Operations Acquired or to be Acquired.* File the financial information required by Rule 8-06 of Regulation S-X.

Instructions to paragraph (b) in Part F/S:

1. *Issuers should refer to Ride 257(b)(2) to determine whether a special financial report will be required after qualification of the offering statement.*

2. *If the last day that the financial statements included in the offering statement can be accepted, according to the age requirements of this item falls on a Saturday, Sunday, or holiday, such offering statement may be filed on the first business day following the last day of the specified period.*

3. *As an alternative, an issuer may — but need not — elect to comply with the provisions of paragraph (c).*

(c) Financial Statement Requirements for Tier 2 Offerings

(1) In addition to the general sales in paragraph (a), provide the financial statements required by paragraph (b) of this Part F/S, except the following rales should be followed in the preparation of the financial statements:

(i) The issuer and, when applicable, other entities for which financial statements are required, must comply with Article 8 of Regulation S-X, as if it was conducting a registered offering on Form S-1, except the age of interim financial statements may follow paragraphs (b) (3)-(4) of this Part F/S.

(ii) Audited financial statements are required for Tier 2 offerings for the issuer and, when applicable, for financial statements of other entities. However, interim financial statements may be unaudited.

(iii) The audit must be conducted in accordance with either U.S. Generally Accepted Auditing Standards or the standards of the Public Company Accounting Oversight Board (United States) and the report and qualifications of the independent accountant shall comply with the requirements of Article 2 of Regulation S-X. Accounting firms conducting audits for the financial statements included in the offering circular may, but need not, be registered with the Public Company Accounting Oversight Board.

PART III — EXHIBITS

Item 1. Index to Exhibits

(a) An exhibits index must be presented at the beginning of Part III.
(b) Each exhibit must be listed in the exhibit index according to the number assigned to it under Item 17 below.
(c) For incorporation by reference, please refer to General Instruction III of this Form.

Item 2. Description of Exhibits

As appropriate, the following documents must be filed as exhibits to the offering statement.

1. *Underwriting agreement* — Each underwriting contract or agreement with a principal underwriter or letter pursuant to which the securities are to be distributed; where the terms have yet to be finalized, proposed formats may be provided.
2. *Charter and bylaws* — The charter and bylaws of the issuer or instruments corresponding thereto as currently in effect and any amendments thereto.
3. *Instruments defining the rights of securityholders* —

    (a) All instruments defining the rights of any holder of the issuer's securities, including but not limited to (i) holders of equity or debt securities being issued; (ii) holders of long-term debt of the issuer, and of all subsidiaries for which consolidated or unconsolidated financial statements are required to be filed.

(b) The following instruments need not be filed if the issuer agrees to file them with the Commission upon request: (i) instruments defining the rights of holders of long-term debt of the issuer and all of its subsidiaries for which consolidated financial statements are required to be filed if such debt is not being issued pursuant to this Regulation A offering and the total amount of such authorized issuance does not exceed 5% of the total assets of the issuer and its subsidiaries on a consolidated basis; (ii) any instrument with respect to a class of securities that is to be retired or redeemed before the issuance or upon delivery of the securities being issued pursuant to this Regulation A offering and appropriate steps have been taken to assure such retirement or redemption; and (iii) copies of installments evidencing scrip certificates or fractions of shares.

4. *Subscription agreement* — The form of any subscription agreement to be used in connection with the purchase of securities in this offering.

5. *Voting trust agreement* — Any voting trust agreements and amendments.

6. *Material contracts*

(a) Every contract not made in the ordinary course of business that is material to the issuer and is to be performed in whole or in part at or after the filing of the offering statement or was entered into not more than two years before such filing. Only contracts need be filed as to which the issuer or subsidiary of the issuer is a party or has succeeded to a party by assumption or assignment or in which the issuer or such subsidiary has a beneficial interest. Schedules (or similar attachments) to material contracts may be excluded if not material to an investment decision or if the material information contained in such schedules is otherwise disclosed in the agreement or the offering statement. The material contract filed must contain a list briefly identifying the contents of all omitted schedules, together with an agreement to furnish supplementally a copy of any omitted schedule to the Commission upon request.

(b) If the contract is such as ordinarily accompanies the kind of business conducted by the issuer and its subsidiaries, it is made in the ordinary course of business and need not be filed unless it falls within one or more of the following categories, in which case it must be filed except where immaterial in amount or significance: (i) any contract to which directors, officers, promoters, voting trustees, securityholders named in the offering statement, or underwriters are parties, except where the contract merely involves the purchase or sale of current assets having a determinable market price, at such market price; (ii) any contract upon which the issuer's business is substantially dependent, as in the case of continuing contracts to sell the major part of the issuer's products or services or to purchase the major part of the issuer's requirements of goods, services or raw materials or any franchise or license or other agreement to use a patent, formula, trade secret, process or trade name upon which the issuer's business depends to a material extent; (iii) any contract calling for the acquisition or sale of any property, plant or equipment for a consideration exceeding 15% of such fixed assets of the issuer on a consolidated basis; or (iv) any material lease under which a part of the property described in the offering statement is held by the issuer.

(c) Any management contract or any compensatory plan, contract or arrangement including, but not limited to, plans relating to options, warrants or rights, pension, retirement or deferred compensation or bonus, incentive or profit sharing (or if not set forth in any formal document, a written description) is deemed material and must be filed except for the following: (i) ordinary purchase and sales agency agreements; (ii) agreements with managers of stores in a chain organization or similar organization; (iii) contracts providing for labor or salesperson's bonuses or payments to a class of securityholders, as such; (iv) any compensatory plan, contract or arrangement that pursuant to its terms is available to employees generally and that in operation provides for the same method of allocation of benefits between management and non-management participants.

7. *Plan of acquisition, reorganization, arrangement, liquidation, or succession* — Any material plan of acquisition, disposition, reorganization, readjustment, succession, liquidation or arrangement and any

amendments thereto described in the offering statement. Schedules (or similar attachments) to these exhibits must not be filed unless such schedules contain information that is material to an investment decision and that is not otherwise disclosed in the agreement or the offering statement. The plan filed must contain a list briefly identifying the contents of all omitted schedules, together with an agreement to furnish supplementally a copy of any omitted schedule to the Commission upon request.

8. *Escrow agreements* — Any escrow agreement or similar arrangement which has been executed in connection with the Regulation A offering.

9. *Letter re change in certifying accountant* — A letter from the issuer's former independent accountant regarding its concurrence or disagreement with the statements made by the issuer in the current report concerning the resignation or dismissal as the issuer's principal accountant.

10. *Power of attorney* — If any name is signed to the offering statement pursuant to a power of attorney, signed copies of the power of attorney must be filed. Where the power of attorney is contained elsewhere in the offering statement or documents filed therewith, a reference must be made in the index to the part of the offering statement or document containing such power of attorney. In addition, if the name of any officer signing on behalf of the issuer is signed pursuant to a power of attorney, certified copies of a resolution of the issuer's board of directors authorizing such signature must also be filed. A power of attorney that is filed with the Commission must relate to a specific filing or an amendment thereto. A power of attorney that confers general authority may not be filed with the Commission.

11. *Consents* —

(a) Experts: The written consent of (i) any accountant, counsel, engineer, geologist, appraiser or any persons whose profession gives authority to a statement made by them and who is named in the offering statement as having prepared or certified any part of the document or is named as having prepared or certified a report or evaluation whether or not for use in connection with the offering statement; (ii) the expert that authored any portion of a report quoted or summarized as such in the offering statement, expressly stating their consent to the use of such quotation or summary; (iii) any persons who are referenced as having reviewed or passed upon any information in the offering statement, and that such information is being included on the basis of their authority or in reliance upon their status as experts.

(b) All written consents must be dated and signed.

12. *Opinion re legality* — An opinion of counsel as to the legality of the securities covered by the Offering Statement, indicating whether they will when sold, be legally issued, fully paid and non-assessable, and if debt securities, whether they will be binding obligations of the issuer.

13. *"Testing the waters" materials* — Any written communication or broadcast script used under the authorization of Rule 255. Such materials need not be filed if they are substantively the same as materials previously filed with the offering statement.

14. *Appointment of agent for service of process* — A Canadian issuer must file Form F-X.

15. *Additional exhibits* —

(a) Any non-public, draft offering statement previously submitted pursuant to Rule 252(d) and any related, non-public correspondence submitted by or on behalf of the issuer.

(b) Any additional exhibits which the issuer may wish to file, which must be so marked as to indicate clearly the subject matters to which they refer.

SIGNATURES

Pursuant to the requirements of Regulation A, the issuer certifies that it has reasonable grounds to believe that it meets all of the requirements for filing on Form 1-A and has duly caused this offering statement to be signed on its behalf by the undersigned, thereunto duly authorized, in the City of _____, State of _____, on __ _____*(date)*.

(Exact name of issuer as specified in its charter) _____

By (Signature and Title) _____

This offering statement has been signed by the following persons in the capacities and on the dates indicated.

(Signature) _____

(Title) _____

(Date)_____

Instructions to Signatures:

1. *The offering statement must be signed by the issuer, its principal executive officer, principal financial officer, principal accounting officer, and a majority of the members of its board of directors or other governing body. If a signature is by a person on behalf of any other person, evidence of authority to sign must be filed with the offering statement, except where an executive officer signs on behalf of the issuer.*

2. *The offering statement must be signed using a typed signature. Each signatory to the filing must also manually sign a signature page or other document authenticating, acknowledging or otherwise adopting his or her signature that appears in the filing. Such document must be executed before or at the time the filing is made and must be retained by the issuer for a period of five years. Upon request, the issuer must furnish to the Commission or its staff a copy of any or all documents retained pursuant to this section.*

3. *The name and title of each person signing the offering statement must be typed or printed beneath the signature.*

INDEX